Significant Emotions

ALSO AVAILABLE FROM BLOOMSBURY

Significant Emotions

Rhetoric and Social Problems in a Vulnerable Age

ASHLEY FRAWLEY

BLOOMSBURY ACADEMIC
LONDON • NEW YORK • OXFORD • NEW DELHI • SYDNEY

BLOOMSBURY ACADEMIC
Bloomsbury Publishing Plc
50 Bedford Square, London, WC1B 3DP, UK
1385 Broadway, New York, NY 10018, USA
29 Earlsfort Terrace, Dublin 2, Ireland

BLOOMSBURY, BLOOMSBURY ACADEMIC and the Diana logo
are trademarks of Bloomsbury Publishing Plc

First published in Great Britain 2024

For legal purposes the Acknowledgements on p. viii constitute
an extension of this copyright page.

Cover design: Olivia D'Cruz
Cover image © Getty/Mayuko Fujino

A catalogue record for this book is available from the British Library.

A catalog record for this book is available from the Library of Congress.

ISBN: HB: 978-1-3500-2680-3
PB: 978-1-3500-2679-7
ePDF: 978-1-3500-2681-0
eBook: 978-1-3500-2682-7

Typeset by Integra Software Services Pvt. Ltd.
Printed and bound in Great Britain

To find out more about our authors and books visit www.bloomsbury.com
and sign up for our newsletters.

Contents

Figures

Tables

Acknowledgements

I began writing this book before a young family and the Covid-19 pandemic had other plans. It's not what I planned or hoped it would be. The reason it exists at all is down to the tireless patience of my husband, children and mother-in-law. 'Thank you' is not enough.

Kathryn Ecclestone, Ken McLaughlin, Daniel Nehring, Frank Furedi and Ellie Lee all graciously read in some cases numerous drafts of various chapters and I owe them an enormous debt of gratitude. I am also grateful for long conversations with my SPIN and PhD students who helped open up new insights and avenues. For this, thanks are owed to Robert Lenton, Anya Williams, Amy Thomas and Eleanor Goldsworthy. Of course, all errors are my own.

Introduction

Our culture attributes immense explanatory power to emotion. Increasingly, social problems are portrayed not simply as threats to physical or material well-being, but as injurious to the state of emotion. On a seeming daily basis, the news media carries stories about a celebrity, policymaker or organization declaring their commitment to promoting mindfulness, or well-being or mental health. Cases for social change are often built on the foundation of claims about the emotional harm suffered by individuals and groups described as vulnerable. When constructing cases for action, emotional risks and benefits are increasingly specified, if not placed front and centre. The case is often made that a range of social problems would disappear, or at least be greatly improved, if those in power would turn their attention to the realm of emotions and the promises of emotion management. Of course, it is not always put so explicitly. Rather, the invitation to conceive of the world through the prism of emotion is often presented as a re-shifting of focus onto 'what really matters'. And increasingly, we are told, what matters is emotion.

That emotions have become central to the fabric of public life is evident in the way that they have permeated discussions of problems, policy and politics over the past decade. Following the controversial election of Donald Trump as President of the United States in 2016, workplaces and educational institutions offered therapy and cancelled classes to deal with the emotional fallout. A widely shared Vox article argued that Trump's election qualified as a traumatic event capable of producing symptoms of post-traumatic stress disorder (Teng, 2016). Months later, CNN ran a headline alleging the American electorate was suffering from 'post-election stress disorder' (Gold, 2017). A psychologist interviewed for the story is described as recommending that 'patients' (in this case, the entire American population) limit their consumption of media and focus on things they enjoy. For many, the election result signified the triumph of the 'politics of hate' to be met with a 'politics of love'. A popular Twitter hashtag surrounding the election campaign was #LoveTrumpsHate.

Similar rhetoric surrounded the UK's vote to leave the European Union in 2016 which many critics saw as driven by hatred and xenophobia. A group of Labour MPs even formed a 'Love Socialism Hate Brexit' group in 2019 to advocate against the move (Lewis, 2019).

In 2020, the populations of many countries found themselves in 'lockdown' as a response to the Covid-19 pandemic. No sooner did policymakers utter the words, 'stay at home' than ads began to beckon from the margins of social media prompting users, 'Working from home? Anxious about the state of things? Talk to a therapist online and find relief' (Frawley, 2020e). Headlines warned of the 'mental health toll' that the virus would leave in its wake, while a press release from Harvard University offered a quasi-symptomatic listing of coronavirus 'reactions' including 'anxiety, worry or panic', 'anger' and 'skepticism or bravado' (Harvard University, 2020). Therapeutic apps offered specialized guided meditations geared towards the pandemic while The US National Alliance on Mental Illness tweeted, 'It's okay to feel sad, angry, or scared because of the #COVID19 outbreak. However you feel is valid' (NAMI [@NAMICommunicate], 2020).

These, of course, were not isolated occurrences. Mainstream politics and lobbying more generally have been saturated with emotion rhetoric for decades. Emotion problems and emotion panaceas regularly intermingle and enmesh with personal, health, political and social issues in public discourse. In 2018 a UK ministerial lead was appointed on 'loneliness' (Prime Minister's Office, 2018) where its amelioration was likened to tackling obesity and smoking (Knapton, 2017). Illustrating a penchant for medical metaphors, a Labour MP refers to a 'silent epidemic of loneliness' facing the country (CBC News, 2018). Reports put out by children's lobby groups routinely connect their world of feelings to a wide range of social problems; for instance, in one report linking 'low wellbeing' to a range of risks and behaviours (Guldberg, 2012). The Royal College of Psychiatrists (2021) warns that 'failure to act on climate change will become a growing mental health problem' and that 'the climate and ecological emergency is a mental health emergency'. The Welsh Wellbeing of Future Generations Act 2015 requires that policies be justified on the basis of their impact on the future well-being of Welsh populations, while policy institutes discuss the importance of 'wellbeing inequality' (What Works Centre for Wellbeing, 2017).

After I finished my first book, *Semiotics of Happiness* (2015), tracing the rise of happiness promotion as a panacea for social problems, I noticed that few seemed interested in the ameliorative potential of 'happiness' anymore. Claims-makers appeared largely to have moved on. But the way in which they did so struck me as peculiar. Now they were stressing well-being, mental health and the promising nature of mindfulness for social change. While differing in significant ways, at their heart, they all seemed to be telling a similar story. Elucidating that story helps give an answer to the question of why, when one emotion problem wave recedes, do there seem to be so many more rippling towards the shore?

This book is my attempt to provide an answer. Drawing together public pronouncements aiming to promote self-esteem, happiness, mindfulness and mental health in personal, public and institutional life, I examine the ways that these coalesced around particular themes and diverged in important ways. Most are characterized by a mix of strong claims to ancient wisdom, coupled with science and 'intuition'. They tend to be led by gurus who relate quasi-magical experiences of conversion to the new concept and who benefit commercially and financially from promoting new interventions with their personal twist. They promise 'deceptively simple' solutions to a wide range of complex problems and inform audiences about new victims and new forms of suffering. In particular, I explore their marked tendencies to rise and fall in a wave that follows each idiom's discovery, adoption, expansion and exhaustion. Unlike many other fads, when they are exhausted, they may lose their novelty and no longer make headlines nor litter policymaker speeches, but they leave a residue in the culture. Each discourse adds its tropes to the cultural repertoire, available for making sense of new claims about emergent social problems. More importantly, the deeper story that they tell about human nature and subjectivity and its relationship to social problems is reaffirmed in each telling and remains after they have gone.

I argue that the persistent recurrence of these fads narrates a society stuck between what *is* and what *ought to be*. That is, the gap between the promises of the modern world and the world *as it is* has come to seem like an unbridgeable chasm. The persistent inability to move beyond some of the most wicked issues of the present has led to their gradual naturalization and relocation within the human soul. Therapeutic fads seem to tell this story, over and over, each with a new twist.

Faced with an inability to move beyond the present, claims-makers promising to remedy problems at their 'root', at the level of the human mind, find an enthusiastic reception. However, as each wave passes, from mind cures and mental hygiene to the promotion of self-esteem and beyond, the problems promised finally to be solved are still there. As they persist so too does the underlying story which places human subjectivity at the centre of a system of social problems. Indeed, the capacity of the subject is questioned even more. The conclusion is not, 'perhaps we have misunderstood the problem,' but rather, 'human subjectivity is far weaker than we imagined'.

The idea that therapeutic discourses are trying to produce 'ideal neoliberal subjects' with a variety of associated capabilities has become so often repeated in critical explorations of the phenomenon that it now sounds clichéd.[1] Yet it is necessary to look more deeply at what precisely this invitation to subjectivity entails. As I argue throughout this book, the ideal subject being constructed across many of these discourses is not the free-willing, autonomous subject capable and indeed desirous of being left alone by the powers that be. That subject is not a goal but a risk. It must first be revealed as illusory before correct, 'safer' and 'healthier' forms of subjectivity can be built. In the pages that follow, I reconstruct from these specific public discourses about emotion a vision of ideal subjects that learn precisely to doubt their autonomy. They must learn instead to see themselves as *heteronomous* subjects – subjects that are always looking for external sources for rules and guidance regarding the correct conduct of life. If no such rules and guidance exist, they must demand them. These are subjects who recognize that they possess a will that, left to its own devices, is easily led astray and likely to lead to poor decision-making and even personal and collective calamity. Instead, individual will must be carefully crafted and guided by a range of expertise. In short, subjects must learn to doubt their autonomy and to see themselves instead as heteronomous in the project of managing a life and world that are ultimately beyond control.

The problem of emotion

It is important to note that in my usage throughout this book, therapy/therapeutic and emotion necessarily diverge from specialist definitions. As Furedi (2004) describes, therapy has become a cultural phenomenon rather than simply a set of clinical techniques; it is a way of thinking rather than a means of curing psychiatric disorders. Therapeutic culture emerges when assumptions and practices extend beyond the clinic and come to shape 'public perceptions about a variety of issues' (Furedi, 2004, p. 22). From this perspective, I view the signifiers studied in the chapters that follow as therapeutic vocabularies. That is, although perhaps once obscure or possessing a variety of meanings, these vocabularies come to be increasingly bound up with psychological knowledge. They become subject to new discourses and practices, rationalized and scientized. Redefined and sometimes commodified, they are culturally re-dispersed through mass media, institutions and eventually everyday life. In this way, terms like 'syndrome' and 'trauma' transcend clinical boundaries and have come to populate the language of a wide range of institutions and social life. From this perspective, emotions are not precisely delineated objects, but heterogeneous cultural vocabularies – signifiers whose broad referent is the inner world of individual feeling (though they can and do extend far beyond). And it is that inner world that is increasingly seen as uniquely problematic.

In this way, this is not necessarily the 'age of emotion' so much as it is the era of the ascendancy of the problem of emotion. The realm of emotion is often portrayed as a uniquely problematic space, vulnerable to deterioration if left unchecked. While stress, depression and loneliness regularly make headlines, even the domain of so-called 'positive' emotions is not immune to problematization. As I describe in the chapters that follow, the concern for self-esteem was implicitly with its low level (Furedi, 2004). The concern for happiness was the suspicion that people were not happy enough (Frawley, 2015c). Mindfulness came to imply mindlessness. And mental health has come to mean 'mental ill-health'. Emotional well-being is not celebrated, but portrayed as constantly under threat, something that must be 'promoted' and a state that is unrepresentative of 'normal' for the vast majority of the population. In an article praising the Royals' launch of Heads Together, a mental health awareness campaign, one commentator alleges that, following the death of his mother, Prince Harry's 'normal emotional distress was left untreated, and festered into something more serious' (Orr, 2017). While there is frequently a tacit recognition that a range of emotions are normal and healthy parts of the human experience, even these 'normal' and 'healthy' reactions require education and 'treatment' to avoid becoming problematic. As the article on Prince Harry continues, 'Simply being aware of one's emotions is the first step towards regulating them.' And this awareness is not something that can be achieved on one's own but should be 'taught in schools' and 'seen as just as necessary as PE'.

I focus on outwardly 'positive' emotions because they show most clearly the way that the problematization of emotion extends into such vast swathes of social life. Moreover, because they are not initially clearly problematic, they show most starkly the ways in which subjects are invited *first to doubt their capacities* before the correct ones can be built using behaviours and outlooks alleged to be 'scientifically proven' to work. To do this, I use and attempt to build on the contextual constructionist approach to social problems (Best, 1993a, 2019, 2021), which I discuss in greater detail in Chapter 1. In particular, this book is a response to Best (2015) and Best and Loseke's (2018) call to move beyond case studies of social problems to make sense of how problems are connected and, as I argue hereafter, can flow from one to the other.

Those working in the areas whose news media manifestations I dissect in the pages that follow, and especially those who have worked hard to put forward more social conceptualizations in their respective fields, will find much of this book frustrating to read. However, this is not a critique of the masses of literature surrounding the idioms I describe – though some of this literature inevitably enters when examining the origins of popularized claims. Critiquing decades of literature across the varied and overlapping domains of self-esteem, happiness, well-being, mindfulness and mental health, not to mention in some cases millennia of religious and philosophical thought, would be impossible, and moreover beside the point. There may be as many ideas of the meaning and proper pursuit of these phenomena as there are people who have given them any thought. But only some of these ideas become detached from their scientific or other foundations, which become hazy referents useful more for their rhetorical air than underlying rigour; only some go on to guide public understandings of social problems and find their way into policy pronouncements on how to solve them. This is a study of what these signifiers become when they are swept up into public spheres of claims-making.

News media and rhetoric

The collective definition of social problems does not occur in vague locations of 'society' or 'public opinion', but rather in particular public arenas in which social problems are framed and made sense of discursively (Hilgartner and Bosk, 1988). These arenas include various branches of government, courts, television and movies, the news media (television news, magazines, newspapers and their online manifestations, radio, blogs), political campaign organizations, social action groups, books dealing with social issues, the research community, religious organizations, professional societies and private foundations, and of course now, social media (Hilgartner and Bosk, 1988; McCombs and Valenzuela, 2020; Tran, 2013). Importantly, the more public the arena, that is, the greater the reach and the more 'mass' the medium (Loseke, 2003), the more claims-makers will need to compete for public attention. They compete for attention not only with other potential problems, but other claims-makers representing similar claims, hoping that their own definitions and preferred solutions will emerge as authoritative or at least set the terms of the debate. The potential of the mass media to reach the broadest audiences means they attract a cacophony of such individuals and groups seeking a space on the public agenda, or the list of problems considered most pressing.

For these purposes, it is useful to distinguish between 'primary' and 'secondary' claims-making (Best, 1990). Primary claims exist 'in the background', at the level of formulating definitions, often before reaching the more public spheres of claims-making. Social problem construction relies upon a process whereby individuals define conditions as problematic, but crucially, they must also seek to convince others of the truth of these claims. Thus, secondary claims-making refers to the process of collective definition as it is inevitably shaped by the need to convince others beyond one's initial and more restricted audiences. More public claims tend to be impressed by a rhetorical need to sound convincing within a particular historical and cultural context.

In doing so, claims-makers must mobilize effective rhetoric. This is because it is usually not enough for a claims-maker to draw attention to what they perceive as a troubling condition, they want something to be done about it. For instance, public money should be spent, individuals should rethink the way they live their lives, policymakers should develop action plans, etc. Therefore, it is crucial that they formulate claims that will be persuasive to audiences and that will stir them into action, or at least avoid resistance. Indeed, a great many claims have been forwarded about the phenomena described throughout this book, but only a small fraction of them have been successful, that is, widely repeated, across the news media. Claims are shaped by the process of competition in the various public arenas in which they are articulated. Those claims that gain salience and those that fall away reflect not only the particularities of the people who make them, but also the particular contexts in which they have appeared. In other words, rhetoric operates within specific cultural contexts that render some claims believable and others out of bounds (Altheide, 2009; Best, 1987). Claims appearing in the news media and their tendencies to adopt common rhetorical strategies and to coalesce around particular themes provide 'a window into collective sentiments, preferences, and identity pronouncements about epistemic communities' (Altheide, 2009, p. 66). For claims-makers, knowing that they must convince broad audiences means that their claims tend to conform to what they believe (or hope) will be strongly held cultural values. Widely repeated claims allude to success in achieving a rhetorical 'fit' with the extant beliefs of this surrounding culture. In other words, they resonate. Since claims-makers draw on existing cultural understandings in the process of formulating claims that will be perceived as persuasive by members of those cultures, claims that are constantly reaffirmed and which become taken-for-granted assumptions about the nature of the problem can provide a window into the cultural moment that produced them.

News media in particular are central to successful mobilization around new social problems, potentially attracting attention, rallying public action and influencing or expanding policy debates (Best, 1990; Gamson, 1990; Hilgartner and Bosk, 1988; McCarthy et al., 1996; Nelson, 1984). While newspaper readership has declined in recent years, newspapers retain public trust over other media (Allcott & Gentzkow, 2017). They have an expectation of covering the most important issues; simply being covered confers a sense of importance (McCombs & Valenzuela, 2020). Their broad reach continues to make them significant for agenda-setting, with the majority of news links shared on social media coming from mainstream news media sources, providing the 'lifeblood' of topical social media conversations (McCombs and Valenzuela, 2020; Newman, 2011, p. 6). Their ability to set the agenda that politics and other media tend to follow (Fawzi, 2018; Langer & Gruber, 2021; Weaver & Choi, 2017) lends them enduring centrality to claims-making campaigns towards the present and thus an ideal place from which to capture a variety of voices, views and commonly repeated claims. It is here where one will find claims from gurus and scientists and bloggers, tech companies and corporations, all trying to capture attention using language that they hope mass audiences (and the media gatekeepers giving access to them) will find convincing. Within this clamour of competing claims, I take my lead from those that 'rise to the top' – those that become commonly repeated in the intensely competitive public arena of news media claims-making before tracing them back to their 'primary' formulations.

While examining constructions in the news media will inevitably fail to encapsulate all public and less public discussions of the issue, identifying claims that survive and indeed thrive in this sphere provides a window into at least some of the taken-for-granted meanings and relationships of the historical and cultural contexts that produced them. The news media also contribute to the broader cultural availability of particular frameworks for making sense of social issues and thus contribute to their expansion and exhaustion which I flesh out in the chapters that follow. However, this sample was a starting point, and additional keyword searching and document gathering was carried out to further elucidate themes identified in the sample (Altheide & Schneider, 2013). For more details on the methods used, see the Methods Appendix at the end of this book. Note also that I offer a mostly country-specific analysis focusing on the UK or at least the majority English-speaking world, though many claims originate in the United States and thus examinations of historical context necessitate a focus on their development and cross-national diffusion from there. This approach offers a focused and in-depth case study of the particular cultural, social and political factors that fostered the growth in popularity of the discourses I describe in these particular contexts. However, future research may consider the way that these phenomena inevitably change as they diffuse into different social, cultural, political and linguistic contexts.

To reiterate then, what gets repeated and what falls away in this competitive atmosphere tells us something about the culture with which those successful claims resonated. In this way, this is not really a study about happiness or mental health, etc., but about a culture that appears increasingly hospitable to claims cast in these terms.

Outline of the book

The book is divided into two parts, the first exploring contextual, processual and rhetorical factors that foster the rise of positive emotional fads and the second detailed case studies of mindfulness and mental health, respectively.

In Chapter 1, I briefly consider 'emotional turns' in several domains of public life and the turn to positive emotion before sketching a number of precursors to the case studies detailed in later chapters including New Thought and mental hygiene movements. The origins of the residual emphasis upon intuition, ancient wisdom and rationalization can easily be gleaned from these movements as well as their coincidence with periods of political impasse. I also describe the theoretical perspective through which I view social problems and their underlying ethnopsychology.

Chapters 2 and 3 detail the main argument that I adopt across this book, exploring key historical and cultural phenomena that have led to the current cultural and political impasse. Here, I argue that ideas of subjectivity are intimately tied to the possibilities of the time period. As possibilities for social change became increasingly closed off, so too did the potential of the human subject. Drawing on the work of Marshall Berman, David Chandler and Julian Reid among others, I introduce the necessity of the heteronomous subject in a context where subjects must learn to live dangerously but never act as such. The world is posited as increasingly beyond the control of human subjects. How could such damaged and dangerous subjects ever risk (again) taking the reins of history?

In Chapter 4, I explore the structure that therapeutic fads tend to take, using self-esteem and happiness to illustrate their rise and fall before diffusing into the ethnopsychology. I draw out the way that claims-makers position emotion management as the first necessary step to any social change. I also consider the way that attempts to use emotion to enchant social life and affect a romantic escape from the present inevitably become the very things they were supposed to prevent.

Chapters 5 and 6 introduce mindfulness as the first case study, following its trajectory across its prehistory, discovery, adoption and current signs of exhaustion. I explore the way that mindfulness was not only offered by conceptual entrepreneurs as a 'word for all seasons', but also the way that the discourse constructed a new problem that only they could cure – subjects that are perpetually on autopilot, automatic and unaware. Yet even as the discourse exhausts, the necessity of intervening first at the level of emotion maintains an air of common sense.

Chapters 7–9 detail the final case study of the book, mental health in higher education. As mental health has a varied and heterogeneous history, a specific domain was selected as the main focus. Here many of the core features of the earlier discourses are maintained including a tendency to assume and consciously seek to inculcate a diminished sense of subjectivity. Tendencies towards inflated claims to scientific foundations are also there. However, in place of gurus, the discourse is populated with 'wounded healers' who turn mental health into a source of meaning, but also career paths largely in the third sector. More importantly, I argue that it is in this discourse that the problematization of subjectivity appears most acute and widespread. Through recourse to a medicalized rhetoric and more shorn of mystique than previous discourses, there is a potential for staying power that surpasses them.

Finally, the conclusion attempts to offer a means of stepping out of the endless ocean of therapeutic fads through contesting the naturalization of the degraded subject and attempting to grapple with the material world that is the product of human minds and hands, and can be changed through the application of both.

PART ONE

Context, Process, Rhetoric

1

Emotional Turns

Emotion appears to exert unique influence over collective understandings of individual and social life. There have been a series of 'emotional turns' across social and economic policy and academic disciplines through which emotion has become increasingly central to their outlook, goals, methods and subject matter. But it is not just emotion that has captured scholarly, public and policy interest, it is emotion as a problem. Emotional disorientation is alleged to lie at the root of a host of social problems. Even when not explicitly stated as such, attending to social issues at the level of emotion implicitly problematizes this realm. The unspoken message is that there is something wrong, but that 'something' is ultimately rooted in human subjectivity. Thus, attending to this realm is posited as the first step in problem amelioration. In this context, emotion problems and solutions emerge as a series of fads – ebbing and flowing programmes for how the subject, once and for all, can be fixed. Partially fuelling these fads are underlying ethnopsychological beliefs in the frailty of the human subject. To understand and challenge the seemingly never-ending waves of therapeutic fads, it is necessary to penetrate deeper, to understand the underlying phenomena that drive them. That is the goal of this book.

In this and the next two chapters, I set out key aspects of the historical, cultural and political context that push forward emotion problem waves. To do so, in this chapter I briefly consider 'emotional turns' in several domains of public life before turning to rising concerns surrounding apparently 'positive' emotions. I then sketch a number of much earlier precursors to the case studies detailed in later chapters including New Thought and mental hygiene movements. This is useful as the origins of the residual emphasis upon intuition, ancient wisdom and rationalization can easily be gleaned from these movements as well as their coincidence with periods of political impasse. This contributes to my overall argument that therapeutic fads are driven by this sense of impasse, by an inability to bridge what is and what ought to be, which has been naturalized and located within the human mind. The second half adds to the overview I gave in the introduction of my particular approach, describing the theoretical perspective through which I view social problems in more detail and the way in which they both draw on and contribute to a particular underlying ethnopsychology.

Emotional turns

Perhaps the most obvious 'emotional turn' has been in the field of policymaking. Rising at least since the interwar period (Rose, 1999) and accelerating from the 1980s (Furedi, 2004), emotion management has become an increasingly central aspect of government policymaking around the world (see e.g. Jupp et al., 2017; Nolan, 1998; Pupavac, 2004a, 2004b, 2006; Yang, 2015). In the UK, successive governments have taken an interest in the emotions of their citizenry. The UK Government announced in February 2019 that schoolchildren would be taught a 'range of innovative techniques' including mindfulness, relaxation and breathing exercises to 'help them regulate their emotions' (Department for Education, 2019). Governments promise to measure well-being over GDP, while New Zealand unveiled its first 'wellbeing budget' in 2019 (New Zealand Government, 2019). For several decades, there has been an increasing focus on parental emotions and behaviours, which are positioned as threats to children's and infants' bodies and minds (Macvarish & Lee, 2019, p. 5). Governments have also been receptive to claims about adverse childhood experiences or 'ACEs', which are linked to parental failures from physical abuse to 'emotional neglect' and, in turn, to a range of social ills (Macvarish & Lee, 2019; Science and Technology Committee, 2018). Psycho-emotional interventions in families go hand in hand with initiatives to measure and teach children 'wellbeing' and give teachers mental health training (Ecclestone, 2018). In the late 1990s and early 2000s, American author and psychologist Daniel Goleman's concept of 'emotional intelligence' was influential on the development of the Social and Emotional Aspects of Learning programme (2003–11) which aimed to teach 'emotional skills' alleged to be central to effective learning (J. Evans, 2018, p. 10).

Conceptualizations of social class and inequality, perhaps perennial concerns of capitalist society, have also seen an 'emotional turn' in social policy and social movements. In 2022, the Conservative Party unveiled a highly controversial 'mini-budget' widely perceived as promising tax breaks for the wealthy amid a 'cost of living crisis' for the average British citizen. In response, Labour MP Rosena Allin-Khan tweeted, 'The Conservatives' cost-of-living crisis is wrecking the British economy – we all know this will damage people's mental health. That's why a Labour Government will revolutionize access to mental health treatment' (Allin-Khan, 2022). While initially citing economic problems, the discourse suddenly shifts from material costs to mental health damage, where the alleged problem is then promised to be tackled. Social movements increasingly emphasize the necessary emotional aspects of social change. Lady Gaga announced that 'we're in the midst of an #EmotionRevolution', coinciding with her speaking at a summit of the same name at the Yale School of Management in 2015 (Hathaway, 2015). Mirroring top-down initiatives is the increasingly 'bottom-up' use of emotion, for instance, the emotionalization of social movements (Sotirakopoulos, 2016). Anti-austerity protests in Spain and Greece in 2010 rallied under the banner of the 'indignant' while think tanks measure 'wellbeing inequalities' around the UK (Abdallah et al., 2017). The emotional has become political.

Political fascination is fed by growing academic fascination with emotions, with a constant stream of academic publishing on emotion, from happiness economics to positive psychology and the founding of dedicated journals like *Emotion*, the *Journal of Happiness Studies* and *The Journal of Positive Psychology*. The Web of Science database lists forty-six articles with the word 'emotion' in the title in 1970. By the end of 2021 there were 5,424. As stated at the outset, so significant have emotions become over the past several decades that numerous disciplines have begun to reflect on 'emotional turns' in their respective areas, where emotion becomes increasingly central to their research methods and focus.[1]

The turn towards positive emotion

Yet the impact of these turns pales in comparison to that of the founding of Positive Psychology, with its turning of the discipline's attention to the realm of ostensibly 'positive' emotions. The emotion fads detailed in the chapters that follow owe much to the founding and spread of this subdiscipline. Following his appointment as President of the American Psychological Association (APA) in 1998, the psychologist Martin Seligman outlined his plans for a 'new science of human strengths' that he termed 'positive psychology' (Seligman, 1999, p. 560). The new subdiscipline would aim to be a 'science of positive subjective experience, positive individual traits, and positive institutions', seeking to 'improve quality of life and prevent pathologies that arise when life is barren and meaningless' (Seligman & Csikszentmihalyi, 2000, p. 5). Positive psychology, its founders claimed, would help turn attention away from undue focus upon pathology and a 'model of the human being lacking the positive features that make life worth living' (p. 5).

In the 1990s, Seligman organized a Positive Psychology Network whose express purpose was to expand the influence of the subdiscipline into nearly every institution and aspect of personal and public life, affecting a 'major contribution to human well-being' on par with the success of modern medicine in its 'advocacy of healthy physical conditions' (Seligman, 1998). Unlike other self-help movements, positive psychology sought to distinguish itself by strong claims to scientific foundations. It would aim to 'produce and organize research findings that would help parents, teachers, reporters, and leaders create and participate in effective and healthy schools, families, workplaces, neighborhoods, and even perhaps nations' (Seligman, 1998). Meetings were organized around task forces and individuals were selected from around the world to spread the message in areas including education, social policy, urban planning and the law. Throughout these activities, the claim to help people steer away from taking the wrong paths to well-being was accomplished on the basis of a claim to being a new 'science' of happiness.

As a project in diffusion, it has been stunningly successful. As I described in my first book (Frawley, 2015c), schools introduced lessons in happiness, companies hired 'chief happiness officers' and brought in positive psychologists to coach their employees. Describing the introduction of happiness coaching at corporations including Disney and McDonald's, one advocate surmises that happiness interventions spread 'because the message works' (Reid, 2008). The message: that positive emotions require scientific expertise, the absence of which lies at the heart of a variety of problems. People require intervention not only when things go wrong, but also for things to go right.

In both the positive psychology movement and in public discourses of emotion more generally, a disorientation with regard to one's inner emotional life is often positioned as the root of poor choice-making that allegedly leads to personal and social ills. By promoting positive emotions, it is claimed that better behaviours and choices will result. In this way, the promotion of self-esteem in the 1980s and 1990s promised answers to problems ranging from educational underachievement to teenage pregnancy (Furedi, 2002, p. 29; Hewitt, 1998, p. 50). Promoting happiness and well-being in the 2000s was argued to prevent future mental illness and other problems through a kind of emotional inoculation (Ecclestone, 2012; Ecclestone & Lewis, 2014). Positive psychology promised not only to study and measure emotions objectively but also to explain 'why we get so much wrong' (Mooney, 2006). While the initial novelty of promoting positive emotions is founded on the purported aim to focus on the bright side of life, it is not long before headlines hint at the flipside, like when prominent UK happiness advocate Richard Layard claimed that 'unhappiness is Britain's worst social problem' (Laurance, 2005).

In this way, the turn towards emotion has not been a simple celebration of the emotional side of the human condition nor an antidote to the cold rationality that allegedly dominated disinterested scientific studies for too long. Instead, what is often posited is the problem of emotion. The final chapters of this book detail how, as the problematization of emotion deepens, emotions ironically no longer seem so significant. Rather, the realization of positive emotions appears increasingly elusive, feelings themselves become 'symptoms', part of the broader and all-encompassing domain of 'mental health', which in turn has gradually come to signify its opposite.

Old wine in new bottles?

While a significant source of primary claims for a variety of emotional fads, the positive psychology movement is only one of the most recent waves problematizing 'positive' or at least 'neutral' emotions and experiences. Indeed, positive psychology has been accused of presenting nothing more than 'old wine in new bottles' (Kristjánsson, 2012; Pérez-Álvarez, 2012, p. 185). In this way, it follows a much more long-standing trend. Stretching into at least the nineteenth century, generations of experts in living have claimed to facilitate positive states of being including the New Thought movement, mental hygiene and humanist psychology (Schrank et al., 2014). One of the earliest of these, the New Thought movement, emerged in the nineteenth century as a quasi-religious grouping of smaller movements sharing a romantic emphasis on ancient knowledge, anti-materialism and religious spiritualism (Cabanas & Sanchez-González, 2012).

New Thought proposed a variety of techniques including the practice of gratitude and examining negative thoughts, which, although representing a secularization of Calvinism, also call to mind medieval magical thinking through which imagination can influence the world and affect change (Pérez-Álvarez, 2012). Phineas Quimby, founder of the movement, summarized: 'the trouble is in the mind, for the body is only the house for the mind to dwell in' (Quimby, 1921, p. 78). As Cabanas and Sanchez-González (2012, p. 176) describe, six exercises were in common use among its proponents:

(1) the scrutiny of one's own thoughts in search of the beliefs that caused our discomfort, (2) the mental rejection of any discomfort or pain from the body, (3) the training of the imagination to generate pleasant feelings and to explore one's own desires, (4) the repeating of positive affirmations to oneself to 'scare away' the negative ones, (5) prayer, or (6) the practicing of gratitude and forgiveness.

The New Thought movement ultimately waned into the twentieth century. However, with a sharp rise whose beginning coincides with New Thought's decline in the 1910s, the mental hygiene movement emerged, aiming to 'facilitate the attainment of physical and mental health through perfect adjustment to society by developing and preserving those human values and achievements which contribute to a balanced mental life for the individual' (Schrank et al., 2014, p. 97). Unlike New Thought's quasi-religious and magical underpinnings (Pérez-Álvarez, 2012), the mental hygiene movement represented a strong step towards the rationalized/scientistic thinking that later reaches its apex in positive psychology and related movements. Yet, as the case studies in this book demonstrate, positive emotion problems tend to share a common tendency to locate issues within problematized subjects, naturalized via discourses of emotional and mental disorientation, coupled with a persistent quasi-spiritual orientation towards the solutions to individual and social problems.

The essentially conservative orientations of these movements and their coincidence with moments of political and social impasse are well illustrated by a footnote in Karl Marx's *Capital*, first published in the late 1860s in which he remarks that, 'One may recall that China and the tables began to dance when the rest of the world appeared to be standing still' (1976, p. 164). Marx is referring to the Taiping Rebellion which had broken out in the 1850s, a time when European resistance movements were being harshly suppressed. At the same time, some former Owenites (a group of utopian socialists) were establishing a spiritualist circle in whose increasingly popular seances table-turning was a common feature. By the time of Marx's writing, the Rebellion had been defeated while spiritualism was reaching new heights. The turn towards spiritualism had been marked by its own set of losses; the Owenites had become increasingly marginalized within working-class movements and the writings of this early spiritualist circle 'evince an effort to reckon with political defeat' (Armstrong, 2017, p. 19).

In other words, in the 1850s, tables appeared to dance of their own volition because people were unable to see or mobilize their own powers in the world. They thus projected them onto objects outside of themselves.[2] 'In the absence of progress, European citizens turn mystical' (Leslie, 2004, p. 7). In an argument that I explore in greater depth in Chapter 2, this projection is key to understanding the never-ending rise and fall of emotional panaceas to social problems. As the ability to move forward politically appears increasingly unviable, the invitation to turn inward for answers and to seek freedom through imagination becomes more powerful.

Into the twentieth century the trend towards naturalizing social problems and locating them within the human spirit, soul and mind would become more rationalized. In Nikolas Rose's (1999) explication of the relationships between the rise of the 'psy' disciplines and the remaking of selfhood, he points to the mental hygiene movement as exemplary of a new relationship between governments and individuals through which the internal world is increasingly implicated in 'social problems from crime to industrial inefficiency' (p. 21). The movement offered solutions in the form of mental health promotion through 'early intervention, out patient treatment and prophylactic measures' (p. 21). As he writes:

> In this seemingly peripheral area of concern, a new way of conceiving of the relation between madness and society was being born. Within this new conception, it would not be a question of organic predispositions, exciting causes, and virtually incurable lapses into insanity. Madness was now thought of in the terms of social hygiene. Mental health could be maintained by proper adjustment of the conditions of life and work; poor mental hygiene and stress could promote neurosis in large numbers of people. The effects were not those of social scandal and florid symptomatology, but unhappiness, inefficiency, incompetence, maladaptation, and antisocial conduct. The effects of this on institutional efficiency were considerable; skilled advice could prevent inefficiency, restore the maladjusted, and promote efficiency and contentment.
>
> (p. 21)

Thus, no longer concerned with exotic states of mind, the purview of surveillance was opened to include large swathes, if not the entirety, of the population. Scientific management of mass emotion was increasingly seen to hold the key to social ills. However, mental hygiene's entanglement in the eugenics movement ultimately spelled its doom in the post-war period. Yet, once more, another rhetoric arose in its place, that of 'mental health', making similar claims about the role of individual psychology in social harmony and social change.

Similarities and slippages between and across these earlier movements and those that I describe throughout this book suggest that movements emerging from American popularizations seem to be playing out the same deeper narrative, retelling the same impasses, in different guises. In short, there is a persistent, spreading and increasingly uncontested belief that the cause and solution to social problems lie within some defect within the human mind. The enduring message is that the first necessary step to personal and social change is to attend to damaged, damaging or at least inadequate aspects of human subjectivity. Such messages become particularly powerful in times of social, political and economic deadlock – a deadlock that continues to characterize our era of 'no alternative'. As I explore in the next chapter, it is this impasse that underlies these continual unhappy returns.

Emotion problem waves

There is a large and heterogeneous literature across history, anthropology and sociology that variously reflects upon, feeds or predates the broader 'emotional turns' discussed above. These literatures have explored connections between emotions and morality, social control, social organization and social change (e.g. Bendelow & Williams, 1998; Elias, 2000 [1939]; Lemmings & Brooks, 2014; Lutz & Abu-Lughod, 1990; Stearns & Stearns, 1985). Yet one key approach eschews study of the 'presumed interiority' of emotions in favour of 'discourses about emotions' or 'emotional discourses'; that is, studying emotions to explicate 'social life and power relations' (Lemmings & Brooks, 2014, p. 4). In this way, joining studies of emotional discourses and social problems to study 'problematic emotions' (Best & Loseke, 2018, p. 178) illuminates the social relations that underlie them. The focus is not emotional manipulation, through for instance emotive rhetoric or encouraging a particular affective orientation (e.g. Ahmed, 2014; J. L. Dunn, 2004; Loseke, 2009), but rather the discursive reconstruction of emotions into problems themselves.

To study this, I adopt a contextual constructionist approach to social problems (Best, 1993a, 2019, 2021). From this perspective, social problems are not defined by their harm, but rather the activities of claims-makers who make assertions about the existence of harm which become powerful in relation to the surrounding social, historical, political and cultural contexts. As discussed in the introduction, in the intensely competitive atmosphere of public claims-making about new social problems, claims must employ rhetoric that (their advocates hope) will resonate in these contexts. Those that do are repeated. The particularly successful are adopted onto the public agenda of problems routinely referred to as the most pressing of the day. Of course, my own effort represents an exercise in social construction, though one that hopefully draws out new aspects of the phenomena in question obscured by their naturalization.

This book attempts to answer calls to develop this theory in new directions by synthesizing case studies and exploring the connections between claims (Best, 2015, 2019; Best & Loseke, 2018). Conceptualizing their rise and fall as a series of therapeutic fads rolling through discovery, adoption, expansion and exhaustion reveals striking similarities and elisions across positive emotion keywords. Claims-makers touting the benefits of inculcating self-esteem often referred to its connection with 'happiness'. Those claiming to be able to promote happiness often referred to well-being and mental health, so that their meanings became difficult to parse. Concurrently, the past decade and a half has seen the rise of promoting 'mindfulness', both positing and solving its own problems as well as offering a tool to promote happiness, well-being and mental health. They also share many common features and interesting divergences, as the chapters that follow detail.

Ethnopsychology

All of this points to an underlying ethnopsychology. Ethnopsychology, a concept drawn from anthropological literature dating back to the 1950s, refers to psychological categories and accounts of selfhood, motivation, cognition and emotion peculiar to a culture (White, 1992). They form the culture's 'common sense' about human nature and human motivation. Prominent as a field of research in the 1970s and 1980s, studies of ethnopsychologies raised questions about the universality of Western psychological constructs and assumptions (Kitayama & Cohen, 2007). Only in a particular culture – though one that is increasingly diffusing globally (Nehring et al., 2020) – can 'self-esteem' and 'happiness' emerge as significant emotions and mindfulness and attention to mental health promise catch-all solutions.

Common-sense understandings of human psychology and human nature form the cultural backdrop against and out of which therapeutic vocabularies emerge. Hewitt uses the term 'myth' to describe the self-esteem problem's encoding of culturally specific expectations of human behaviour as well as its ethnopsychological norms. Self-esteem narratives tell 'the story of people who in the end become what their culture urges them to be' he writes (Hewitt, 1998, p. 20). 'Every culture contains a set of ideas and beliefs about the world, how their minds work, and the emotions that are natural to them. Cultures differ, sometimes in profound ways, in their beliefs about the psychology of human beings' (p. 21).

In a shift that I make sense of in terms of a post-liberal destruction of liberal subjectivity in Chapter 2, expectations of self-reliance and stoicism have given way to injunctions to constant help-seeking and emotional expression. While studies tend to be polarized in terms of their embrace or rejection of the increased centrality of emotion in understandings of self and society (Brownlie, 2014), as Wright (2008, p. 324) observes, the depoliticization and individualization of social problems are widely seen as the central impulse of the therapeutic paradigm. In Pupavac's (2006, p. 27) rendering:

The Anglo-American therapeutic ethos essentially conceptualises social problems as rooted in a defective ethnopsychology: improve the psychological well-being of people and how they interact with each other and the social environment will be improved. Conversely when the psychological well-being of people is threatened, their behaviour and their relationships deteriorate, according to the model, creating a vicious cycle in which the social environment is damaged.

For Furedi (2004), ethnopsychology points to prevailing attitudes about the state of people's emotions. Increasingly, he argues, this state is defined by vulnerability. Myriad mental health awareness campaigns reminding us of the magnitude of disability reveal the strong value that Anglosphere culture places on awareness of emotional vulnerability. Increasingly, the term 'vulnerability' has expanded to encompass not only those who suffer extreme hardship, but everyone (Frankenberg et al., 2000). The public realm and everyday life have become saturated with therapeutic vocabularies and narratives; for example, people routinely refer to themselves as 'traumatized', or 'a bit OCD'. In many ways, the extant cultural stock of meanings and emotional vocabularies reflects successful claims-making in the past. Each wave makes way for the next. New people are trained, spaces in institutions are created and research funded. Ethnopsychological constructions of social problems as essentially rooted in a naturalized emotional vulnerability become a ready-made script on which a culture's members can draw to make sense of the world. But how did this come to be?

2

Emotion after the Death of the Subject

It is not only that emotions tend to be culturally emphasized. It is that, over time, their uses and meanings change, and sometimes, their positioning in cultural life changes too. Most importantly for the purposes of this book, their positioning in chains of cause and effect changes. The way that a culture talks about emotion tells us something about the way that culture views the subjects that comprise it – what is natural to them, what they can and cannot do. At the same time, differing views of subjectivity reflect something of the real possibilities of the time. These differing possibilities are reflected in the stories a culture tells about itself and the inner world of its inhabitants.

The purpose of this chapter and the one that follows is to contextualize historically shifts in thinking about the role of subjectivity in social and economic life and social change. These shifts ultimately underpin the problematization of apparently positive emotions that forms the focus of this book. In other words, historical changes and possibilities ripple through subjectivity, and in turn, discursive constructions of emotion. Crucially, this chapter sets out the main argument of this book: discourses of problematized apparently 'positive' emotions continually recur because they discern and explain an unspoken gap between the world as it is and the world as it has been promised to be. In this, I follow Berman (1982), Malik (1996), Heartfield (2006), Chandler (2014) and Chandler and Reid (2016a) in arguing that the uneven realization of Enlightenment promises and ideals in practice has led to a profound disillusionment and uncertainty with regard to their import and role in public life. Hereafter, I claim that this gap has come to be seen as an unbridgeable chasm. This inability to bridge what is with what ought to be has been increasingly explained by defects within the human soul, in human subjectivity as such.[1] There are myriad cultural forms that narrate this impasse and discourses of emotion are just one of many potential examples. As explanations that located the sources and solutions to intractable problems in the scaffolding of society have receded into history, the eye of the social engineer turns more and more towards the people. There is something wrong with them. They will not follow the rules, they will not choose right, and thus threaten to derail a fast-moving modern world. The inner lives of these individuals must be made positive – that is, 'positive' in the sense of 'made good' and 'positive' in the sense of 'filled with content'. Towards the present, there is also a perceptible desire for stasis. As human beings seem to be pulled into an ever-changing future apparently beyond their capacities for control, theories and ideas emerge which beg humanity to hold on to the present against the forces of change. These theories naturalize the present and position social change as something inhuman, acting back on an unchanging humanity and damaging it. In what follows, I attempt to describe and explain some of how this came to be.

Mind the gap

As Heartfield describes (2006, p. 5), 'The freely willing human Subject is the cornerstone of contemporary society.' It underpins employer and marriage contracts, the ability to vote in elections and drive on roads. These subjects are able to exercise freedoms because they are assumed to be rational or at least 'thoughtful and reflective' (p. 8). '[A]s a Subject, one expects to decide for one's self exactly what one is – or is not – prepared to do' (ibid. p. 6). Yet, while the freely willing subject and the principles that spring from it might be routinely referred to and assumed, there is a sense that they are wearing thin.[2]

For instance, in William Davies's (2018) *Nervous States*, he attempts to describe how and why, in our present political and cultural moment, feelings appear to trump facts. According to Davies, various developments have led to society being gradually overrun by strong, scarcely controllable emotions emanating from the masses.[3] Trump's election and Brexit were only the most visible expressions of a lashing out by those victimized by society. They were, he contends, a kind of self-harm inflicted in a futile attempt to exert control over one's situation akin to actions observed in sufferers of PTSD. He argues that an updated knowledge of human nature drawn from, for instance, neuroscience and evolutionary psychology can help us explain why human beings are more likely to act and behave emotionally rather than rationally. These sciences allegedly reveal that a thin bubble of rationality precariously protects an inner nature of emotional vulnerability. Thus, if politics is to move forward and contain these potentially destructive tendencies, it is necessary to lean into them and imbue facts with feelings and empathy.

Implicit within this narrative is a sense of pessimism regarding human subjectivity that also underpins and reverberates throughout contemporary discourses of emotions. It is telling that when Davies talks about the fading away of the Enlightenment dream of a society governed by reason, he takes Thomas Hobbes's emphasis on self-preservation and the threat of mutual violence as his representative anecdote. The right to life and measures to secure it (as opposed to, for instance, the right to free expression) are positioned as foundational. Yet doing so reifies a pessimistic desire for safety and protection over other more optimistic visions that also emerged from the same Enlightenment legacy. As Marshall Berman has observed, 'The *philosophes* were the first group of thinkers to see clearly the vast range of possibilities for human self-expression in the world' (1972, p. 69). The first light of the modern industrialized world seemed to reveal possibilities that most human beings had previously ascribed only to the heavens. At the same time, these possibilities seemed unevenly realized or altogether imaginary.

We are still grappling with this tension between the possibilities of the human subject and the reality of what can and can't be realized today. Berman's contrast between the pessimism of French seventeenth-century mathematician, philosopher and defender of religion Blaise Pascal and the overoptimism of the Enlightenment *philosophe* Voltaire is instructive here. When Pascal looked out into the world, he did not see endless possibilities for self-realization that modernity appeared to promise. Instead, 'The activities men engaged in did not constitute an expression of the self, but rather a displacement and a disguise; not a fulfilment, but an endless emptiness' (Berman, 1972, p. 58). Human beings were naturally infected with the vice of insincerity, Pascal thought; most of their lives and supposed fulfilments were simply illusions. 'The mutual deceit on which society was founded was simply the sum of all individual deceptions' (p. 59), he thought. Only when locked away from society in an inert world of quiet contemplation could man truly be himself. And yet still he was not happy. 'I have discovered,' Berman quotes Pascal concluding, 'that all of the unhappiness of men arises from a single fact, that they are unable to stay quietly in one room' (p. 69). But what Pascal failed to realize, Berman says, was that the 'emptiness man felt in the void might reveal not the emptiness of his nature, but the unnaturalness of the void' (p. 64). In other words, the unease one felt in the 'void' only evidenced the futility of trying to find fulfilment inside of one's head alone.

By contrast, Voltaire sought 'to take the part of humanity against [Pascal] this sublime misanthrope', retorting that, 'man is fortunate [...] that he attaches *ennui* to inaction, in order to force us to be useful to others and to ourselves' (Voltaire in Berman, 1972, p. 66). Voltaire contended that 'man's need for occupation and action' is not a '*divertissement* from himself' but rather his 'authentic self-fulfilment' (Berman, 1972, p. 66). Humanity realizes itself when it acts upon the world. However, if Pascal was too eager to reject the modern world and humanity's ability to fulfil itself within it, Voltaire was too quick to embrace it as it was during his time. Even though Voltaire thought that man proved himself by being occupied, he did not seem perturbed enough by his own admission that most occupations of his time were so 'empty of meaning that it basically did not matter what men did' (p. 68). While Voltaire's views softened over time, he possessed and never fully shed a 'distrust of the masses', identifying them with 'passion' and the educated classes with 'reason' (Gay, 1959, p. 226).

This tension between the pessimism of Pascal and the (highly selective) optimism of Voltaire is a representative anecdote that well illustrates an ongoing tension played out across the therapeutic discourses described in the chapters that follow. If the world fails to live up to ideals, do we abandon those ideals or the world or both? Do we seek refuge in a world of 'quiet contemplation'? Do we explain humanity's persistent failures and problems as things that arise out of humanity itself or do we – can we – see humanity as providing the solution? Neither of these thinkers, nor their societies since that time, have succeeded in fully recognizing or resolving these conflicts. As Berman (1972, p. 69) continues, just as much as Pascal was dismayed by modernity, Enlightenment *philosophes*:

> Elated by the beauty and grandeur of their vision [...] lost sight of the great gap between what they saw and where they stood, between what was possible for man and what was real for men, between the human world as it might be and European society as it was.

Why have we not been able to bridge the gap that separates the idealization of the subject and a future in which its freedoms might be more widely and fully realized? Dimly perceiving this gap but unable to reckon with it, Pascal threw man into its abyss. Embrace the void. It's just the way things are, the way 'man' is, and the difficulty is in learning to live within it. Voltaire built a bridge that only some could cross. It seems now that we are tending back towards that abyss rather than learning how to build sturdier bridges.

Since their time, the human subject has been ideally raised to commanding heights only to be tossed down again. Growing with ever-greater fervour and sophistication over two and a half centuries has been the notion that the human mind is the seat of neither free will nor reflective action, but is rather ruled by a cacophony of conflicting forces operating mostly beneath the surface of conscious thought. The vast majority of humanity has not been allowed into the world of reason, but permanently shut out. It has become increasingly commonplace to argue that if one wants to solve problems, one must seek to ascertain and manage those subterranean forces. How did this happen?

All subjectivity melts into air

Subjectivity at least since the Enlightenment has been one of the central problems of philosophy. At its most general, it refers to conceptualizations of selfhood and what it means to be human, and out of these, the limitations and possibilities of human action and freedom. Theories of subjectivity bring together and attempt to make sense of ontology and epistemology – the study of existence or being, and the study of how, whether, and in what ways we can come to know it (D. E. Hall, 2004, p. 3). It was René Descartes's seventeenth-century distinction between body and mind, between man's animal nature and his divinely given higher faculties of reason, that 'enthroned the thinking Subject as the arbiter of certain knowledge' (Heartfield, 2006, p. 27). As Bowler (2008) describes, during the Enlightenment there emerged a sense of uniqueness to human life that could not be reduced to man's animal past or 'organic origins' (p. 58). In many ways, human beings are less well adapted than animals to the natural world, but they are profoundly different in their ability to hold the forces of nature at bay, to 'objectify' them, understand them and 'mediate their impact' (Bowler, 2008, p. 43). For Enlightenment man (and indeed, women were generally considered by nature irrational and thus excluded from this vision), the goal became not to embed oneself fully in nature but rather to detach oneself as much as possible from it so as to facilitate a more effective channelling of passions and the fuller exercise of the human intellect. This ideal was made possible by the unique position of many Enlightenment *philosophes* in society. Privileged and distanced from toil, it was a vision of human nature that sat well with freedoms that they had recently acquired and sought to codify.

While varied and often contradictory in their claims, Enlightenment philosophers essentially agreed that it was in man's nature to be rational and were optimistic about the potential for human reason to instigate worldly improvements. The seventeenth-century founder of liberalism, John Locke, wrote in 1689 that the natural state of men is 'a perfect freedom to order their actions [...] without asking leave, or depending upon the will of any other man' (2003, p. 101). Locke and other Enlightenment figures possessed a strong belief in the relationship between human reason and the perfectibility of man and society. Jean-Jacques Rousseau idealized fictional characters like Robinson Crusoe, individuals possessing the capacity to overcome adversity through the strength of will and ingenuity. However, it was Immanuel Kant who introduced the notion of the 'subject' as a 'universal aspect of human consciousness and conscience' and from whom is drawn the identification of subjectivity with consciousness today (Balibar, 1994, p. 6). For Kant, human beings possess the capacity to rationally decide between right and wrong, take responsibility for those choices, and construct universal laws on this basis. Human beings are free only insofar as they live under laws which are an objectification of their own reason.

However, the very etymology of 'subjectivity' implies the *subjection* or submission of human beings to an authority, whether full or partial, legitimate or illegitimate, internal or external to the individual (Balibar, 1994, p. 8). Thus, the very word that Enlightenment thinkers used to articulate and justify human freedom contained within it a contradiction between subjugation and liberation. It is this struggle that represents the '*becoming*' of human freedom and which makes subjectivity itself so representative of the movement of history. Indeed, there is a persistent tension stretching throughout human history between being in possession of free will and the lived reality of being subjected to forces beyond one's control. When these forces appear insurmountable, the subject emerges in emaciated form. This tension looms larger historically as fate appears to recede into new possibilities (and dangers) for human action.

It was from traditions ignited largely during the Enlightenment that the modern world took its view of human subjects as free-willing, conscious agents capable of making choices and taking responsibility for their actions. All too often, this conceptualization was rooted in a static and exclusive view of human nature that served to justify the existing order. But the fluid nature of the modern world, so well described by Marx and Engels with their phrase, 'all that is solid melts into air' (Berman, 1982, p. 21), meant that subjectivity became increasingly historicized, rendered dynamic and thrown open. In its most radical forms, it came to encompass a notion of the conscious human subject with a potential not simply to respond to but also control the forces of history.

Fate, freedom and subjectivity

Throughout at least western philosophers' attempts to make sense of the relationship between the individual and the world, there is a perceptible tension between stasis and dynamics, between rest and movement, being and becoming. As I noted at the outset of this chapter, towards the present, there is a perceptible desire for stasis. These tensions are conditioned by the real possibilities of our times. For much of human history, a static conceptualization of subjectivity prevailed. As Malik (1996, p. 43) writes, 'The pre-Enlightenment view of the world was characterized by its irrational premises, static nature and parochial scope. Man's relation was fixed to God and to nature.' Social divisions were seen as natural and people subservient to fate.

Yet paradoxically, it is precisely these tensions that reveal the openness of the human subject. For instance, in G. W. F. Hegel's *Lectures on the Philosophy of Religion*, he describes the role of fate in ancient Greece as something that stood 'above all', so powerful that even the gods were subject to it (Hegel, 1988, p. 339). Nonetheless, Hegel thought, the Greeks did possess some freedom in their wilful submission to fate. In this submission, while they undoubtedly felt deep sorrow and grief when things did not go as they had hoped, they could not be dissatisfied. This is because dissatisfaction, for Hegel, is what results when there is a mismatch between what one desires and what is. And fate, for the Greeks, is simply the world as it is. Thus, they are able to achieve inner peace by telling themselves, 'there is nothing to be done about it; I must be content with it' (p. 340). They withdraw into 'pure being, pure rest' (p. 340). In this way, Hegel alluded, the ancient mind is fundamentally different from that of the modern; the former experiences peace in submitting to fate which is inescapable, whereas the latter experiences 'vexation' (p. 340) at disharmony between what is and what ought to be.

However, these differences are not simply confined to the realm of subjectivity and ideas. People really were thrown about by forces beyond their control – disasters, famines and plagues all characterized the reality of pre-modern life. This subjection to fate on the part of the Greeks is reflected in the view of happiness presented in Herodotus's *Histories*, written in the fifth century BC. Herodotus narrates the poet Solon's visit to King Croesus, whom Herodotus describes as being at the height of his prosperity and power. Croesus shows Solon his riches and after seeing them all, asks the poet,

> Stranger of Athens, we have heard much of thy wisdom and of thy travels through many lands, from love of knowledge and a wish to see the world. I am curious therefore to inquire of thee, whom, of all the men thou hast seen, thou deemest the most happy?
>
> (Herodotus, 2013, p. 12)

Solon proceeds to tell him two stories of men he deemed happiest, men who had lived fortunate lives followed by noble deaths. He finishes by telling Croesus that no man can truly be happy so long as he lives: 'Call him [...] until he die, not happy but fortunate' (p. 14). Indeed, several times Croesus is confronted with the inability to cheat fate which, in spite of his riches, brings him to calamity. Fate, Solon had told him, can bring people great fortune followed by immense sorrow. Happiness can only be judged from the point where one can nobly accept his fate.

While Aristotle ultimately disagrees with this conceptualization of happiness,[4] for him, human beings and their relationship to nature remain somewhat bounded. For Aristotle, everything from objects to humans has a certain essence or defining form. Just as a seed contains the potentiality of the tree it will become, or a lump of marble a statue, so too with human beings. Form is brought into actuality through a process of change towards a potentiality that exists within that thing, a *telos*, which for humans is contemplation or politics (Lloyd, 1968). One's move from *is* to *ought* is the becoming of a good or excellent version of the kind of thing one is. For human beings and society, this move is the realization of *eudaimonia*, or a life lived in accordance with virtue. In other words, to live well is to live up to and in accordance with the best of a pre-determined essence. However, the achievement of *eudaimonia* is not entirely the result of virtuous activity but partially determined by factors beyond one's control like friends, a good birth, wealth and power (Engstrom & Whiting, 1996, p. 104). In this way, there remain strong elements of fate determining the possibilities of the subject, and the subject in turn appears more determined.

From the perspective pervasive of this era, 'we only act ethically when we act in fulfilment of our preordained purpose, in concert with our duty to our society and its subunits' (D. E. Hall, 2004, p. 8). The orientation of activity was not towards a transformative future because the future was not something that could be controlled.

However, modernity and its developing productive forces allowed a glimpse of a transformative future led by human action that had scarcely been available in previous eras. These new possibilities radically transformed conceptualizations of the relationship between human beings, nature and fate. Radical thinkers of the Enlightenment period began to envision a world of unending material and moral improvement with human beings at its centre. Like Aristotle, many *philosophes* of the Enlightenment era agreed that what differentiated human beings from animals was their capacity for reason – the ability to reflect on experience and rationally choose how to act. But unlike Aristotle, they lived in a world that could at least glimpse a potential for 'infinitely extensible' improvement (J. A. Passmore, 2000, p. 158). Modernity had overseen a gradual move from perfection as an absolute ideal towards an unlimited 'perfectibility'.

For the past two centuries, a belief has grown that it is possible to transform both human beings and society. Perhaps the most enthusiastic representative of this outlook during the eighteenth century was the Marquis de Condorcet, who wrote one of its most optimistic defences.[5] His *Sketch for a Historical Picture of the Progress of the Human Mind* (1796) consists of nine epochs through which the progress of human achievements has advanced followed by a tenth characterized by a bright and boundless future springing from human reason. He denies that there can be an *a priori* definition of a perfect human existence. Rather, 'the perfectibility of man is absolutely indefinite [...] [and]

has no other limit than the duration of the globe upon which nature has placed us' (p. 11). His conviction that we must study history to uncover 'obstacles' (p. 23) that have impeded the course of progress speaks to a sense that most of what holds humanity back is located in the past, and the future, he assures us, 'will be happy' (p. 22). Reason need only identify and overcome these impediments and humanity would be freed.

Condorcet praised the ancient Greeks for achieving a level of civilization scarcely paralleled thereafter but lamented its basis in slavery so that the objective of 'liberty and happiness' was shared with 'at most but half the human species' (1796, p. 78). Where others argued that liberties would only lead to vice, Condorcet contended that the 'progress of virtue has ever accompanied that of knowledge' (p. 81). Radical even for a *philosophe*, he argued that human rights be extended to all humanity, including women and other races. He spoke approvingly of those who had rallied the 'friends of mankind' with a cry of '*reason, toleration, and humanity*' (p. 198, emphasis in original).[6]

Where such ideals had not been fully realized, he pointed to social rather than natural impediments (albeit allowing for a residual basis of natural inequality which could not be eradicated).[7] On this he writes that while 'there frequently exists a considerable distinction between the rights which the law acknowledges in the citizens of a state, and those which they really enjoy; between the equality established by political institutions, and that which takes place between the individual members' (Condorcet, 1796, p. 259), these are rooted primarily in the unequal material conditions and education a society affords its members. In sum, Condorcet saw few limits to the course of human improvements and looked forward to a future of indefinite perfectibility.

Of course, there are obvious ways in which this vision went terribly wrong. But it is important for the moment to point out that almost as soon as these ideas were articulated they attracted criticism and even revulsion. Condorcet himself alludes to this at various places throughout the text. However, the most well-known criticism came four years after his death in Thomas Malthus's *Essay on the Principle of Population* (1798), which explicitly criticized Condorcet as well as similar ideas put forth by the anarchist thinker William Godwin. In sharp contrast to Condorcet, Malthus anchored human nature not in the mind but rather in the more animalistic needs for food and sex. It was these 'fixed laws of human nature' that lay to rest the question of whether 'man shall henceforth start forwards with accelerated velocity towards illimitable [...] improvement' (Malthus, 2013, p. 2). Famously, he posited that 'the power of population is indefinitely greater than the power in the earth to produce subsistence for man' (p. 10); the two foundational aspects of human nature together check the progress of humanity. 'Necessity, that imperious all pervading law of nature, restrains them within the prescribed bounds' (p. 11).

While Malthus thought the leisured classes could enjoy comforts, he was adamant that the lower orders must not. 'Man cannot live in the midst of plenty. All cannot share alike in the bounties of nature' (Malthus, 2013, p. 136). Man is not by nature rational and industrious but rather, 'inert, sluggish, and averse from labour, unless compelled by necessity' (p. 283). Thus not only was inequality a fact of human existence, but it was also a preferable state of affairs since suffering encourages hard work and passions that lead to 'intellectual wants' and 'desire of knowledge' (p. 294). However, the sphere of influence for this knowledge, warns Malthus, lies not in the future but in the present. Against the forces of change, Malthus dug his heels in. 'Life is, generally speaking, a blessing independent of a future state' (p. 303).

Compare the language of Condorcet, replete with reference to 'indefinite', 'perfection', 'boundless', 'happiness', etc., to that of Malthus: 'impossibility', 'fixed laws of our nature', 'diminishes' 'redundant population', 'misery'.[8] For Malthus, freedom only leads to the basest instincts of our nature to outrun each other bringing society to ruin.

Condorcet's open subject was suited to the open future he perceived taking shape on the horizon whereas Malthus's eyes were fixed firmly on the present which he projected forward forever. Observers like Malthus heard such lofty claims of reason, equality, freedom and fraternity, but when they looked out into the world they saw a reality characterized by unreason, inequality, unfreedom and war. Against Condorcet's 'fanciful', 'imaginary' and 'amusing' future, Malthus posited the present as eternal and natural, the real 'facts' that matter. '[S]ince the world began, the causes of population and depopulation have probably been as constant as any of the laws of nature with which we are acquainted' (Malthus, 2013, p. 97). The problems of society are really just the problems of nature. And ever it shall be.

Dropping the subject

In this way, when confronted with a contradiction between present reality and high-minded ideals, those like Malthus naturalized the present state of affairs and used this as a justification for why it could not be changed. In this I want to make a similar argument regarding the death of subjectivity implied by contemporary therapeutic discourses as Malik (1996, p. 39) does in relation to the discourse of race. *It is not weak subjectivity that determines the structure of the present world, but the structure of the present world that leads to a conception of weak subjectivity.*

For Malik (1996), the ideal of universal equality came up against the reality of inequality, which demanded explanation. 'The difficulty in reconciling belief in the abstract principle of universality with the actual, concrete, particular expressions of humanity reveals one of the central problems of Western philosophy' (p. 265). 'As the intelligentsia grew increasingly apprehensive of social transformation it began to distance itself from the emancipatory logic of Enlightenment discourse' (p. 266). Rather than recognizing the limitations put on equality by the economic base of society, increasingly the answer came in the form of an eternalized human difference. It was something within the nature of human beings that accounted for social divisions. While beginning as a recognition of the particularity of human social life, it was gradually essentialized. The notion of the 'universal', or of a common human essence, became 'nature'. Recognition by those like Rousseau of human particularity (i.e. that in order to understand society, you must understand it as it is expressed in particular people and vice versa) degraded into the particularities of 'human difference'. This was biologized, he argues, in the discourse of race and culturalized in what German philosopher Johann Gottfried Herder called the *volksgeist* – or the unique spirit of a people.[9] The result was discourses of race and cultural difference that became eternal categories. While the stress on social and cultural specificity offered an important check on *philosophes'* tendency to eternalize and universalize their own cultures, it also fostered denial of a common human essence (p. 79). In the face of the particularity of the present, they dropped the universal human subject.

Similarly, as the discussion of Voltaire alludes to above, while rational activity, the ability to exercise one's reason and creativity in the world, might have been the ideal, it was not the reality for large portions of humanity who continued to live in physical and mental drudgery. What is more, reason did not seem to light the way to 'happiness' as Condorcet assumed, but created instead a soulless bureaucratic rationality. Condorcet's mathematical writings were criticized by Romantic literary critic Charles Augusten Sainte-Beuve who saw 'his vision of a life regulated by the certainty of predication [...] as a recipe for "universal mediocrity," in which there would be no place "for great virtues, for acts of heroism," a bright new world whose unfortunate citizens would all die of boredom' (Pagden, 2013, p. 2).

From a perspective that reached its apex in the Romantic movement, the Enlightenment had not unleashed reason as a path to freedom but precisely the opposite; it had released 'everything that conspired to deprive the autonomous individual of self-knowledge and self-control' (Pagden, 2013, p. 11). The early Romantics, as Pagden describes, 'some of whom had grown up in the shadow of the Enlightenment', were eager to replace its 'cold rationalism, soulless secularism, and bleak, rootless cosmopolitanism' with 'a vivid attachment to home, hearth and heart' (p. 12). For them, the Enlightenment had sacrificed humanity to the 'Empire of Reason' (p. 12). Moreover, its dissolution into The Terror seemed to prove right the most pessimistic visions of human nature.

Isaiah Berlin quotes the conservative Joseph de Maistre saying, 'Over all [the] numerous races of animals man is placed, and his destructive hand spares nothing that lives' (de Maistre, 1993, p. 137). Religious subjugation had been necessary to check humanity's basest instincts. And yet the entire trajectory of the Enlightenment had been the 'separation of man from God' (De Maistre, 1993, p. 148).

With the rising tide of critique that the Enlightenment had been the 'inversion of everything it had promised to be' it was not long before the 'excesses of the 19th century' too were laid at its feet (Pagden, 2013, p. 12). The hubris of the Enlightenment subject had nearly brought society more than once to ruin. Maybe all this time the problem was not the world, but humanity's persistent and misguided attempts to control it. From this perspective, not only was a society led by human reason not desirable, it was also not possible. However, not every critique would travel in this direction.

3

An Open Subject?

In the previous chapter, I sketched out the way in which the possibilities of a time period were reflected in the possibilities of the human subject. As the possibilities of society seemed more open, so too did human subjectivity. Both society and humanity were infinitely perfectible. Yet the real world did not bear this out, and doubts about the subject began to rise. In this chapter, I consider more optimistic visions that placed the causes of this inability of modern society to live up to its own ideals – to enshrine ideals of equality, reason, freedom and brotherhood while fraught by inequality, drudgery, unfreedom and war – in society rather than something innate within humanity itself.

Condorcet's inkling, described in the previous chapter, that the cause of the failure to realize fully Enlightenment ambitions and ideals lay in society rather than nature would be taken to its logical conclusions by Karl Marx. While Marx was undoubtedly a critic of some of the over-optimism of the *philosophes*, his criticism was very different from that of the Romantics and in many ways represents the last sigh of Condorcet's enthusiasm.

For Marx, while the society of his time was certainly freer than it had been in the past, it still contained a sense of 'fate', or of being thrown about by forces beyond one's control. As Berman (1982) summarized of this outlook, which he claims was also held by Nietzsche, Tocqueville, Carlyle, Mill and Kierkegaard:

[They] understood the ways in which modern technology and social organization determined man's fate. But they all believed that modern individuals had the capacity both to understand this fate and, once they understood it, to fight it. Hence, even in the midst of a wretched present, they could imagine an open future.

(p. 27)

It was Marx who arguably took these ideals furthest, beyond the society that, in his view, could not possibly realize them. Throughout his analysis of the capitalist system, most famously across three volumes of *Capital*, he does not locate the origins of its problems within mistakes in public policy, nor human greed, nor human weakness at all. Instead, he takes for granted the rational human subject that had animated the liberal Enlightenment imagination, albeit in a thoroughly historicized form. Marx was scathing of those who sought to root and explain society by appealing to abstract notions of 'human nature' set outside of it. Man is 'no abstract being squatting outside the world. Man is *the world of man*, the state, society' (Marx, 1994, p. 57 emphasis in original). As Screpanti (2007, p. 12) sums up, 'Man is neither good nor evil in nature because man does not live in nature'; there is no such thing as a fully developed human being wandering about outside society.

What differentiates human beings from animals is their relationship to nature, which is characterized by conscious activity and transformation. Marx and Engels (1998a) write:

> While human beings can be distinguished from animals by consciousness, by religion or anything else you like. They themselves begin to distinguish themselves from animals as soon as they begin to produce their means of subsistence.

(p. 37)

As Marx famously put it elsewhere, what differentiates human beings from the 'best of bees' is that the 'architect builds the cell in his mind before he constructs it in wax' (1976, p. 284). Human beings objectify their creativity with and in the material world around them. 'Man not only effects a change of form in the materials of nature; he also realizes [...] his own purpose in those materials. And this is a purpose he is conscious of [...]' (p. 284). While spiders and bees may make beautiful things, they are more or less the same across individuals and time. However, the work of a human being is conscious and capable of being carried out according to a plan which, while produced as a result of being a member of society, is nonetheless capable of being wholly different from that of society's other members.

What is more, the work they carry out changes what they are as human beings. When 'developing their material production and their material intercourse', human beings also alter 'their actual world, [...] their thinking and the products of their thinking' (Marx & Engels, 1998a, p. 42). In this way, as Screpanti (2007) puts it,

> Human "nature", for Marx and Engels, is plastic, i.e. strongly influenced by the economic, social and cultural context in which man is historically

placed; but it is self-poietic too, in that the economic, social and cultural contexts are in turn determined by human actions. According to them the transition to a better mode of social organization such as communism would contribute to liberate men [...].

(p. 12)

The nature of human beings is to create their own nature. Revolution would, for the first time, make this an entirely conscious project.

In his early years, Marx had been a member of the Young Hegelians, a group of followers who took Hegel's ideas in radical directions after his death. One of these was replacing Hegel's mystical notion of 'Spirit' as the subject of history with 'man' (Knowles, 2002, p. 19). They were inspired by the French Revolution and even compared themselves to the 'Encyclopaedists', the Enlightenment *philosophes* (McLellan, 1969, p. 34). However, they grew to consider that 'the liberals had [...] abandoned the course of freedom' which necessitated an alternative (McLellan, 1969, p. 34). If Marx had at all doubted this abandonment, he was utterly convinced of it by the 1850s when he observed liberal society collapse into authoritarianism following the failed revolutions of 1848. In a speech given in 1856, he told attendees that these events had revealed that beneath all the promises of history having reached its end, they only served imperfectly to hide the 'abyss' that lurked beneath its crumbling crust (Marx, 2019, p. 633).

While the previous century's French Revolution may have opened up possibilities for new freedoms, human beings were not yet fully free because they remained alienated (separated) from their conscious ends. This is because, in capitalism, man's conscious activity is split up; his ends are pursued indirectly via commodity production which, while needing to produce useful things, produces these not for their usefulness but for the end of profit accumulation (though he is keen to stress, it should be noted, the progressive side of this process in that it provides a foundation for a 'higher form' of society).[1] In the famous introduction to his *Critique of Hegel's Philosophy of Right* (Marx, 1994), Marx describes how religious vestiges nonetheless remain in rational, modern society because, religion 'is the fantastic realization of the human essence since the human essence has not acquired any true reality' (p. 57). It remains alive not because of some innate inclination towards religiosity but because human beings still inhabit a world that requires such comforting illusions. Thus, perceiving the 'abyss' that separates the present from the future, he urged readers to cross it and 'pluck the living flower' (p. 58).

If human beings can use reason to understand the forces of history, he thought, they can control them. They can do this because they are both the subjects and objects of revolutionary processes. History itself had produced new subjects in the present and would continue to do so in the future. That is, humanity, and workers specifically, had made the world and were products of it. As he continued in his 1856 speech, 'We know that to work well the new-fangled forces of [present] society, they only want to be mastered by new-fangled men – and such are the working men. They are as much the invention of modern time as machinery itself' (Marx, 2019, p. 634).

Across their work, Marx and Engels also expressed a particular distaste not only for naturalization of the social order but also for what they often called 'shallow moralizing', instead attempting to base their critiques in scientific reasoning. While the success of this endeavour is open to question, it is a testament to the depth of their commitment to the use of human reason to light the path towards the future whose first steps were already visible in the present. Even amid the wretched present, Marx and Engels placed their hope in the human subject.

Take for instance Marx's remark in his notebooks that 'Monetary greed, or mania for wealth, necessarily brings with it the decline and fall of ancient communities' (1973, p. 222). It is easy to misread this as an observation regarding ethics[2] or simple human frailty, that civilizational decline is wrought by a defect within ancient minds and morals. However, the point is quite the opposite. '[G]reed itself is the product of a definite historical development, not *natural* as opposed to *historical*' (p. 222). For Marx, greed arises from the historical emergence of money as the representative of wealth. While hunger for commodities can be sated (there is only so much bread one can eat), money contains within it the potentiality of all pleasures. Thus, two forms of greed emerge: hedonism, the desire to possess this potentiality, and miserliness, a desire not to negate it by turning it back into something particular (i.e. spending it). In this way, the emergence of money as the representative of wealth makes it possible for it to become alienated from productive activity where the former is pursued at the expense of the latter. 'Hence the wailing of the ancients about money as the source of all evil' (p. 222). However, this problem cannot be fixed by a course of moral improvement. The pursuit of wealth's representative over and above real wealth, that is, productive activity, is an irrational outcome of rational behaviour. Indeed, within the capitalist system, what had been embryonic for the ancients emerges full-fledged – one's survival as a capitalist depends upon it.[3] In other words, there may be a problem, but the problem does not arise out of the human head but rather from the particular social organization of the time.

This draws forth one further aspect of Marx's understanding of subjectivity and its role in forging the path to the future that will be of subsequent importance: his appraisal of the critiques that the Romantic movement had launched at capitalism and modernity. This critique laments aspects of capitalism such as its sterile quantification and longs instead for an emphasis on virtue and sentiments, often looking back to an imagined and idealized past in which its allegedly dehumanizing elements had not yet emerged (Löwy & Sayre, 2002).[4] In response to this outlook, Marx wrote:

> In earlier stages of development the single individual seems to be developed more fully, because he has not yet worked out his relationships in their fullness, or erected them as independent social powers and relations opposite himself. It is as ridiculous to yearn for a return to that original fullness as it is to believe that with this complete emptiness history has come to a standstill.
>
> (1973, p. 162)

While Marx appreciated romantic literature and tropes and often drew on them himself, he warned of the weaknesses 'of criticism which knows how to judge and condemn the present, but not how to comprehend it' (1976, p. 638). In other words, while he saw a role for feeling and sensation in recognizing that something amiss is 'weighing' upon the living, he distrusted the elevation of emotion over reason.

This is evident in his discussion of the way that capitalists themselves often feel this weight. Marx describes how the capitalist acts as 'capital personified' whose 'motivating force is not the acquisition and enjoyment of use-values, but the acquisition and augmentation of exchange values' (1976, p. 739). He is compelled by external laws[5] to continue expanding his capital to preserve his existence as a capitalist. As a mere 'function of capital', his 'own private consumption counts as a robbery committed against [its] accumulation' (p. 739). However, as capitalism develops, a certain amount of expenditure upon luxury becomes necessary, for instance, in the securing of additional credit. It is no longer a threat to and may even help drive accumulation.

The capitalist, formerly an ascetic, begins to be drawn towards 'sin' (1976, p. 740) – he wants to enjoy and consume some of his riches and is even able to look back on his miserly past as quaint. Yet, Marx points out, he is never fully able to enjoy his profligacy. It 'has always lurking behind it the most sordid avarice and the most anxious calculation' (p. 741), even though capitalism has developed to a point where it is more able to accommodate both. For the miser, pleasure was a distraction from accumulation, for the modern capitalist, accumulation (while it enables it) is a mere distraction from pleasure (Berman, 1999), or to put it in more romantic terms, 'what really matters in life'. He begins to eschew mere money and searches for meaning and enjoyment.

However, as Berman describes, this nascent desire for freedom and happiness quickly turns in on itself, is devoured, assimilated and turned to the capitalist's own advantage (1999, p. 52). 'Where pleasure becomes a business, it must acquire up-to-date business methods – that is, must duplicate all the compulsive calculation, all the cutthroat competition, all the frenzied self-alienation it was meant to allay' (p. 52). Thus, all the obsessions and necessities of capitalist society – to extend the working day, to push wages as far down as workers will accept – are 're-enacted beneath a façade of idyllic calm' (p. 52). Hence that Marx called the romantic outlook capitalism's 'legitimate antithesis', its space of acceptable condemnation, because it is easily absorbed, does not threaten capitalist society, and will instead 'accompany it [...] up to its blessed end' (1973, p. 162).

In these ways, Marx had not only an open vision of the future but an open vision of the subject capable of building the bridge to get there but only through a rational understanding of the task before it. There is no escape through emotion alone. An open conceptualization of subjectivity was necessary because, as Marx understood, if society is an outgrowth of human nature, then there is no point attempting to change it. Yet previous revolutions (political as well as industrial) had done much to wash away former ways of life and with them their representatives of human nature. Human beings had rebuilt entirely new ones on their old foundations and would continue to do so.

It might be said that there are many similarities between Aristotle's *eudaimonia* and Marx's conceptualization of 'species-being', or a being that realizes itself through conscious activity (Marx & Engels, 2009, p. 76). However, for Marx, this is not the end goal of individual nor civil life. He argues that human beings remain, in the past as well as the present, engaged in the 'creation of the conditions of their social life' and 'have not yet begun, on the basis of these conditions to live it' (1973, p. 162). For Marx, 'only a conscious political revolution, with its eyes fixed on the future, could make men fully free' (Mazlish, 1972, p. 337). Where modern interpreters of Aristotle stress that eudaimonia is the end and not a means, and wealth, if at all necessary, is simply a means to get there (Bruni, 2006, p. 19), Marx thought production 'for its own sake means nothing but the development of human productive forces, in other words, the *development of the richness of human nature as an end in itself*' (Marx, 1969, pp. 117–18 emphasis in original). All history in which human beings had produced indirectly, *been moved about by forces beyond their control*, is merely 'prehistory'. Human beings, at last able to objectify their consciousness directly, begin an open future. With this possibility, history does not end. History begins.

But history did not begin.

A difficult subject

It is this 'problem of the self' (Rose, 1999, p. xvi), or a more dynamic consideration of human nature and the shaping of human subjects, that was a key animating force of classical sociological thought. In the twentieth century, 'almost every serious social thinker who reflected on their present found themselves having to address the relations between social arrangements and the types of human being who inhabited them' (Rose, 1999, p. xvi). For C. Wright Mills (2000 [1959]), grasping the contingency of human nature was central to the sociological imagination and was part of the brilliance of much early social scientific thought from Marx to Mannheim. The best social thinkers had endeavoured to ask not what aspect of human nature underlies a given problem, but what varieties of human beings are brought into existence by an ensemble of relations, epoch, discourse or social transformation? Yet Mills's summation of these insights hints at the pessimistic turn that apprehension of the contingencies of human nature had taken in the twentieth century. In our time, he writes, we have come to realize that the limits of human nature are 'frighteningly broad' (2000, p. 6). In other words, open subjectivity had led to the destructive belief that, as Hannah Arendt argued of the outlook that characterized totalitarianism, 'everything is possible', or the notion that 'everything that exists is merely a temporary obstacle that superior organization will certainly destroy' (1973, p. 387).

Instead of history beginning, the twentieth century was heralded, famously, as its end (Fukuyama, 1989). The authoritarianism into which the USSR degenerated before dissipating, the Great Depression, two world wars and the Holocaust – all stark warnings about what happens when human hands attempt to, as Marx put it, 'make their own history' (2008, p. 15) in the full light of reason. Condorcet's optimism is now seen as paradigmatic of colonialism's 'civilizing missions'. The Enlightenment faith in progress, reflected in the Marxian hope of transcendence of the present and triumph of human reason in a radically new society built on its basis, seems perilously naive.

Twentieth-century intellectual movements looked to the 'Subject of absolute self-creation' as the root of fascism (Lacoue-Labarthe in Heartfield, 2006, p. 19). Humanism had led to its opposite because it had disastrously depicted man as the centre and substance of history; too often that 'man' was a white European (Heartfield, 2006, pp. 19–20). The problem was not simply that subjectivity was conceived too narrowly, but rather that 'subjectivity itself could be intrinsically domineering and exclusive' (p. 20). Where conservative thinkers had been keen to denigrate optimistic views of humanity, even progressive thinkers began to question, 'whether Man was indeed the central figure of the human story, and whether he deserved to be' (p. 21).

A final representative anecdote is illustrative here in the form of the late nineteenth/early twentieth-century economist and sociologist, Vilfredo Pareto. While Pareto was writing before the above trends, he perhaps best exemplifies the psychologized path such doubts would take towards the present. He illustrates well the apparent exasperation that results from observing the ideal of a rational order on the one hand and its apparent failure to exist on the other. Pareto had trained as an engineer and developed complex mathematical equations of capitalism in equilibrium drawing on the physical sciences. From this perspective, market distortions can only occur from the outside – from the realities of human society and individual behaviour. While Pareto was aware that his mathematical assumptions did not exist in reality, it is difficult not to imagine him comparing his perfectly functioning machine, guided as if by an invisible hand, to the reality of human society and government that increasingly diverged from it. The disappointment apparent in his social theory is profound. Pareto harboured deep doubts about human rationality, focusing instead on 'derivations' or sentiments rationalized after the fact (Lyttelton, 1973, p. 19). It is perhaps telling that later in life, he abandoned economics to develop his social theory – a theory which tended to explain social facts in terms of their psychological and biological bases and 'sentiments' (Lyttelton, 1973; Mirowski, 2003, p. 121). Tellingly, he had been an early supporter of Benito Mussolini and wrote offering the latter guidance. While Pareto's support would later wane, his effect on Fascism remained palpable, if only in its 'powerful strain' of 'exasperated and disillusioned liberalism' (Lyttelton, 1973, p. 18).

Yet if Pareto remained a liberal in some respects, it was a liberalism that was decidedly economic rather political. While he was greatly enamoured with at least the language and methods of science, he was a staunch critic of both socialism and democracy, based as they were on a rational human subject that was illusory. The liberal utopia of free trade and free enterprise never came to fruition, Pareto thought, because its defenders were too afraid to use force (Lyttelton, 1973). Justice and coercion were necessary for society to subsist. The notion that man's ends were of his own free will and making was regarded as a dangerous illusion that would only bring society to ruin.

Henryk Grossman (2015 [1941]) criticized Pareto for failing to deal adequately with dynamics in the capitalist system focusing instead on a conceptualization of reality as a system of 'continuous oscillations around a central point of equilibrium' analogous to Lagrangian equations in mechanics (ch. 5). For Pareto, the 'system tends to re-establish itself, to return to its original position' (Pareto in H. Grossman, 2015, ch. 5), an assumption that comes less from reality than from his chosen mathematical metaphors. 'Pareto employs the concepts of "statics" and "tendency to equilibrium" without investigating whether they make sense in economics', Grossman argues (ch. 5). His social theory was also decidedly cyclic rather than progressive, a revolution of elites and those close enough to usurp them. Again, there is a tension between stasis and dynamism, harmony and the destabilizing forces of movement and a deep desire to dig one's heels in. Pareto preferred the static perfection of a model over the tumultuous dynamism of reality. Faced with the unreality of his models and the reality of human subjects who did not act the way they 'should', Pareto dropped the rational human subject. In a manner that echoes our present moment, the awe at science remains, but the subject who wielded it is gone.

The (diminished) subject is all there is

It is interesting to note that contemporary emotion management is frequently traced precisely to the Enlightenment and its emphasis on the rational, free-willing and self-governing subject. For instance, Burnett (2012) attributes the rise of public and policy interest in 'happiness' in recent decades to modern 'myths' of individualism, humanism, instrumentalism and rationalism, which he roots in Enlightenment demands for happiness through reasoned, calculated and political means.[6] Rationalization of emotion is seen to represent the continuation or at least rediscovery of Enlightenment emphases on instrumental reason, independence and responsibility, which create a vision of life primarily under individual control (Cabanas & Sanchez-González, 2012, p. 172).

From these perspectives, liberal, or reactivated 'neoliberal' modes of understanding the relationship between individuals and governing institutions, which stress the importance of self-organizing principles, create continuous demand for technologies of individual self-governance, often to shore up against proliferating uncertainties (Binkley, 2011, 2014; Cabanas, 2018; Cabanas & Illouz, 2019; B. Evans & Reid, 2013, 2014; Rose, 1999). While varying in their theoretical inspiration (and tendency towards optimism, pessimism or ambivalence), many such approaches draw on Foucauldian notions of 'governmentality', or techniques facilitating the exercise of power over populations, largely through autonomizing and responsibilizing projects of the self (Foucault, 2008 cited in Rose, 1999, p. 5). Numerous analyses have thus seen more explicit attempts at emotion management, for instance through resilience, happiness and well-being promotion, as implicitly encouraging adoption of subjectivities congruent with the needs and operations of neoliberal governance (Binkley, 2011, 2014, 2016; De La Fabián & Stecher, 2017; C. Wright, 2013). Thus, happiness interventions in China and Greece, for instance, have been understood as attempts to inculcate neoliberal values like individualism and entrepreneurship, becoming a pacifying rhetoric of adaptation to existing circumstances (Mentinis, 2013; Yang, 2013). From this perspective, emotion management represents a continuation or renewal of liberal visions of minimal government, attempting to create ideal, self-governing neoliberal subjects who will accept and adapt to uncertainty and not call upon expensive state, employer or other supports.

These approaches capture important facets of the rise of emotions as the causes of and solutions to social problems. Emotion management does embody a contradiction whereby escape from the iron cage of bureaucratic rationality through emotional re-enchantment of everyday life is attempted precisely *through* (and thus collapses back into) rationalization and endless measurement of emotion (Sugarman, 2007). Freedom and meaning of life are indeed presented to individuals as projects of the self, with the self representing the limits of one's sphere of influence (and even then, only to a limited extent). The internal world of the self, under the careful management of experts and expertise, becomes the site of individual and social goals.

However, there is a tendency within some critique to assume that the Enlightenment subject is simply being reactivated. But as I have tried to show in this and the previous chapter, these discourses reflect not so much a reactivated faith in a self-governing subject than a persistent disbelief in the capacities of the vast majority of humanity to enact such a form of subjectivity. There is also a tendency not to question *why* the subject has become the object of so much attention. Why do such ideal subjects need to be 'built' in the first place?

Foucault himself warns that late liberal or what he terms 'neo-liberal' discourses are not simply a rehashing of old forms of liberal economics nor its vision of *homo oeconomicus* (Foucault, 2008, pp. 130, 147). Instead, the subject has been transformed in important ways. As Chandler (2014) and Chandler and Reid (2016b) argue on the basis of studies of the idiom of 'resilience' in international development, not only do contemporary regimes of governance not create self-governing subjects, they expressly seek to destroy any illusion that uninitiated subjects harbour any such capacities.

> In spite of its claims to make humans more adept and capable in their dealings with the world, the promotion of resilience requires and calls forth a much degraded subject, one defined by much diminished capabilities for autonomy and agency, so crucial to the formation of human subjectivity.
>
> (Chandler & Reid, 2016b, p. 1)

What is posited in its place is a considerably emaciated version of what had been forwarded in the most optimistic liberal visions.[7]

Considering the subject of resilience discourses sheds considerable light on the visions of subjectivity portrayed in problematized apparently positive emotions, particularly as the first step in claims-making is not usually the identification of a clearly defined problem but rather the identification of a new area of life as the legitimate domain of expertise, as subject to lay error and in need of expert fixing. Subjects are not initially propped up, they are expressly put down. Chandler refers to such discursive formations as 'postliberal' rather than 'neoliberal' (although there is some variation across publications) to highlight a 'shrinking world', the 'end of the liberal problematic and the final stage of the Enlightenment project which gave birth to the human subject' (Chandler, 2013, p. 8). In this vision of subjectivity, 'There is no teleology of progress as an external measure of growth in human well-being, there is no universalist framing and there is no longer the understanding of the liberal subject – as either a rights – or an interest-bearing rational and autonomous actor' (Chandler, 2016a, p. 89).

In contemporary regimes of governance, the Enlightenment subject of someone like Condorcet, who looked out on the world and bent it to its will, has gone. Indeed, it is often positioned as the very problem for which therapeutic interventions are needed (Frawley, 2020c). The 'civilizing missions' inspired by those like Condorcet are remnants of a damaging past for which a new 'development as freedom', championed by Indian economist Amartya Sen, is positioned as the anecdote (Omar, 2012). Sen's work has been influential on dominant understandings of development, for instance in the United Nations Development Programme (UNDP), and is greeted as an emancipation from liberal modernity's allegedly narrow concerns with economic growth (Chandler, 2013). While initially powerful in the international arena, these discourses have long since been 'brought home' (Frawley, 2015c).

The 'freedom' championed in the regimes of governance represented by these outlooks differs from that of its liberal forebears in important ways. Foucault (2008) describes how the free-willing subject was naturalized in early liberalism as a means of contesting the imposition of the will of the sovereign. Adam Smith's famous 'invisible hand' acted as a means not only of saying that kings should not intervene, but that they could not. No single overarching power could have access to the information that individuals enacted when they pursued their own self-interest. Human beings were 'island[s] of rationality' within an uncontrollable economic process (p. 282). This was a powerful subject that emerged as it freed itself from an old bond.

However, the problems apparent in this economic system, once taken for granted in liberal political economy, soon came to be seen as insurmountable before being denied and externalized. Monopoly for instance had long been accepted as an inevitable problem endemic to the functioning of capitalism, even by liberals. However, neoliberals of the twentieth century soon began to place its origins outside of a properly functioning market, in the governments and institutions surrounding it (Foucault, 2008). This externalization extended the purview of governance beyond the market, which was seen as possessing an internally coherent logic, if an external fragility. Like Pareto, they began to see the market as something too perfect for mere humans; their role as regulators was not over market activity, but of the activities and behaviours of the humans and (all too) human institutions surrounding it.

From this perspective, now pervasive of governance, self-reliance is not the goal, but is explicitly problematized and connected to a wider network of social problems. Far from creating ideal, rational, self-governing subjects who do not need the enlightened sovereign to guide their will, subjects must be expressly warned away from autonomy, itself positioned as a threat for which discourses of emotion management ostensibly offer protection (Chandler & Reid, 2016a). The goal instead is what I would term, following Berman (1999, p. 44), 'heteronomy' – a will conditioned by external forces that encourage the 'correct' outlook on life and deter the making of 'wrong' choices. Like Smith's subject, Marx's subject was in the process of freeing itself from old bonds and had a world of new freedoms at its feet. In both conceptualizations, the subject appears considerably more robust.

Yet now, in the face of seemingly diminishing possibilities, instead of rationality, the subject is characterized by, for example, 'information weakness'. Far from assuming the rational decision-making *homo oeconomicus*, the inner world of the subject is problematized and situated within a context of 'superstition, culture, ethics' which introduce irrationality into decision-making, revealing the liberal faith in a 'reasonably well-informed' public as misplaced (Chandler, 2016a, p. 83). Recognition of social context resolves into a focus on how social and cultural context introduce irrationality into decision-making. Irrational outcomes of the market are no longer understood in terms of capitalist social relations, but rather as resulting from barriers to adaptive efficiency erected by human differences.

In this way, when problems arise, investigations cannot begin with the system but rather with identifying inducements to making the 'wrong choice'. As Chandler (2016a) continues:

> The logic of the argument is that social and economic problems are the result of poor adaptive capacities or poor choice-making, especially by young people who lack the adaptive capacities for good choice-making. Development no longer takes the form of economic and social transformation but of capability-building; empowering the poor and the marginal to make better choices and thereby to become more resilient to external threats and pressures [...].
>
> (p. 94)

Freedom then does not emerge from a simple exercise in removing barriers. This is why claims-makers and policymakers are so keen to turn their attention not only to what could go wrong, but also in making things 'go right'. Freedom is 'empowerment' to make 'correct' choices. What might have been considered foundational to the liberal subject, that once freed (e.g. from despotism, etc.) human beings would be able to live in accordance with reason, is now denaturalized (though, as previously footnoted, this possibility was always implicit within it). Policymaking does not assume that freedom is all that is required for a rational autonomous subject. Instead, 'freedom is the ongoing process of empowering the individual' which is to be measured not in external outputs 'but internal processes of valuation and decision-making'

(Chandler, 2016a, p. 92). *The subject has become the object*. In his discussion of the manifestations of these phenomena in Sen's 'development as freedom', Chandler writes:

> There is no goal beyond the human subject and no agent beyond the human subject and no measurement beyond the human subject. But the human subject does not set goals; the human subject has no agency and no measuring capacity itself. In adaptive capability-building the subject is denied its own capability as a subject. The human subject is the end to be achieved, through the process of development, justice, democracy and so forth – the project of humanizing is the human.
>
> (p. 93)

In this way, postliberal discourses are not about enabling the capacity to choose how to live. Echoing the Hobbesian outlook, it is not one's exercise of freedoms but the right to life that is considered foundational. Autonomy is not the enabler or end point, but actually a 'threat to life' (Chandler & Reid, 2016a, p. 1). One is enjoined to 'live dangerously' in the sense of accepting a world of dangers and risks, but never to act in dangerous ways. As Evans and Reid argue, postliberal governance equips the subject 'only ever to adapt to a world outside its control' (2014, p. 203).

Thus, outer yardsticks of progress are turned inward. Therapeutic discourses tend to downplay the role of material advancement in human fulfilment. Foucault noted already in the late 1970s that the goal was not to create the ideal consumer. My previous study of happiness detailed the strong desire for claims-makers to recast progress in subjective as opposed to material terms (Frawley, 2015c). The project of progress has become an internal rather than external one. How do we make subjects content to 'stay quietly in one room'?

It is a naturally 'inclusive' project because there is nothing outside of it, Chandler says (2016a, p. 87). Enlightenment positivism lives on in the positive need to fill alleged information gaps. But it bears the unmistakeable marks of the triumph of its most doubtful aspects and exponents. It is a thoroughly naturalized science that is not about creating something new outside and beyond the subject. It is about the unending project of discovering innate incapacities and vulnerabilities, the management of which humanity had variously grasped but from which they have been led astray as in, for example, estrangement from religious practice, or which new professional discourses can help alleviate. The remaining chapters of this book explore this outlook in action within therapeutic discourses of happiness, well-being, mindfulness and mental health.

What these projects reveal is a deep-rooted certainty that there is something very wrong with the human subject. Subjects must first be convinced of their incapacity because the progenitors of these postliberal discourses are themselves convinced that it is some failure and defect within subjectivity that is responsible when things go wrong. Indeed, lack of awareness of this and continued ill-advised self-reliance can quickly lead to things 'spiralling out of control'.

This oversight in current understandings of therapeutic cultures which root the outlook in a simple rehashing of Enlightenment ideals of autonomy and self-government therefore risks deepening the malaise. While attacks on the modern, 'neoliberal' subject through celebrating more romantic portrayals based in, for instance the recognition of vulnerability (e.g. Fineman, 2010, 2015), show up the exclusions often implied by liberal visions, they are also inflected by suspicion of human potential to transform the world through the exercise of reason. The problem wasn't that liberal thinkers espoused ideals of rational subjectivity that were too narrow and exclusive; it's that they possessed such illusions at all. As Ecclestone argues (2017, p. 59), the result has been that both governance and the critique of governance have taken an emotional turn. This is particularly apparent in mindfulness discourses (Chapters 5 and 6), wherein some critics have balked at the commercialization of mindfulness, positing instead what they see as a fuller 'civic or social mindfulness' (R. Purser E. et al., 2016, p. x). In this orientation, mindfulness practice is redirected towards developing critical awareness of institutions and processes that engender social suffering. However, the starting point for solving the intractable problems of our times is not struggling toward rational understanding (and bringing others over to that understanding), but more non-specific projects in empathy or awareness raising. The logic is, 'First we must promote X before Y can ever be achieved' where X is a reconfigured and corrected emotional outlook and Y is solving some intractable problem. The assumption remains that there is some block within the human subject rather than that block existing outside in the world that subjects inhabit. The start and end points remain at the level of attitude and behaviour; the sphere of influence of the human subject remains narrowly embodied.

Conclusion

My intention is not to posit the rational subject as 'real' and other conceptualizations mythic. Rather, subjectivity is fluid and responsive to the unevenly experienced possibilities of our times. The 'demotion' of the rational human subject has not simply been mistaken. Instead, it has come up against limits. Whether these limits are exterior or interior, temporary or eternal, have been the abiding questions. As Heartfield (2006, p. 100) argues, commentators since the Enlightenment had become 'increasingly troubled by the widening gap between the theoretical Subject and the reality'. For some, this brought forth the possibility and need to transcend the gap. For others, it showed up the natural limits beyond which human beings must not trespass and the need to develop new ways to live within it. The persistent inability to transcend what were conceptualized as external limits means that this gap has been increasingly naturalized and explained away as all but inevitable – a void intrinsic to human existence and reflective of human weakness. Compounded by the experiences of the twentieth century, it is reflected in a pervasive pessimism about both human subjectivity and the movement of history as a necessarily destabilizing force.

What remains is the subject that learns to accept the abyss and live comfortably within it. It is this positing of the subject as the problem of our times and its solution its own emotional containment that lies at the heart of the problematization of emotion. It is why even positive outlooks must be inculcated and positive emotional signifiers filled with the correct emotional contents. Whereas focusing on problems implied the ability of the subject to 'get on with it' once the barrier had been removed, the notion that intervention is also needed for things to go well, even in the absence of problems, betrays profound doubts about subjects left to their own devices. The result is to say that if there is some failure to live up to our goals, the impediment is not out there in society but in subjects themselves.

4

Waves of Emotion

Introduction

In the 1980s and 1990s, self-esteem was promoted as a 'social vaccine' (Hewitt, 1998, p. 59) capable of preventing a wide variety of personal and social problems. It had spawned a global industry of books, training programmes, audio tapes and educational curricula. Policymakers widely affirmed the importance of self-esteem and its role in the causes and solutions to social problems and social movements sprang up dedicated to spreading its influence (p. 68). In his (2007 [1995]) book *The Optimistic Child*, psychologist and later founder of 'Positive Psychology', Martin Seligman, criticized the growth of self-esteem as an all-purpose explanatory model for almost any social problem, calling it 'self-contradictory' and 'puffery' (p. 28). Within a decade, he had published *Authentic Happiness* (2002), promoting a new discourse making similarly expansive claims. There, Seligman compared the preventive power of teaching positive emotions to the discovery of handwashing and immunizations for physical diseases (2002, p. 26) – a 'social vaccine', if you will. Happiness soon spawned an industry of self-help books, training programmes, audio guides and educational curricula.

As self-esteem was questioned as a social problem panacea, happiness emerged as a powerful new discourse that performed very similar functions. Later chapters explore the rise of mindfulness and mental health promotion, about which similar claims were made regarding their preventative power and role in the causes and solutions to social problems. In short, there are strong parallels across therapeutic vocabularies in terms of advocacy, rhetoric and marked tendencies to rise, expand and give way to new vocabularies which nonetheless mark out very similar claims.

In this chapter, I consider the process through which such problems rise and fall and explore commonalities in their rhetorical formulations, focusing on the cases of self-esteem and happiness. I draw on John P. Hewitt's *The Myth of Self-Esteem* (1998) which details self-esteem's rise in the mid-1980s and comparative decline in the late 1990s and my own studies of happiness as a social problem in the 2000s (Frawley, 2015c, 2018b). Recall that I take my lead from the most commonly repeated claims and most commonly cited and appearing claims-makers in samples of news media discourse as a mass medium through which claims-makers seek to persuade the broadest possible audience.[1] These discourses rise and relatively decline in waves moving through a prehistory, or developments that occur before the emergence of concerted claims-making in the public sphere, discovery, adoption, expansion, exhaustion and finally, cultural diffusion. As one wave recedes and another rolls forward, the new is inflected with many of the hallmarks of the old.[2] For instance, the promises are more tentative and more successful claims are foregrounded. Yet, when each emotion problem fails to live up to its promises, its tendency to place the subject at the heart of social problems remains. Instead of questioning the way problems have been understood, for instance, as lying within the brains and behaviours of individuals, the questioning of the subject is only deepened. It is not, 'perhaps this is not the problem' but rather, 'the problem is worse than we thought'.

Theorizing emotion problem waves

The constructionist approach to social problems (see Best, 2017; Blumer, 1971; Spector & Kitsuse, 2017) has helped shed light on how a variety of emotions have come to be problematized. Recall that from this perspective social problems are social processes involving efforts to arouse concern about putative conditions (Best, 2017, p. 10). Indeed, 'concern' itself alludes to social problems as invitations about how one should feel. For instance, Loseke (2009) has discussed the articulation and circulation of 'emotion codes' in political speeches, that is, invitations regarding what emotions one should feel and to whom they should be directed. Yet social problems do not only invite us to feel in particular ways, they also draw out emotions as problems themselves. Berns (2011) has discussed how grief has become gradually commoditized and in this process, redefined as a problem to be overcome with expediency. Moreover, while researchers usually produce case studies of social problems, exploring relationships between social problems has become increasingly significant (Best, 2015, p. 19; Best & Loseke, 2018, p. 178). There have been many studies of the problematization of particular emotions in isolation. But there has been less attention to how these claims are connected. When viewed together, it is clear that many of these signifiers are elided. For instance, well-being and

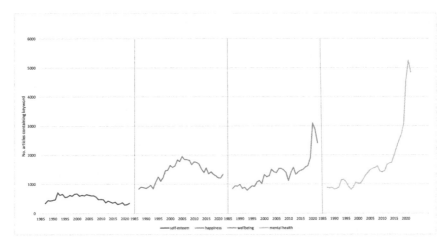

FIGURE 4.1 *Positive emotion keywords in Anglosphere Newspapers of Record (1987–2022).*

mental health have been so frequently elided in the British education system that in their common usage they appear synonymous (Ecclestone & Hayes, 2019). They also show similar tendencies in their manner of emergence and relative decline in the public sphere. Figure 4.1 shows the number of times each keyword appeared in Anglosphere (the United States, Canada, the UK, Australia) newspapers of record from 1987 to 2022.[3]

Happiness and self-esteem rise and relatively decline, while well-being and mental health appear to be ascending – the latter much more rapidly. What drives these trends?

Therapeutic fads

That social problem frames tend to be cyclic or at least volatile has been widely commented upon (see e.g. Peyrot, 1984 on drug abuse; Spector & Kitsuse, 2017 on general problem development cycles). Volatility and recurrence are key features of moral panics (Goode & Ben-Yehuda, 2009, p. 41). For social problems more generally, Best describes how public concern for social problems often comes in 'waves' (Best, 2017, pp. 312–16). The appearance of highly resonant and exploitable master frames often leads to social movements clustering around particular issues (Benford, 2013; Snow & Benford, 1992, p. 133). Yet there are many features of moral panics that do not quite capture the life course of emotions as social problems, particularly their short-termism and tendency towards hostility. Instead, and particularly for the discourses of positive emotion discussed throughout this book, their ostensible positivity is foregrounded as a key feature. Rather than inviting suspicion or hatred of deviants, the invitation in such discourses is a sense of excitement and an air of radicalism.

While like moral panics, the shifting concern from one idiom to the next does indeed appear to recur in waves, perhaps the most illuminating framework is Best's (2006a) discussion of fads which cycle through 'emerging', 'surging' and 'purging' as they are discovered, enthusiastically, often evangelically, adopted and quietly discarded. There are clear elements of faddishness to the keywords depicted in Figure 4.1. Yet unlike many fads, emotion frames seem unparalleled in the pervasiveness of their ability to permeate institutions. Unlike management or educational fads like 'whole language' reading approaches, happiness seemed to spread quickly affecting everything from parenting to architecture (Frawley, 2015c). While self-esteem and happiness ultimately declined in importance, they were never fully 'purged' from public life. Indeed, there are remnants of happiness claims in the more recent concern for mental health in Higher Education (HE) discussed in the last chapters. While many fads appear to drop from public consciousness, therapeutic fads leave a mark on the cultural vocabulary. They are readily accessible when making sense of new social issues, even if their significance is demoted by the next 'big thing'. They may not be able to grab attention nor form a convincing banner behind which to rally, but they evoke a 'common sense' about how the world works, what matters and why things go wrong.

In what follows,[4] I draw together aspects of social problems and social movements literature to flesh out emotion problem waves as recurring through phases including a prehistory, preceding their entry onto the public agenda; discovery, when concerted claims-making emerges; adoption, when more and more individuals and groups in society adopt the agenda; expansion, the stretching of the agenda to fit wider arrays of concerns; and exhaustion, where they no longer appear able to galvanize attention. These phases are followed by their diffusion into the cultural repertoire of therapeutic vocabularies.[5]

Prehistory

The prehistory phase consists of the existence of various signifiers before they are drawn out as significant emotions and drawn up into public claims-making. It is the origin or invention phase. It also includes existing ethnopsychological beliefs about human subjectivity, themselves the result of successful claims-making in the past. More deeply, as I have argued in Chapters 2 and 3, these beliefs about subjectivity speak to extant possibilities at a given time.

Pinpointing the prehistory of a new emotion problem is complicated by the fact that history is used as a rhetorical tool in claims-making. In response to charges of being 'just a fad' many advocates will object that their quest has 'always' been important, represents basic elements of human nature, or an ever-present quest for emotional self-realization. Prehistories thus can be dauntingly expansive, but once 'discovered' in the public sphere, only some histories are mobilized into commonly repeated claims. For instance, the sudden uptick in attention to happiness in the 2010s was attributed variously to contemporary society's disorientation from its true purpose (often rooted in Ancient Greece via recourse to Aristotle's *eudaimonia*) and scientific discoveries confirming the eternal truth of ancient wisdom (Frawley, 2015, pp. 176–7). Even self-esteem, of much more recent vintage, was rhetorically historicized and universalized. For instance, the feminist writer Gloria Steinem begins her best-selling *Revolution From Within: A Book of Self-Esteem* (1992) defending against charges of faddishness by tracing the roots of self-esteem to Ancient Greece, Buddhism, Hinduism and even Ancient Egypt. In this way, rather than representing the 'prehistory' of the present problem, contemporary concerns are eternalized and written onto the past.

For their ascent onto the public agenda however, the prehistories of emotion keywords can be marked out by more recent rises in interest, though in somewhat less public arenas. Public (e.g. news media) claims-making may exist, but it lacks concerted attention. At any given time, society is bubbling with potential new social problems. While not all will catch on, social problem invention has become a growth industry in the West, particularly in relation to children (Ecclestone, 2017). With large amounts of funding doled out for the identification and eradication of new harms and growing pressures for academic research to make an 'impact', boundaries between academic and advocacy research become blurred. Hewitt uses a market analogy to describe relationships between problem invention, discovery and adoption. For Hewitt, problem invention represents the 'wholesale' self-esteem market (Hewitt, 1998, p. 52). In 'wholesale' form, claims are unpolished and not all will become public issues. But if successful, wholesalers can benefit from feedback loops through which specialized knowledge, becoming commodified, is marketed and sold to individuals and institutions in the form of self-help books, training programmes and other therapeutic products. Thus, incentives for problem creation are myriad.

Prehistories of emotion problems tend not to be characterized by bottom-up demands made by lay people for new expertise about the management of emotions of whose problematic nature they had previously been unaware. Indeed, this phase is often characterized by advocating acceptance of the new area as being a worthwhile object of expertise at all. Many of the first claims about happiness did not posit a pressing problem of happiness in society. Rather, they focused on the notion that happiness was scientific. In the late 1980s, psychologists emerged in the press claiming that happiness was a 'stable', 'understandable' and 'universal phenomenon' that could be measured through specialized tools (e.g. Albery, 1988). However, they stopped short of claiming there was a specific problem to which this information should be directed. Similarly, a key moment for self-esteem came in the mid-1960s with the development of tools through which it could be putatively measured (Hewitt, 1998, p. 40).

For the contemporary problematization of emotion, it is this rationalization, or the transformation of previous discursive formations into scientized vocabularies and/or the creation of new ones, that potentially sets the course from prehistory to social problem. Emotional turns in academia therefore potentially act as feeders for problematization in the public sphere. In later phases, claims-makers are at pains to emphasize the scientific authority of their claims, referring back to these discourses, positioning their claims at the intersections of scientific discovery, intuition and ancient truth.

As a wholesaler of problematized positive emotions, positive psychology has been particularly important over the past two decades. Following his appoint as President of the American Psychological Association in 1998, American psychologist Martin Seligman outlined plans for what he termed a new 'science' of human strengths which would focus on those things that make life worth living and 'prevent pathologies that arise when life is barren and meaningless' (Seligman & Csikszentmihalyi, 2000, p. 5). While considerable research had focused on happiness and other quality of life data since the post-war period, it had been unevenly politicized. It was visible in American President Lyndon Johnson's Great Society initiatives in the 1960s but faded following regime change (Andrews, 1989, p. 402; Frawley, 2015c, pp. 69–71). By contrast, positive psychology was from its inception explicitly aimed at global institutionalization, including a formal network intending to influence 'education, social policy, urban planning, and the law' (Seligman, 1999 cited in Frawley, 2015c, pp. 127–30).

Past claims-making campaigns had expanded the influence and institutionalization of psychology into more and more areas of society, the state and social problems (see e.g. Dineen, 2001; Furedi, 2004; Nolan, 1998). This fostered receptivity to the activities and organizations of positive psychologists. Positive psychologists created new and multiplied existing 'social problems clusters' (H. Griffiths & Best, 2016), that is, claims-making efforts involving similar individuals and groups as advocates.

Problem waves oversee expansion of these clusters and create new areas of claim receptivity and invention. When the old fad fades, those who had been dedicated will be eager to invent or adopt something new. They also create pools of existing vocabularies on which claims-makers draw to construct new claims. A public that cared about self-esteem was also likely to care about happiness. Indeed, there is considerable overlap between self-esteem and happiness discourses (evident in the subtitle of Hewitt's book: *Finding Happiness and Solving Problems in America*). As the self-esteem movement waned, the happiness movement grew. Claims-makers like Martin Seligman positioned happiness as a discourse finally capable of solving the problems for which self-esteem proved ill-equipped.

Discovery

What Hewitt calls the 'retail' stream represents the first phase proper of issue 'discovery', where dedicated advocates take up the issue, campaigning in public arenas in hopes of affecting the public agenda. Five areas are key: 1) issue ownership; 2) the positioning of the discourse at the intersections of scientific knowledge, ancient wisdom and intuition; 3) 'deceptively simple' storytelling; 4) the creation of new victims and new ways to think about suffering; and 5) promising radical and even 'revolutionary' approaches to social problems.

Issue ownership

The passage from wholesalers to retailers is a key moment for problem discovery. Claims do not emerge abstractly of their own accord from existing cultural repertoires; people must make them and find them compelling. Individuals become dedicated issue 'owners' (Best, 1999, p. 46), 'go-to' experts, crafting the discourse's origin stories, bringing together a variety of claims to create a new, pressing problem, and providing information about causes and cures. Even with ownership, claims can arrest due to inopportune moments in the political sphere or news cycle or lose out to other claims. However, well-connected, well-resourced and organized issue owners are better able to move an issue from prehistory to public problem. Such dedicated advocates can wait for new opportunities to launch and if necessary, re-launch their claims.

Problem discovery can also be marked by the emergence of what Hewitt (1998, p. 49) calls 'conceptual entrepreneurs' who promote particular emotions as solutions to individual and social problems (Hewitt, 1998, p. 49). Typically focusing on a single idea or concept, conceptual entrepreneurs differ from moral entrepreneurs who focus on notions of 'right' and 'wrong' and from other claims-makers who seek recognition of conditions they define as troubling. Instead, conceptual entrepreneurs promote a particular solution to social problems whose definitions and troublesome nature they usually take for granted. According to Hewitt, conceptual entrepreneurs:

1   engage in claims-making to convince others of the importance of their
    discoveries,

2   strongly and sometimes unequivocally emphasize scientific
    underpinnings of claims and claims-makers (even if firm research
    foundations have yet to be established),

3   promote specific programmes based on the central idea, often with
    their own 'twist', and

4   stand to gain in financial or social status from their activities (1998,
    p. 50).

Conceptual entrepreneurs play an important role throughout the problem's
life course. Their promotion of specific programmes for personal and financial
gain is particularly evident in the adoption and expansion phases as more and
more people begin to ride the problem's wave and visibility. However, claims-
making often begins with a dedicated conceptual entrepreneur developing
their own twist on a larger philosophy or body of work. For instance, John
Vasconcellos, California Assemblyman and prominent self-esteem advocate
in the 1980s and 1990s, extracted self-esteem as a solution to social
problems from Carl Rogers's humanist psychology (Fishel, 1992) and positive
psychology had similar origins (Cabanas & Illouz, 2019). Once constructed,
these formulations often act as solutions in search of problems. At the same
time, locating solutions within subjectivity alludes to subjectivity as the source
of social problems.

A key difference between movements drawing attention to positive
emotions as problems and what one might typically imagine as characteristic
of social movements is their top-down nature. That is, rather than being
'grassroots' or 'bottom up' orientations whose visibility may depend on
creating 'social or moral disorder news' (Gans, 2004, p. 81), they tend to
be taken on by insiders already in positions of power and with ready access
to (or who are themselves) members of the media and policymakers. The
first 'discoverers' of happiness as a social problem were nearly all insiders
(Bache & Reardon, 2016; Frawley, 2015c) or from that 'set of groups that can
routinely influence government decisions and can insure that their interests
are normally recognized in the decision making process' (Useem & Zald, 1982,
p. 144). Hewitt (1998, p. 58) describes how the curative power of self-esteem
was discovered early on by California legislators led by Vasconcellos who set
up the 'California Task Force to Promote Self-Esteem and Personal and Social
Responsibility', a move widely ridiculed by the public at the time (Hewitt,
1998, p. 58).

Established actors even sometimes mimic grassroots social movement
rhetoric and activities. Indeed, the creation of ersatz grassroots movements

campaigning policymakers for agendas that are already set is becoming increasingly common, and is even offered up 'for hire' by various businesses (E. T. Walker, 2014). In 2011, 'Action for Happiness' was founded, inviting the public to 'Join the movement. Be the change' (Frawley, 2015c, p. 135). In spite of the rhetoric of radicalism, the movement was founded by prominent insider owners of the issue since the early 2000s, including policy adviser, Geoff Mulgan, Richard Layard, government advisor since the 1990s and member of the House of Lords, and Anthony Seldon, headmaster of prestigious boarding school, Wellington College, and knighted in 2014.

'Science', intuition and ancient wisdom

The discovery of a new emotion problem is typically characterized by strong claims to scientific foundations. Self-esteem entrepreneurs gradually 'canonized' some researchers, praised their achievements and substituted their authority for facts (Hewitt, 1998, p. 52). Happiness advocates were even more resolute. One self-help author disparages books of previous eras: 'Some self-help books are practitioner-led', he warns, while his 'is based solely on empirical studies' (Marsh, 2009). Newspaper reports referred to a science 'as hard as rocks' underpinning happiness claims (S. Griffiths, 2007). Correlative studies of happiness were described as having 'scientifically established' (e.g. Toynbee, 2003) the true meaning of happiness. Reports underscore expert credentials, use strongly scientific language and imbue common sense observations with a scientific aura (Fernandez-Rios & Novo, 2012; Hedges, 2009; Perez-Alvarez, 2013). Findings of heavily invested advocates are described as though they are disinterested scientific discoveries (Hedges, 2009; Whyte, 2013).

Particularly at early stages of problem development, scientific developments are often in their infancy. Yet, in public claims-making, their scientific basis tends to be communicated unequivocally. Cabanas and Illouz (2019) relate a conversation that transpired in 2008 (reported in Seligman's book *Flourish* (2011)) between Seligman and Richard Layard in which the latter expressed a desire to bring positive psychology into UK schools. When Seligman intimates that further evidence is needed, Layard responds that it is necessary to act when political will is present, not when the science is clear-cut. For Layard, the evidence was 'satisficing' (Cabanas & Illouz, 2019, p. 73). However, when one looks at Layard's claims-making in the public sphere up to that point, it is not at all clear that the evidence was 'satisficing'. Indeed, he titled his book, which pointed to schools as key sites of change, *Happiness: Lessons from a New Science* (2005).

Perhaps the clearest example of claims-makers' becoming enamoured by the appearance of science is psychologist Barbara Fredrickson's 'positivity ratios'. Fredrickson and Losada (2005) had used a complex system of differential equations to calculate what they claimed was the precise ratio (2.9013) of positive to negative feelings needed for human flourishing (Frawley, 2015a, p. 67). Before anyone noticed that the equations were essentially meaningless (N. J. L. Brown et al., 2013), the paper had been cited hundreds of times and spawned an industry (Anthony, 2014). This scientific grounding is important in modern pluralistic societies whose inhabitants share few certainties that once might have been grounded in common religion, culture and history. Evoking the language of science and coupling it with positive emotion offers a seemingly value-free rhetoric from which a variety of claims-makers (and policymakers) can construct rationales for action.

Even when the science proves disappointing, claims-makers are disinclined to relinquish the concept, falling back on intuition and anecdote. That emotion management works simply makes 'intuitive sense'. For instance, the California Task Force on self-esteem culminated in the production of a book about the importance of self-esteem to solving problems, entitled *The Social Importance of Self-Esteem* (Mecca et al., 1989). In the first chapter, sociologist Neil J. Smelser describes the results of the Task Force as 'disappointing' with the most consistent results showing 'that the associations between self-esteem and its expected consequences are mixed, insignificant, or absent' (Smelser, 1989, p. 15). Still, the authors were resolute. Lack of evidence is enlisted as a strength. Since it causes so much, he reasons, it is difficult to see how it causes any one variable. In place of evidence, he cites methodological difficulties and an 'intuitive' case for its social significance (indeed, he uses the word 'intuitive' or 'intuition' ten times across the chapter), concluding '[T]he link that we all know exists is shrouded in error' (Smelser, 1989, p. 16). In spite of the admission throughout the book that there is little to no evidence to prove a causal link between social problems and self-esteem, the Task Force concluded with a press release headed 'Poor self-esteem plays a role in causing social problems, University of California scientists find' (UC Berkeley, 1989).

Claims-makers are able to rely on intuition because emotion problems do not rise to prominence on their strength of evidence. In Snow and Benford's (1988) terms, they possess 'narrative fidelity', or 'resonate with cultural narrations [...] the stories, myths, folk tales that are part and parcel of one's cultural heritage and thus function to inform events and experiences in the immediate present' (p. 210). Part of their power comes from a cultural intuition that ultimately a disorganization at the level of individual emotional life is significant, if not the most significant factor, in making sense of why things go wrong. While the rhetoric of science is drawn upon for its authority, once the case is made, the underlying intuition becomes fact. Over time, claims become increasingly separated from their shaky evidence bases, becoming 'facts' about the phenomenon through repetition. For instance, claims that the UK has the 'unhappiest children in the developed world' or that Vanuatu is home to the happiest people, though emerging from skewed studies that were roundly criticized (or in the case of Vanuatu, advocacy research created by an environmental organization), through wide repetition became self-evident and commonly cited truths (Frawley, 2015a, pp. 92–4; 122–3).

Yet claims to science are counterbalanced with a healthy dose of magic. Issue owners sometimes characterize their discovery of the problem in quasi magical, romantic tales of inspiration. Martin Seligman relates an 'out of the mouths of babes' apocryphal tale of the 'epiphany' that led to the founding of positive psychology involving his then five-year-old daughter telling him not to be 'such a grouch' (Seligman, 2002, p. 28).[6] He would later say that he 'did not choose positive psychology. It called me', likening the experience to Moses and the burning bush (Cabanas & Illouz, 2019, p. 16). John Vasconcellos reverses this depiction in his linkage of self-esteem to his Roman Catholic upbringing, through which he was conditioned to think of himself 'as a sinner, guilt-ridden and ashamed' (Mecca et al., 1989, p. xv). Gloria Steinem describes her discovery of the power of self-esteem in a story where she learns to stand up to an officious hotel guard. She concludes that 'It's a feeling of "clicking in" when that self is recognized, valued, discovered, esteemed—as if we literally plug into an inner energy that is ours alone, yet connects us to everything else' (Steinem, 1992, p. 26). She describes self-esteem as a kind of primordial force, 'a oneness with all living things and with the universe itself,' that precedes 'patriarchy, racism, class systems, and other hierarchies that ration self-esteem' (p. 33).

Although early happiness and self-esteem conceptual entrepreneurs described the origins of these movements as personal epiphanies, considerably more propulsive forces were found in the form of initial large investments. The California Task Force was successful in earmarking $735,000 over three years to study self-esteem and its relationships to social problems (Mecca et al., 1989, p. xvii) and Vasconcellos himself would go on to become a California state senator. Positive Psychology's foundations were set by a series of large cheques 'appearing' on Seligman's desk (Cabanas & Illouz, 2019, p. 18). Already by 2002, positive psychology had amassed $37 million in funding (p. 18). Seligman for his part would publish mass-market books, offer life-coaching by conference call to hundreds of people at a time at a cost of $2,000 per head and found a for-profit website offering monthly exercises on how to be happy (Ehrenreich, 2010, p. 149).[7]

Finally, as alluded to in the prehistory section, scientific truth is married to ancient wisdom, the latter allegedly confirmed by sufficient scientific advancement. This has the effect of lending claims eternal validity. Jonathan Haidt's (2005) *Happiness Hypothesis* tours ancient and Eastern philosophy drawing out those aspects deemed confirmed by modern science and thus worthy of carrying forward. According to Haidt, while many philosophers were good psychologists, they ultimately lacked 'a deep understanding of human nature', which he sees psychology as uniquely positioned to offer (Haidt, 2005, p. 215). Humanity is portrayed as having become alienated from the true meaning and proper pursuit of emotions through the distorting effects of consumerism, modernity or (western) civilization. According to a self-esteem advocate, 'We're unwilling to do the real work to achieve a sense of self-worth. What psychology is coming to recognize more and more is that our sense of self-esteem and self-worth comes from our interaction with other people, not our acquisition of things' (Nesbitt, 1993). Happiness advocates' romantic rejection of consumerism is even stronger, its most widely repeated claims alleging the scientific 'discovery' that 'money can't buy happiness' (Frawley, 2015c, p. 152). As with self-esteem, the 'pursuit of money', audiences are warned, is not on the list of 'seven key factors now scientifically established to affect happiness' (Toynbee, 2003). In this way, emotion discourses offer a pseudo radical rejection of materialism in favour of a romantic return to what 'really matters' in life, conceptualized as something inside of individuals. As I detail elsewhere drawing on Löwy and Sayre (2002; Sayre & Löwy, 2005), this romantic rejection in favour of a promised return to pre-capitalist values is a potent force in rationalized Western societies longing for re-enchantment (Frawley, 2015a).

'Deceptively simple'

Successful competition amongst the cacophony of claims in the mass media 'marketplace' (Hilgartner & Bosk, 1988, p. 57) depends on good storytelling. Competition makes rhetoric important, and claims often take the form of rhetorical arguments incorporating grounds (claims about the existence and nature of the problem), warrants (statements about why action is necessary) and conclusions (recommendations for action) (Best, 1987, 2021).

These chains of argument often implicate emotions in simplified causal relationships. Emotions are presented as 'deceptively simple' solutions to complex problems, hinting that their outward banality belies an inner nature of arcane complexity. Simplicity also implies cost-saving. In promising to tackle intransigent and costly issues, they justify high upfront investments in their interventions based on much larger future savings and warn of dire costs should their advice not be heeded. 'Leave things as they are,' one happiness advocate warns, 'and the state will increasingly have to pick up the bill for how consumer capitalism effectively produces emotional ill-health–depression, stress, anxiety' (Bunting, 2005).

In this way, highly complex problems are explained in simplistic – and soluble – terms. Remove the impediment in human behaviour, and all will be well. For instance, even the 2008 financial crisis was attributed by some advocates to misguided pursuits of happiness by both individuals and governments. Bankers had become 'addicted' to a 'power game that keeps them happy' (Howse, 2013). 'If we genuinely cared about personal and societal happiness in this country', one economist alleged, 'we probably wouldn't allow our elected representatives and powerful unelected civil servants to obsess about the opinions and sensibility of foreign bond holders so much' nor 'carry on borrowing billions of euros every month to keep afloat the zombie banks [...]' (Kirby, 2010). Complex issues like the workings of the capitalist economy are explained as mistaken beliefs about happiness ameliorable through emotion management. Moreover, if emotions can explain and solve problems, they also explain success. Seligman has even claimed that 'flourishing' explains why certain societies are more advanced and better developed than others (Cabanas & Illouz, 2019, p. 138).

Since claims-makers tend to be members of the cultures with which they are communicating, claims tend to be increasingly inflected with taken for granted cultural notions (Best, 2017). As alternative vocabularies for making sense of social problems have dwindled and emotion culture increasingly takes the form of therapeutic culture (González, 2012, p. 5), it is little surprising that disordered emotions are ascribed immense explanatory power within these simplified causal chains.

Magic bullets and social vaccines

The promised solutions offered by emotion management often take the form of 'magic bullets' possessing wide curative potential with few, if any, downsides or risks. Andrew Mecca of the self-esteem Task Force claimed in 1988 that 'Virtually every major social problem we have [...] can be traced to people's lack of self love: alcohol and drug abuse, teenage pregnancy, crime, child abuse, chronic welfare dependency and poor educational performance' (Davis, 1988). Happiness research was forwarded as relevant to nearly every aspect of individual, political and cultural life, from schools (Daneshkhu, 2007) to architecture (Street-Porter, 2006), to fractured relationships and declining religion (Elliott, 2007). As Richard Layard claimed in 2010, 'Everyone is concerned with avoiding poverty, ill health, conflict and enslavement. But these things are nothing but versions of unhappiness. So what we're all really concerned with, although we might be afraid of the simplicity of the term, is happiness' (Simons, 2010).

Positive emotion promotion is also touted as preventing problems before they start. 'Social vaccine' was a phrase explicitly used by self-esteem advocates in the 1980s and 1990s. Schools teaching self-esteem would 'prevent teen pregnancy, truancy, teen suicide, dropping out, and drug and alcohol abuse' (Uzelac, 1989). Similarly, happiness promotion was promised to inoculate people from future problems, 'a powerful ally in the prevention and remedy of physical and psychological problems, as well as better enabling us to thrive and flourish on all major fronts' (*The Times*, 2003).

In this way, conceptual entrepreneurs are able to offer a vague but easily exploitable formula through which the adoption of their preferred programmes is positioned as a necessary precursor to the amelioration of nearly any social problem—first we must promote *x* before *y* can ever be achieved. That is, first the particular emotional orientation must be inculcated before the intractable problem can be broached. As Cabanas and Illouz (2019, p. 88) observe of positive psychology, these discourses affect an inversion of Abraham Maslow's well-known 'Pyramid of Needs', which had assumed a 'secured economic base' was necessary in order to achieve higher faculties of personal growth. Maslow's theory had once provided legitimacy for a variety of organizational demands characteristic of post-war capitalism. However, Cabanas and Illouz argue that it was gradually unable to answer 'to the rising demands and necessities of the emerging economic corporate setting' (p. 90) by the end of the twentieth century. The model came to be increasingly questioned. Yet the result of this questioning was not so much to do away with it, but to stand it on its head. Happiness, they argue, is now widely viewed not as the outcome of success, but a requirement of success. First you must promote psychic security and economic security will follow. Yet with inner fulfilment frequently positioned as superior to material entanglements, it is not surprising when economic security itself is quietly shunted aside.

New victims, new suffering

In spite of claims to focus on the positive side of humanity, positive emotion problem waves tend to posit new categories of victims and expand old ones. Promoters of self-esteem were not concerned with celebrating this capacity within individuals but rather were preoccupied with the belief that without explicit advice, individuals were unlikely to achieve it. A headline in a Canadian newspaper alleges fostering self-esteem is a 'full-time job for families', and warns that 'building your family's self-esteem takes effort' (Gervais, 1998). Self-esteem is a problem affecting everyone, even those who appear to have no problems at all. An article in *The Irish Times* posits self-esteem as the cause of shyness, timidity, being quiet, attention-seeking, aggression and bullying but also warns that even those who appear not to have any problems could be hiding a 'potential problem' in their high achievement (McTiernan, 1994).

'Equally important,' the article continues, is for 'us parents to look at ourselves and our relationship with each other' as 'failings' here can 'infect your children'. Even the most 'clued up' parents therefore require the checklists offered in the claims-maker's new book.

Similarly, while the founding of positive psychology promised to deflect the discipline away from a concern with deficits toward a 'new science of human strengths' (Seligman, 1999, p. 560), public claims-making quickly moved to problematizations. Headlines proclaimed that 'Unhappiness is "Britain's worst social problem"' (Laurance, 2005); it was claimed that the average person is 'consistently wrong' (MacLeod, 2005) in their pursuits of happiness and required expert guidance to live better. The public was described as hapless without intervention, likened to 'hamsters' on a treadmill striving to attain something that the new expertise could at last offer (Frawley, 2015a, pp. 133–5). People need expert guidance not only when things go wrong, but also for things to go right.

Emotion revolutions

Finally, novelty is key to gaining and sustaining fickle media and public attention. The notion of focusing on the 'brighter side' of life helps propel these formulations into the spotlight. Moreover, self-esteem and happiness were portrayed as revolutionary challenges to scholarship, institutions and even capitalism as a whole. Self-esteem's 'discovery' by feminism entailed its construction as a challenge to racism, patriarchy, class and other hierarchies— as a 'revolution from within' (Hewitt, 1998, p. 63). Economist and UK labour peer, Richard Layard, was described as challenging the fundamentals of economics and 'quietly effecting a revolution in this miserable, materialistic, overworked country' (Jeffries, 2008). Yet this radical break with the past resolves in a romantic return to eternal truths and unchanging human nature (Frawley, 2015c, pp. 140–1). Claims-makers often find their answers in previous eras before true happiness and its associated values were lost. Not only Aristotle, but non-western cultures were frequently evoked, often seen as 'living time capsules for pre-capitalist values' (Frawley, 2015, p. 177).

Adoption

Experiential commensurability

Therapeutic vocabularies tend to be adopted across a bewildering array of domains. In contrast to owners who discover the problem, adopters jump on the bandwagon, spreading the message once it has already become available in the public sphere. They also use the new emotional vocabulary to make sense of and refresh existing problems and demands. The experiential commensurability, or resonance at the level of personal experience (Snow & Benford, 1988), of positive emotions constructs common ground between advocates and audiences (Frawley, 2018b). As Hewitt writes, 'The very currency of the language [of self-esteem] affords an opportunity to describe victimization in terms that may elicit sympathy, [...] provid[ing] common ground between victim and potential sympathetic allies' (1998, p. 96).[8] The exploitable language of positive emotion allows claims-makers for many different causes to draw on its novelty to bring attention to their causes as well as to expand the domain of alleged suffering of putative victims. For instance, it is not only diagnosable illnesses that are worthy of attention, but also various forms of unhappiness and the many experiences that can be drawn together beneath its wide umbrella. 'There is only one indicator that matters', asserts one claims-maker, 'are people happier?' (Toynbee, 1998).

Exploiting existing spaces

Solutions in search of problems find enthusiastic adopters in institutions generally prone to fads, for instance, in education and medicine which have high expectations for progress or management which is highly competitive (Best, 2006a). Education has been particularly receptive to emotion problem claims (Ecclestone & Hayes, 2019; Ecclestone & Rawdin, 2016). Happiness education exploited existing institutional niches and 'built upon' the firm belief that emotion and individual factors were fundamental to learning (Cabanas & Illouz, 2019, p. 74). Underlying this receptiveness is a strong cultural belief in the vulnerability of children, but also of adults, through which parental ability has been cast increasingly into doubt (Frankenberg et al., 2000; Furedi, 2001; Lee et al., 2014). Suspicion of the adult generation deflects many concerns about childhood onto education (Furedi, 2009). It is also fed by the ongoing construction of childhood in 'crisis' (Ecclestone, 2017; Guldberg, 2009; Myers, 2012) and the ease with which western audiences connect to claims about threatened children (Best, 1993b). Returning to institutional niches, Nolan describes how, following the conclusion of the California self-esteem task force, similar task forces proliferated across the country (1998, pp. 153–7). The continued existence of the institutional spaces created by this cultural and institutional receptivity depends on occupants' refreshing claims about problem severity, underscoring the importance of their endeavours; when the current therapeutic fad wanes, they will be on the lookout for the next wave.

Swift institutionalization

Spector and Kitsuse's definition of successful problems relies upon their 'institutionalization as official categories' (2017, p. 72). Problematized positive emotions have tended to be institutionalized quickly. This is because like discovery, adoption also proceeds from the top down—from policy insiders, think tanks, various 'therapeutic entrepreneurs' (Ecclestone, 2018) existing institutions and finally, public consciousness. Policymakers have strongest incentives for involvement in issues perceived as high salience but low conflict (Nelson, 1984, p. 94). The positive valence of positive emotion incentivizes adoption over rejection and criticism since few would risk accusations of wanting to make children unhappy or have low self-esteem. Criticism tends therefore to be sporadic and unorganized, creating a path of least resistance to institutionalization. Fluid and expansive, they offer 'something for everyone'. As a result, adoption is not only swift but also bipartisan. The happiness agenda was initially embraced in the UK by New Labour but was quickly affirmed by the Conservative opposition (Frawley, 2015c, p. 99). Hewitt describes how self-esteem created strange bedfellows in feminist authors, 'touchy, feely, dopey' therapeutic entrepreneurs, and followers of Ayn Rand (1998, p. 61). Though adopters may do so for different reasons, the agreeability fostered by couching claims in the rhetoric of positive emotion drives their widespread adoption.

Therapeutic industries

The appeal of conceptual entrepreneurship is most fully realized once the discourse gains a foothold. Institutionalization breeds demands for solutions which conceptual entrepreneurs readily supply. As Hewitt (1998) describes of self-esteem:

> Once the general idea has been 'discovered' by conceptual entrepreneurs and given scientific legitimacy, the way is open for the invention of means to put their discovery to use. If self-esteem lies at the root of many problems and is an efficacious solution, then entrepreneurs are free to create and market programs that will, they claim, enhance self-esteem.
>
> (p. 52)

Conceptual entrepreneurs proliferate. Bookshelves begin to fill with titles promising the true path to attaining the new emotional outlook. Individuals adopt it in life coaching, found for profit websites and consultancies. Individual researchers and advocacy groups appear competing for public funds available to track and control the problem (Cabanas & Illouz, 2019, p. 80). Nolan describes a proliferation of self-esteem organizations emerging in the 1990s, all vying for public funds (1998, p. 53). Feedback loops develop through which new research refreshes public claims and keeps the problem alive.

Technological adaptation is evident in a range of 'emodities', or 'services, therapies and products that promise to enact emotional transformation calculated and exchanged in a market' (Cabanas & Illouz, 2019, p. 115). Hundreds, if not thousands, of happiness promoting and tracking apps have emerged in the past decade. An app, called *Happify*, advertises itself as offering 'science-based activities & games to help overcome negative thoughts and stress' (Happify, 2022). Another, *The Happiness Planner*, promises to aid in 'Mastering happiness, success, and productivity—all in one app!' (Happinessplanner.com, 2022) and includes a function to rate and track of your happiness levels. Free for the first seven days, most features then require a Premium subscription. The life coaching and wellness start-up called *BetterUp* made headlines in 2021 when Prince Harry joined as its 'Chief Impact Officer'. However, it was not long before reports appeared alleging BetterUp had cut employee wages to fund the high profile recruitment (Bosotti, 2022) and was a 'psychologically unsafe place to work' (Steerpike, 2022).

Where the emphasis on positive emotion is initially heralded as a return to 'what really matters' against the cold rational logics of consumer capitalist society, it becomes easily assimilated. Beneath the digitized face of idyllic calm lies the same furious machinery.

Institutionalization into public policy makes clearer these intersections and contradictions between the romantic escape offered by emotion and its assimilation into capitalism. In 2015, Wales passed the Well-Being of Future Generations Act, which set out a number of 'well-being goals' for the country. Sophie Howe, then Future Generations Commissioner for Wales, alludes to the assimilation of well-being into the fluid needs of the economy when she writes in 2018:

> There is potential for technology to be used to free up valuable time for our workforce to reinvest in patient-centred care, the human touch that our NHS has prided itself on. Perhaps the large numbers of clerical and admin staff who are still engaged in booking appointments and whizzing paperwork around the system could instead be wellbeing advocates focused on working with people to find out what is impacting on their health and what opportunities there are for addressing it outside the NHS system. Or providing a friendly ear for the large numbers of older people who would otherwise be lonely and isolated and therefore more at risk of needing health and social care services.

> (Howe, 2018)

In other words, those whose jobs might be impacted by technological change can be retrained as 'wellbeing advocates', sopping up their excess labour and redirecting it to other state goals (here, reducing usage of the NHS). The unemployed or soon-to-be are transformed from potential risks into assets. Yang (2015, p. 4) describes similar uses of therapeutic discourses in China where laid-off workers are given 'training in the basics of counseling' and re-employed as 'companions for chatting'. 'In this way,' she concludes, 'potential "enemies" of the state, those who may harbor *yinhuan* [hidden risks and dangers] as a result of economic restructuring, become subjects and advocates of psychotherapy.'

Expansion

The popularity of the new idiom means that no organization wants to be left behind. More and more adopters expand the scope of its influence to fit their needs and demands. Once this solution becomes 'accepted', nearly every problem is pulled into its scope. As Hewitt writes, everything starts to 'look like a nail' (1998, p. 91). As Seligman's spurning of self-esteem illustrates, its existence as a panacea for social problems may also begin to be noted.

Expansion occurs in a number of ways. Asserting the preventative power of positive emotion expands its impact beyond those currently experiencing problems to the entire population. Early happiness claims urged concern for mental illness be extended to include unhappiness (e.g. Layard, 2003; Le Fanu, 2001). Another means of expanding numbers is in calculating public health costs. 'Unhappiness is an expensive business' writes one advocate; 'Mental ill-health is the biggest single cause of incapacity and costs the country an estimated £9bn in lost productivity and benefits' (Bunting, 2005). The message is that even if you are not ill, you may be unhappy. And even if you are not unhappy, you may be paying for someone who is.

Expansion also occurs in terms of meanings attributed signifiers, facilitated by their flexible syntax, or the ease with which they can be utilized by many groups and concerns (Snow & Benford, 1992). Hewitt calls self-esteem a 'word for all seasons' with many and sometimes contradictory meanings attributed to it (Hewitt, 1998, p. 99). Happiness came to encompass stipulating behaviours like volunteering, healthy eating and even 'pro social spending' (e.g. Hamburgh, 2016). However, while the ability to expand facilitates their proliferation, it can also act as a drawback if claims-makers attempt to go beyond experiential commensurability. As one critic warns, 'most of the happiness gurus don't mean what you mean by happiness at all. They want you to be the right sort of happy' (Finkelstein, 2009).

Here, the tendency for one emotional panacea to give way to the next is clearest. Claims-makers often elide and employ new terminologies to facilitate the expansion of existing claims. Self-esteem advocates routinely drew on a wide range of emotions, sometimes using them synonymously. Self-esteem's emphasis on 'feeling good' permitted extensions to happiness and depression and to draw on related claims and statistics to make their case (Hewitt, 1998, p. 140). Happiness advocates employed additional terminologies including flourishing, eudaimonia, well-being and mental health—themselves potential candidates for the next wave (Frawley, 2015c).

The numbers of individuals and groups claiming to deal with the problem expand and become more diffuse. While psychologists may require a licence, there are few restrictions on the creation of therapies and training others in administering them (Hewitt, 1998, p. 53). While claims-makers cite myriad broader causes of emotional problems, lobbying often focuses on expanding the ranks of those armed to deal with it. One of Layard's most prominent claims was for the training of 10,000 additional psychotherapists for the NHS, who, it was also claimed, would help the unemployed get back to work (Richards, 2005).

Adoption in one institution can lead to expansion into other connected institutions. For instance, claims-makers who had championed happiness curricula in schools later focused on universities (e.g. Grove, 2017). As claims-makers move to new organizations and institutions, they take the agenda with them, sometimes globally. The global spread of positive psychology was facilitated by a conscious project through which its leader recruited 'young, rising academics' with 'leadership qualities (future department chairs)' from across the world to become part of a formal network aimed at furthering its spread (Seligman, 1999 in Frawley, 2015c, p. 128). Global expansion is also facilitated by saturation of local markets leading to expansion into new. A review of positive psychology RCTs (Hendriks et al., 2018) reveals a sharp uptick in global studies from 2014. Indeed, expansion into non-western cultures is explicitly promoted by the authors as a means of overcoming allegations of ethnocentrism. It also works in the opposite direction. While nonetheless 'invented' in the Anglosphere, claims about shifting attention away from economic measures of progress towards more subjective valuations were influential in development before they were 'brought home' (Pender, 2002; Pupavac, 2008).

Exhaustion

Complaints begin to surface that the discourses have been stretched past a breaking point. Their existence as panaceas, once a selling point for adoption, becomes a rationale for abandonment. Yet it is not criticism that leads to exhaustion. Hewitt (1998, p. 115) notes that while self-esteem backlash was becoming more apparent at the time of his writing, criticism had always been voiced. Yet it did little to stop the issue's ascent. Indeed, the absence of evidence resulting from the California Task Force did not dampen its champion's certainty. The same is true of criticism of the happiness movement, of which there has been much (Frawley, 2015b). Evidence (particularly regarding experimental interventions) often takes time to collect and does not emerge until the issue is already beginning to exhaust itself. Criticism is also less organized than advocacy. Without organization, critics are limited in their ability to turn a valence issue into something contentious. Rather, discourses become exhausted largely because they lose their novelty and come to be replaced by new ones. That said, exhaustion is rarely definitive; it is reflected in a protracted decline as claims recede into the cultural backdrop. Frustrated critics may remark, as Coyne et al. (2010, p. 39) put it regarding positive psychology's relevance to cancer care, that it is a 'story line resistant to evidence'. Moreover, much criticism attempts to shift attention to new emotional vocabularies for which advocates become conceptual entrepreneurs, potentially prompting the next wave. Savvy claims-makers position themselves as critics of the old and harbingers of the new.

As with other social problems, once institutionalized, people may lose enthusiasm for policies or perceive conditions as persisting (Best, 2017, p. 312). Part of their exhaustion may ultimately lie in that as magic bullets for social problems they ultimately miss their mark. Hewitt notes the ever-proliferating promises of self-esteem ultimately went unfulfilled. The more 'radical' claims that governments should focus on growing happiness rather than wealth could not possibly be realized given growth's emergence from the basic functions of capitalism (R. Smith, 2010). A lack of growth moreover is not a harmonious 'steady state' but rather a volatile situation of crisis (Frawley, 2015c, pp. 25–6).

However, rather than realizing that this is probably the limitation of emotional solutions to social problems, some claims-makers lament a revolution betrayed. Reflecting on the potential for the related discourse of mindfulness to become yet another means of encouraging individuals to adjust to the status quo, Purser (2015, p. 42) writes that mindfulness 'could become a formidable force for a radical transformation of Western capitalist society' if only it can overcome (among other things) its tendency to individualize and encourage instead 'prosocial behaviours'. The late 1990s and early 2000s saw criticisms that it was not low self-esteem, but high self-esteem that was the problem. Yet in all cases, the assumption that individual subjectivity is ultimately to blame remains.

Cultural diffusion

Problematized positive emotions become exhausted in that they are no longer able to grab the attention of media, policy or other institutional gatekeepers. But they are not fully exhausted. Instead, they recede into the ethnopsychology, remaining available for more perfunctory forms of meaning-making in everyday life. Catchphrases of the self-esteem movement such as 'I am special' remain common in cultural texts (Twenge et al., 2012). While emotion keywords continue to possess a range of lay meanings, claims-making campaigns add new and seemingly authoritative meanings to popular vocabularies (Hewitt, 1998, p. 35). They have become part of the cultural 'common sense'. The belief that the promotion of positive emotions will improve learning and other outcomes was not hindered by a review finding little to no positive (and perhaps some negative) effects (Humphrey et al., 2010). Instead, its authors noted encouraging anecdotes and suggested closer and more intensive adherence to future programmes. The absence of evidence is not enough, because intuition indicates that it must be significant and therefore it is the implementation, not the programme, that is flawed.

It is no longer even necessary to use the words themselves to draw upon these beliefs. Indeed, publicly referring to 'self-esteem' as a solution to a new social problem might inadvertently dredge up vague memories of discredited panaceas past. Yet the vague belief that feeling good about oneself is important, even a necessary criterion for success, is still there.

In policy, one discourse may shift almost imperceptibly to the next. Best (2006a) notes that the 'purging' of fads is often quiet. Without much fanfare the concern with self-esteem shifted to happiness and the concern for happiness shifted to well-being. In both everyday life and key areas of policy, well-being is giving way to mental health. In each iteration, the domain of the therapeutic is widened and the pool of problematic emotions is deepened.

Conclusion

In this chapter, I have suggested that problematized ostensibly 'positive' emotions tend to emerge into the public eye in waves of discovery, adoption, expansion and exhaustion. The need to package claims as uncontroversial by constructing them as valence issues on which everyone can agree, the matter of fact nature with which Anglosphere ethnopsychology treats claims about emotional vulnerability and the centrality of subjectivity to social problems, a growing industry invested in problematizing emotion, and the necessity of novelty in the competitive public sphere of claims-making are powerful underlying forces. Each wave enlarges the base of individual and institutional receptivity, priming for the next.

Yang (2015) argues of similar trends in the Chinese context that interventions aimed at promoting positive emotions probably do not make workers feel any better. Where they are successful however is in dividing collective movements, internalizing problems and creating new needs readily catered to in a growing array of therapeutic services. Far from giving people the tools with which to excel in an increasingly atomized society, therapy culture, enacted in a variety of treatments and strategies for a growing array of emotion problems, encourages a dependent and ever more diminished subject.

As panaceas for social problems, the promotion of positive emotions is unlikely to live up to its promises. Instead, individuals are encouraged to look inward; even if broader social structures are implicated, their start and endpoint in individual psychology is underscored.

PART TWO

Case Studies

5

Mind(fulness) of the Gap

Self-esteem, happiness, well-being and mental health have formed major focuses of attention within the UK media and around the English (and increasingly non-English)-speaking world, as illustrated in Figure 4.1 (Chapter 4). However, within these waves a smaller, but no less interesting and illustrative therapeutic fad emerged in the form of 'mindfulness' in the early 1980s, steadily climbing to prominence over the past decade (Figure 5.1).[1]

Mindfulness can be variously described or defined, but generally refers to a practice or series of practices drawn from Buddhist meditation that is broadly focused on cultivating awareness or attention. As I describe in this and the chapter that follows, precisely of what mindfulness meditation or practice should consist is constructed loosely in public discourses, with meanings and emphases shifting to accommodate new applications and objectives. However, claims-makers typically advocate practices geared towards encouraging awareness of the present moment. Forms of mindfulness practice have been promoted not only as relevant to the private life of individuals, but also as a social vaccine and magic bullet for a variety of social problems. The introduction to a *Clinical Handbook of Mindfulness* promotes the practice as the culmination of an eternal quest: 'Throughout history, human beings have sought to discover the causes of suffering and the means to alleviate it' (Siegel et al., 2009, p. 17). Mindfulness, the authors continue, offers a 'deceptively simple' means of reducing this suffering and sets the path for 'positive personal transformation' (p. 17).

As interest in the practice reaches its apex over the past decade, it seems there are few institutions it has not touched, few benefits it does not give and few problems for which mindfulness cannot be of use. Military personnel are offered 'mindfulness-based mind fitness training' (Stanley, 2022), corporations including Google, Apple and Amazon offer employees various forms of mindfulness coaching, meditation breaks and dedicated rooms in a bid to increase productivity and combat burnout (Crispin, 2021; Gelles, 2015a;

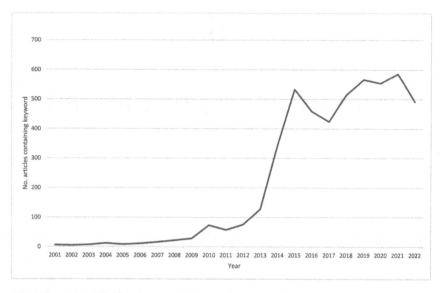

FIGURE 5.1 *'Mindfulness' in UK Broadsheets (2001–2022).*

Quelch & Knoop, 2018). Instruction in meditation is offered to dangerous prisoners to help manage anger and curb reoffending (Booth, 2015b). Police are presented with 'mindfit cop' and mindfulness courses are offered to doctors and nurses in NHS trusts (Booth, 2018). British educators were swiftly swept up in the phenomenon. Then Education Secretary Damian Hinds announced in early 2019 the start of a trial aimed to boost young people's mental health and well-being by teaching school pupils mindfulness practices, including breathing exercises and relaxation techniques to help 'regulate their emotions' (Department for Education, 2019). Mindfulness advocates have claimed it can tackle obesity, mental health problems, addictions and even climate change.

In this chapter I offer a sketch of the rise of mindfulness in US and UK media discourses expanding on my work with Daniel Nehring (Nehring & Frawley, 2020a) and explore some of its prehistory, discovery, adoption, expansion and current signs of exhaustion and cultural diffusion drawing on a sample of 150 articles from major UK news media and additional theoretical sampling on the basis of the most common claims identified in this sample (see Methods Appendix). The purpose is not to offer a detailed critique of the rise and use of mindfulness in every public arena but rather to draw out the way that claims about mindfulness resonating in this arena construct subjectivity and its relationship to social problems.[2] As a therapeutic fad, it draws out perhaps most strikingly the arguments described in previous chapters, particularly in terms of the naturalization and psychologization of the gap between *is* and *ought* to be.[3]

Prehistory

In Wilson's (2014) study of *Mindful America* he traces the underlying feeders of the mindfulness movement to the expansion of higher education introducing students to Eastern religions, Asian immigration and travel of Westerners East, the growth of American-based meditation centres and the popularity of psychology (pp. 30–1). Yet the growing fascination with the 'wisdom of the East' (Lasch, 1979, p. 4) must also be understood in the light of a palpable sense of exhaustion with traditional political ideologies that followed the Second World War. Countercultural movements at the time saw in 'Eastern' spirituality, philosophy and religion an answer to the problems they perceived the West as having created or been unable to solve.[4] Buddhist practices were particularly appealing to young people frustrated with the cold rationality and materialism of modernity (Bodhi, 2011, p. 20). While the association with the young Bohemians of the 'beat generation' waned, more general interest in Buddhism experienced a boom in the West in the ensuing decades (Coleman, 2001, p. 8). It is to these trends that Christopher Lasch refers when he writes of the seeming exhaustion of change by political means at the time of his writing:

> Having no hope of improving their lives in any of the ways that matter, people have convinced themselves that what matters is psychic self-improvement: getting in touch with their feelings, eating health food, taking lessons in ballet or belly-dancing, immersing themselves in the wisdom of the East, jogging, learning how to "relate," overcoming the "fear of pleasure."

> (1979, p. 4)

Claims about the benefits of Buddhist practices were often bound up with a romantic rejection of a perceived cultural emphasis on finding fulfilment in material objects, seeking instead an inner fulfilment perceived as more authentic.[5] One advocate reflects that Buddhist practices will remain popular as more people 'discover that the BMW and the heavily-mortgaged home are not conducive to inner peace' and begin to seek its 'answers and [...] techniques for dealing with a rough-and-tumble world' (McAteer, 1987). By the end of the twentieth century, exponential growths were seen in Buddhist groups, sales of Buddhist-themed books and people from Western backgrounds identifying as Buddhist (Coleman, 2001, p. 20).

Within this general interest, the term 'mindfulness' was sometimes, but not often, foregrounded. One of the first to do so was the British Naval Officer Admiral Ernest Henry Shattock in his *An Experiment in Mindfulness*

(1958). Shattock had gone to Yangon (then Rangoon) to study Satipatthana under Mahasi Sayadaw, a Burmese Theravada monk in the 1950s. The book describes the author's journey East and training at the Thathana Yeiktha monastery as well as his general disenchantment with modern life. Our goal, as he describes in the opening chapter, should be to 'cultivate [a] feeling of abstracting ourselves from an outside world into an inner seclusion where security is self-generating and strength is in acquiescence rather than in activity; and to develop a permanent insulation from the shocks and tensions of modern life' (Shattock, 1958, p. 13). Seeking a solution that could be used by anyone (therefore, he felt, ruling out religion, though somewhat ironically), his 'experiment' was to 'test the reaction of a well-tried Eastern system on a typical Western mind' (p. 19). Upon return to his usual routine, he found that many of the habits he learned gradually faded but claimed he retained a deeper sense awareness and satisfaction and that the practice could easily be generalized and repeated by anyone in the 'quiet of one's room' (p. 152).

While Shattock's book had limited effect on broader public discourses, it was read by early Western adopters of Buddhist practices in the 1960s like Ruth and Henry Denison who were inspired by it to travel to Japan and Burma to study meditation (Boucher, 2005). Meditation was itself experiencing a revival within certain forms of Buddhist practice in the eighteenth century, having waned in significance for several centuries prior. Promoted by charismatic teachers, the spread of Buddhist meditation practices was greatly aided by a mutual interest between such leaders and Western spiritual seekers (Wilson, 2014, p. 23). The Denisons for instance had trained under U Ba Khin who was enthusiastic about promoting meditation to American audiences, selecting charismatic individuals who would spread the practice (Boucher, 2005).

However, a specific focus on 'mindfulness' remained secondary,[6] or bound up with more complicated, overtly spiritual and/or less easily popularly translatable conceptualizations (e.g. Thera, 1968). Yet as 'Eastern' spirituality and philosophy grew in popularity in Western culture (Coleman, 2001), mindfulness increasingly moved into the foreground. In his 1976 book, *The Miracle of Mindfulness* (Hanh, 1975), Thich Nhat Hạnh describes a highly simplistic series of techniques meant to be suitable to anyone. Claims that would later become familiar, such as that mindfulness can be practised throughout one's daily activities, also appear here. Yet the broad application to social problems so characteristic of contemporary mindfulness discourse is missing. While an afterword by American peace activist James Forest claims that until the peace movement incorporates a 'meditative dimension', it will remain 'terribly crippled' (p. 106), the majority of the book is highly personalized. Similarly, although other practitioners and teachers like Nyanaponika Thera foregrounded mindfulness and emphasized its inclusiveness, they remained abstract in terms of claims about its usefulness (Wilson, 2014, p. 25).

A key moment came in the 1970s, when mindfulness was extracted from its broader Buddhist suspension, appearing within academic articles highlighting its potential as a new form of psychotherapeutic practice (Deatherage, 1975; Goleman, 1971; Kornfield, 1979; Walsh et al., 1978). While cultural interest in Buddhism did not subside, this period marks a crucial moment for mindfulness as a standalone phenomenon and aspect of Western psychotherapy, having been distilled from more heterogeneous and sometimes outright religious discourses. Yet, early on, these academic discourses largely fell short of formulating a clear programme based on this central idea. It was with the emergence of the first conceptual entrepreneur that mindfulness moved from a ripple to a wave.

Discovery

The rising popularity of Buddhism in the West and its gradual scientization represent the wholesale market for mindfulness. Its entry into the 'retail' market came in 1979 with the packaging of these discourses into a discrete programme of Mindfulness-Based Stress Reduction (MBSR) by Jon Kabat-Zinn, then Associate Professor of Medicine working in preventative and behavioural medicine at the University of Massachusetts. It was then that Kabat-Zinn founded the Stress Reduction Clinic at the University of Massachusetts Medical School and began offering MBSR as an eight-week programme applying Buddhist meditation techniques for the treatment of stress and pain. A practitioner of meditation since the 1960s and with a PhD in molecular biology (Kabat-Zinn, 2011, p. 286), his potent admixture of science, intuition and ancient wisdom set the path from prehistory to public problem.

Conceptual entrepreneurship

Kabat-Zinn illustrates well Hewitt's (1998) four-part description of conceptual entrepreneurs who 1) engage in claims-making to convince others of the importance of their discoveries, 2) strongly and sometimes unequivocally emphasize scientific underpinnings of claims and scientific credentials of claims-makers (even if firm research foundations have yet to be established), 3) promote specific programmes based on the central idea, often with their own 'twist' and 4) stand to gain financially from their activities.

Teaching a series of practices including mindful movement, breathing exercises, visualizations, sitting meditation and forms of body awareness, Kabat-Zinn's twist was to 'discover' mindfulness as a distinct, secular, medicalized and popularizable practice. It was meditation in a clear eight- (and later four) week training formula with a medical twist. As an article appearing in the 1990s covering, the growing phenomenon described it:

> At the University of Massachusetts Hospital and Medical School, people like Peter can learn to build up mental fitness as well as physical stamina after major illness. In the heart of this temple of high-tech medicine, Professor Jon Kabat-Zinn's Stress Reduction Clinic teaches patients how to help their own recovery through ancient meditation practices, which he has adapted for use in modern medicine.
>
> (Robertson, 1994)

From its inception Kabat-Zinn deliberately sought to spread his discovery as far and wide as possible. In Purser's (2019) critique of *McMindfulness*, he compares Kabat-Zinn to the McDonald's franchiser Ray Kroc in terms of his ability to realize and exploit business opportunities, expanding the reach of mindfulness to new institutions under the broad umbrella of 'mindfulness based interventions' (MBIs) (p. 16). By the early 2000s, MBSR training had spread to hospitals, clinics, schools, workplaces, corporate offices, law schools and prisons around the world (Kabat-Zinn, 2003, p. 149). The initial eight-week training programme, delivered out of the University of Massachusetts Medical School, had been completed by 16,000 patients by its twenty-fifth anniversary (Kabat-Zinn, 2005). It also trained 'legions of teachers' (Wilson, 2014, p. 35) who then acted as agents of diffusion, moving the practice across the country and implementing it into the range of institutions with which they came into contact. Many would go on to create their own teacher training programmes which have since proliferated (see e.g. Selva, 2017) with little standardization in terms of professional qualifications (Demarzo et al., 2015). Soon after the opening of the Stress Reduction clinic, he had developed outpatient treatments in the form of guided meditation audio tapes (Kabat-Zinn, 1982), videotapes for use in hospitals around the United States (Goleman, 1986) and opened a mail order business for mindfulness audio in 1990 (Stress Reduction Tapes, 2022). That same year, Kabat-Zinn authored *Full Catastrophe Living*, a self-help book popularizing his vision of mindfulness which became a bestseller. In less than ten years he would publish four additional titles, cementing his position not only as a conceptual entrepreneur for mindfulness but as a self-help entrepreneur in a more general sense.[7]

Reflecting on the development of the MBSR thirty years later, he shows a consciousness of the rhetorical activity required to convince others of the import of his new programme:

And because naming is very important in how things are understood and either accepted or not, I felt that the entire undertaking needed to be held by an umbrella term broad enough to contain the multiplicity of key elements that seemed essential to field a successful clinical programme in the cultural climate of 1979.

(Kabat-Zinn, 2011, p. 288)

In defending this rhetorical work, Kabat-Zinn frequently invokes the Buddhist doctrine of 'skilful means', implicitly responding to critics who charged that he had exploited Eastern religions:

The intention and approach behind MBSR were never meant to exploit, fragment, or decontextualize the dharma, but rather to recontextualize it within the frameworks of science, medicine (including psychiatry and psychology), and healthcare so that it would be maximally useful to people who could not hear it or enter into it through the more traditional dharma gates, whether they were doctors or medical patients, hospital administrators, or insurance companies.

(Kabat-Zinn, 2011, p. 288)

Skilful means refers to the tradition, which the Buddha is said to have employed, of using pedagogical devices that may not be entirely theoretically coherent or correct but which nonetheless help to separate people from their attachments and begin them on the path to enlightenment (Pye, 2004; Schroeder, 2004). Wilson (2014) and Purser (2019) have observed that this evocation of skilful means, whereby promoters position themselves as acting deceptively for the greater good, is ubiquitous among Western mindfulness advocates. Once mindfulness became firmly established however, its advocates were free to declare it as a Buddhist practice or to joke that it is 'stealth Buddhism' (Purser, 2019, p. 87).

But early on, while maintaining an aura of 'wisdom of the ancients', the scientific credentials of the practice were heavily emphasized in Kabat-Zinn's claims-making to spread the concept. Key to his formulation was the notion of abstracting from ancient wisdom what could be 'scientifically proven' to be useful. As he told journalist Bill Moyers in the early 1990s,

Now the planet has gotten incredibly small. There is no East, and there is no West, and the human race needs all the wisdom it can get. We need to take what's most valuable from all the various consciousness traditions, integrate them into Western behavioral science and mainstream medicine, and study them as best as we can in terms of the most sophisticated and

stringent scientific methodologies. We need to ask: what is it about these
ancient traditions that tells us something about healing and the mind?

(Moyers, 1993, p. 143)

In this way, science was key to Kabat-Zinn's conceptual entrepreneurship (I
will return to its marriage with wisdom and intuition below). This marriage
clearly mattered to reporting journalists who frequently played up the
contrast between the potential 'flakiness' of practices associated with the
1960s counterculture and American New Age movement and Kabat-Zinn's
impressive medical credentials. 'Kabat-Zinn is no lotus-seated yogi – he
has a PhD in molecular biology and runs the Stress Reduction Clinic at the
University of Massachusetts Hospital', reads one such report (Austen, 1994).
Kabat-Zinn himself augmented the scientific basis of mindfulness, as he tells
CNN in 1999, 'And this [research result] is across all the different diagnoses
that people are sent for. So it's not just like the headache patients do well
or the cancer patients do well or the heart disease patients do well. They
all do well' (Salvatore et al., 1999). He continues to claim that his research
shows the techniques were 'unbelievably powerful, and they're very useful
in the boardroom, and they're very useful in the bedroom, and they're very
useful in the playroom, and they're very useful in the operating room'. Yet
this confidence preceded the strength of the evidence. Crane et al. (2010)
note large amounts of research did not begin to appear until the early 2000s.
Indeed, Kabat-Zinn concedes that early academic research was tentative
(Kabat-Zinn, 2003, p. 145). However, like self-esteem and happiness before it,
this tentativeness was downplayed early on.

Finally, there was considerable personal gain to be had. Kabat-Zinn refers
to the ability to make money from mindfulness as 'right livelihood' and is
unabashed about his promotion of mindfulness as a business venture (Kabat-
Zinn, 2011, p. 286; Stress Reduction Tapes, 2022). His 1990 book became a
bestseller, being reissued several times, most recently in 2013 ([2013] Kabat-
Zinn, 2005) – in addition to many more books and myriad mindfulness products
released since then. Mindfulness itself has evolved to become a $1.2 billion
industry by 2018 and mindfulness practice and training are now part of a global
wellness industry worth trillions of dollars (Dawson, 2021; Kim, 2018).

What's the problem?

From its inception, Kabat-Zinn's conceptual entrepreneurship positioned
mindfulness as a solution primarily to stress, a social problem that had
ascended into public consciousness in the 1970s and 1980s (see Wainwright
& Calnan, 2002) concurrently with the MBSR. Indeed, the official name of the

business he founded in 1990 was 'Stress Reduction Tapes' which remains the official (if outmoded) name of his website (Stress Reduction Tapes, 2022). However, the desire for expansion and flexibility is evident in Kabat-Zinn's early claims-making and later claims-makers would find little difficulty positioning the discourse as a solution to a vast array of social problems.

However, being initially positioned as a solution to a specific issue, mindfulness at first diffused mainly via issue communities and networks and the somewhat limited audio-visual artefacts created by Kabat-Zinn. Key turning points occurred in the early to mid-1990s. One of these was a 1993 feature on mindfulness in the PBS series *Healing and the Mind*, highlighting Kabat-Zinn and the Massachusetts Medical Centre. The show followed participants through eight weeks of training and reported results, in the words of one patient, 'like a miracle' (Moyers, 1993). News media reports of the time describe a proliferation of new training programmes inspired by the episode (e.g. Suzukamo, 1996) which has since been described as a key moment in the practice's spread (Crane et al., 2010). For conceptual entrepreneurs, reportage in the media is a key part of gaining recognition and facilitating spread beyond face-to-face and professional networks to previously unconnected individuals and groups.

Another occurred in 1995, when Kabat-Zinn set up the umbrella organization the Center for Mindfulness in Medicine, Health Care and Society. The foregrounding of mindfulness and its connection not just to health but also 'society' signifies the expansion of mindfulness conceptual entrepreneurship and the beginning of a concerted effort to launch mindfulness as a social panacea. While 'charting the course' of the MBSR, the centre aimed not to control how mindfulness spread, but instead asked that those who wanted to adopt MBSR with their own twists did so by renaming it accordingly (Boyce, 2011, p. xiii). New conceptual entrepreneurs emerged offering 'Mindfulness-Based Childbirth and Parenting, Mindfulness-Based Cognitive Therapy, Mindfulness-Based Eating Awareness Training, and Mindfulness-Based Art Training for Cancer Patients, to name just a few' (Boyce, 2011, p. xiii). In this way, the organization fostered a generation of conceptual entrepreneurs for the spread of mindfulness to a diversity of areas from childbirth to prisons (e.g. U.S. Department of Justice, 1998).

Even with dedicated ownership, the story told by mindfulness advocates had to be compelling enough to attract attention and converts, repeated many times across the mass media, and inspire clients to take up the training or become consumers of the phenomenon's rapidly proliferating commodities. Like self-esteem and happiness (and partially concurrent with both), claims-makers tell a familiar tale blending scientific claims with intuition and ancient truth, offer mindfulness as a 'deceptively simple' magic bullet and social vaccine, warn of the costs of inaction and identify new victims and new forms of suffering. In what follows, I make sense of the news media construction of the issue through an analysis of the rhetoric of the most commonly repeated claims in the 150 article sample (see Methods Appendix) using Best's (1987, 2021) framework of grounds (statements about the nature of the problem), warrants (rationales for action) and conclusions (proposed actions).

A conclusion in search of grounds

According to Best (1987, 2021), grounds refer to statements alleging that a troubling condition exists. They may give the problem a name, describe and offer typifying examples of those affected and quantify the scale of the problem. Given that mindfulness began its life as a solution to the problem of stress, it is unsurprising that most claims-making focused less on the construction of a particular issue than on identifying existing problems to which the concept could be applied. Like self-esteem and surpassing it in this respect, it was a hammer in search of a nail.

By far, the most commonly cited problems were depression (50 per cent of articles sampled), anxiety (49 per cent) and stress (43 per cent). However, from the early 1990s, claims-makers emphasized the wide benefits of the concept. More people from more diverse backgrounds are exhorted to seek out mindfulness training and advocates push for the expansion of mindfulness provision via the NHS. One article laments that 'very few patients who could benefit from mindfulness training are currently being referred for the treatment – just one in 20 GPs prescribes MBCT [Mindfulness Based Cognitive Therapy] regularly' (Halliwell, 2010a). However, less than five years later as the success of these claims becomes evident (particularly in the form of MPs pushing for expanded use and prescription (MAPPG, 2015)) demand for the training of more practitioners in mindfulness to meet the new need is taken as evidence of the scale of suffering rather than the success of such claims. Responding to the challenges of regulating practitioner training to meet demand for new teachers, Madeleine Bunting urges, 'Whatever our anxieties – and there are plenty of legitimate ones – this is responding to a real need, and is relieving human suffering' (Sherwood, 2015).

There are nearly as many claimed benefits (fifty-three identified in total) as there are problems for which it can be used (seventy-one). This has led many critics to suppose that mindfulness is about human optimization (e.g. Purser, 2019; Sauerborn, 2022). However, mindfulness claims construct human beings as existing in a state of vulnerability and disorientation without the prescribed specialist training. For instance, mindfulness is portrayed as being able to 'help children learn how to think'. By contrast, the normal state of affairs is, as described by one claims-maker:

We spend much of our daily lives doing things automatically without thinking [...]. When we are on automatic pilot we unknowingly waste enormous amounts of energy in reacting automatically and unconsciously to the outside world and to our own inner experiences. We are also more likely to react to situations in a 'fight or flight' way rather than in a more considered way.

(Jeffries, 2002)

It is not simply about making effectively functioning individuals a bit better. The use of the word 'we' and reference to 'fight or flight' generalizes and naturalizes a vision of an unthinking and reactive subject. Intervention in childhood is positioned as being necessary to manage effectively this fate.

Autopilot, automatic and unaware

Indeed, it is this that forms the distinct problem that claims-makers allege exists and through which mindfulness's ameliorative benefits, beyond relaxation, are said to function. After depression, anxiety and stress, the most commonly cited problem for which mindfulness was said to be useful was a generalized lack of awareness, often described as going through life on 'autopilot', variations of which appeared in 31 per cent of articles sampled. 'Many of us have so much on our minds at any given time that we function quite regularly on autopilot,' argues one journalist (Woods, 2013). 'Mindfulness teaches individuals to be present in the moment rather than being distracted about the past or projecting into the future. It doesn't stop you feeling emotions per se, but it does allow you to deal with them more dispassionately' she continues. One headmaster is described explaining that 'living our lives in full awareness, rather than on autopilot, is a vital skill at school and beyond' (Furnham, 2014). Another headmaster argues that the importance of mindfulness lies in its ability to help us 'stop and think' (Doughty, 2015).

The focus is on the subject, in whom solutions are said to lie, but only with the right preparation. Kabat-Zinn claims that mindfulness is 'an oxygen line straight into the heart of what is deepest and most beautiful in us as human beings' (Booth, 2017). But bringing this out requires careful coaching, particularly given the complexity of modern life. A claims-maker for the Mindfulness in Schools Project explains, 'The speed of life is making it increasingly more important [...]. Being mindful makes it easier to savour the pleasures in life as they occur. We have within us the capacity to change our relationship with what life can throw at us' (Doughty, 2015). Cultivating mindful awareness is said to allow the right choices to reveal themselves. A practitioner is quoted as saying, 'It has given me lots more options in my life, but only when I wake up to them [...]. There's a sense that we drift through our lives. Mindfulness gives you an awareness and therefore a choice as often as you choose to bring it to mind [...].'

Left to their own devices, people are portrayed as ruled by scarcely controllable emotions. A promotion for a 'Guardian Masterclass' in mindfulness tells audiences 'it's easy to lose touch with the way our bodies are feeling and end up "living in our heads". This inspiring introduction to mindfulness includes practical guidance to help you master your thoughts and feelings, rather than be controlled by them' (The Guardian, 2016). If people are not living in their heads, they are ruled by destructive instincts. One advocate claims that 'it takes some effort to fight the instinct to just do something destructive and get to that win-win mentality' (Confino, 2014). Sometimes people are referred to as mindless 'zombies' unthinkingly and precariously moving through the world. For one psychologist, mindfulness has become important due to humanity's reliance on technology. 'Look what happens at work when an IT system goes down or the electricity fails. People wander around like zombies, not knowing what to do' (Furnham, 2014). More in keeping with the preferred aviation metaphors, people's thoughts are said to be constantly 'hijacked', not only by technologies like mobile phones, but also 'emotional issues, regrets, worries about the past and future and other distractions' (Lister, 2010). Technologies appear less as human creations than increasingly out of step with human nature, presenting new dangers and threats.

The long-standing cultural tension between stasis and dynamism reverberates through mindfulness claims-making. In a world in which all that is solid apparently melts into air, mindfulness advocates promise the stability of a 'focus on the moment', where thoughts about the past and future cause upset. A life coach tells audiences:

> We are living and working in times of constant change. Change is nothing new. What is new is that the pace of change is accelerating and mindfulness trains us to focus on the moment rather than allowing our attention to be hijacked by thoughts about the past or worries about the future.
>
> (Woods, 2013)

Related claims included that people suffer from 'mental chatter', variations of which appeared in 14 per cent of articles, and possess brains in a permanent 'primitive' state of 'high alert' due to modern 'crises' such as a 'deluge of work related emails' (Woods, 2013). Writer and comedian Ruby Wax tells a journalist, '[Mindfulness] is being aware of the moment, the now, and using that to calm our over-anxious amygdala – the area in the brain which hosts our emotions – which modern life otherwise keeps in a constant state of high alert' (Lambert, 2013). '[O]ur brains have no braking system', she continues (Lambert, 2013).

In this way, while mindfulness was positioned as a solution to existing problems, a new problem was also identified: a subject characterized by generalized emotional and mental disorientation, whose overarching tendency is to act automatically rather than through reasoned activity. These automatic actions are posited as the root of social problems. This is evident in early interest in mindfulness on the part of the US Department of Justice. In detailing MBSR as an 'innovative' programme in correctional settings, criminal behaviour is described as

related to an inadequate ability to deal effectively with severe stress, deprivation and low self-esteem. Lack of development in this area, including lack of moral development, abnormal states of mind, and strong negative feelings such as fear, frustration, anger, hatred and greed can quickly lead to over aggressive and violent behavior.

(U.S. Department of Justice, 1998, p. 64)

Although a context of 'deprivation' is recognized, the problem arises when individuals fail to develop the correct emotional, moral and behavioural means to 'deal effectively' with it. Decades later, UK policymakers would place similar hope in mindfulness, writing in their report by the Mindfulness All-Party Parliamentary Group (MAPPG) entitled Mindful Nation UK: 'Practitioners may be less drawn into unhelpful habitual reactions and more able to make good choices about how to relate to their circumstances' (MAPPG, 2015, p. 16). Mindfulness parenting programmes aimed at 'disadvantaged families' (the focus on whom is justified by their 'greater risk of stress') are said to be able to reduce parents' 'destructive behaviour' and improve their children's behaviours (p. 32). Recalling the argument discussed in Chapter 2, mindfulness promises to equip subjects to adapt to a world whose structures and tumult appear naturalized and beyond human control.

The tendency towards automatic and unthinking activity without the development of special skills was placed at the heart of social problems and presented as the mechanism through which mindfulness, by providing a means to 'pay attention to what's happening in the present moment' (MAPPG, 2015, p. 6), could provide solutions. As Kabat-Zinn concluded of the report: its ramifications are 'profoundly beneficial. They will be addressing some of the most pressing problems of society at their very root – at the level of the human heart and mind' (Booth, 2015c).

It is argued that a particular mental and emotional orientation must be achieved before larger problems can be broached. Mindfulness is positioned as preparing people to deal with wicked issues, even if how these issues will ultimately be approached remains vague. As one mindfulness teacher argues, 'When we're more able to deal with stress, there's space to be creative, connect with others, make good decisions, and offer an openness of spirit to the world' (Halliwell, 2010). Even policymaking will be improved when policymakers are more 'balanced', as a Labour MP argues,

> If you make decisions from a position of balance and equilibrium, it is far better, not just for personal but political decisions that affect a whole nation. In times when you have political leaders who may not be making political decisions from a position of balance, it doesn't do them, their country or the world much good.
>
> (Booth, 2017)

Reflecting on mindfulness sessions in UK Parliament, Kabat-Zinn argues that the introduction of mindfulness into the political process could improve policymaking; by 'training the mind to be more attentive, politicians may listen better to the needs of the country and the world' (Booth, 2017).

On the other hand, some claims-makers are keen to avoid reductionist approaches: 'Self-care can never be a substitute for political struggle' says a trade union activist (Rigby, 2018). 'Helping to create a more equal society is the best way to address the suffering that results from chronically poor mental health', she continues. Still, mindfulness is positioned between subjects and the political struggle, representing the first step to 'fortify us for the many challenges that lie ahead' (Rigby, 2018).[8] Political struggle to create a 'more equal society' has become fragmented and disoriented. In the meantime, promising to strengthen subjectivity at least offers a concrete form of action. However, the effect is to imply that the main barrier to progress lies in weak subjectivity.

In positioning mindfulness as acting on social problems at their very root, claims-makers enacted the familiar rhetorical strategy of flipping the hierarchy of human needs discussed in the previous chapter, inserting their new concept between individuals and the world. First we must teach people mindfulness and receive its purported benefits before success or solutions can follow.

New victims, new suffering

In this way, claims-makers alleged the existence not only of a problem in the form of automatic and unthinking behaviour, but also constructed subjectivity in particular ways. They also singled out and described groups who could most benefit or who were most at risk and in need of intervention. Table 5.1 shows the most common of these.

Most often it is claimed that everyone could benefit in some way from mindfulness. However, children and young people are most commonly specifically singled out. Children are said to be naturally mindful, but put at risk

Table 5.1 Five most common groups mentioned in news media sample

Groups most in need	% of sample (n=150)
Everyone	26
Children and young people	25
Professionals, managers, business 'leaders', owners	24
Parents	11
Government departments, policymakers, etc.	10

by parents, society and institutions. As Kabat-Zinn is described as explaining, 'Children [...] are naturally mindful because they live in the moment and are not overly concerned about the past or the future' (McMahon, 2014). In light of this, he claims, 'The most important thing we can do is not kill that natural quality of openness and presence, but reinforce it and encourage it to continue to develop' (McMahon, 2014).

Anthony Seldon, then headmaster of the prestigious Wellington College, claims,

> I have seen the pressures grow steadily from schools, parents and, above all, from the children. The frenetic daily dash from home to school, often after too little sleep, a day of ceaseless activity, and then an evening trying to juggle homework with chatter from electronic devices, proves too much for many.'

(Seldon, 2014)

In the face of this, mindfulness will give children the ability to 'cope' with and perform better in school (Matthews, 2014), make better decisions (Reilly, 2016), be 'less impulsive' and 'have some degree of control over their inner world' (McMahon, 2014). Skills that they will 'carry with them into adulthood' (McMahon, 2014).

This focus on children is typical of post-liberal governance and is also evident in broader resilience discourses (Chandler & Reid, 2016a). Indeed, resilience is one of the most commonly referenced benefits of mindfulness practice.[9] Targeting childhood ostensibly offers a means of transforming society through reshaping children's internal worlds (Chandler, 2016a, p. 94). Whenever there is a choice to be made, and particularly at crucial life transitions, interventions emerge to attempt to enable the 'correct' one. Successful mindfulness claims (i.e. those which were widely repeated and ultimately institutionalized) were those that fit well within a policymaking framework that focuses on the 'internal life of individuals as shaped by the immediate context of family and child-rearing' (p. 93) especially as one transitions from childhood into a 'decision-making' subject. Criticisms of the mindfulness movement, particularly in its corporate manifestations, have drawn out this dimension (e.g. Forbes, 2019; Purser, 2019). For instance, Purser (2018, p. 106) writes that 'Neoliberal mindfulness emphasizes the sovereignty of autonomous individuals who can navigate the vicissitudes of late capitalist society by becoming self-regulating and self-compassionate, governing themselves, and by freely choosing their own welfare, well-being, and security.' Yet it is precisely this sovereignty that must first be demolished.

To become good decision-making subjects, people must first learn to doubt their autonomy. The state and institutions do not simply withdraw and allow subjects to make their own choices. This is why a large part of claims-making is devoted to constructing rationality and the capacity for autonomy as uncharacteristic of subjects without intervention. Subjects cannot be autonomous. They must learn to be heteronomous lest their alleged innate capacities for poor decision-making lead to risks to themselves and others. This construction is necessary not just for governance of course, but also in the basic sense that selling a new commodity often requires creating new needs and deficits that its retailers claim they can and must fill.

Mindfulness is thus constructed as something that everyone needs (even if, it is often admitted, not everyone will like or enjoy it). Claims-makers often speak in abstract terms, using the language of 'we' and 'ours'. Kabat-Zinn writes in *Full Catastrophe Living*:

> However, when we start paying attention a little more closely to the way our own mind actually works, as we do when we meditate, we are likely to find that much of the time our mind is more in the past or the future than it is in the present. Consequently in any moment we may be only partially aware of what is actually occurring in the present. We can miss many of the moments we have to live because we are not fully here for them. This is true not just while we are meditating. Unawareness can dominate the mind in any moment and consequently, it can affect everything we do.
>
> (2005, p. 21)

Headlines employ 'you' and 'yours'. 'Take control of your monsters with mindfulness' reads one in *The Telegraph* (Stogdon, 2018). 'Being more mindful, focusing on the present moment, can benefit everyone. It's not just for gurus' argues a claims-maker cited in the article, a former GP who 'now advises on healing'. There are also strong claims to universalism. 'These are universal qualities of being human,' Kabat Zinn tells readers (2011, p. 283). But it is a kind of universalized vulnerability. According to one advocate, 'mindfulness is one of the few things that gets people talking about stuff that is human' (Gelles, 2015b). 'Vulnerability may be a scary word [...] but opening up and being a bit vulnerable is the way to build relationships. [...] People say things where you think, "I'm like that, too"' (Gelles, 2015b).

The demand that mindfulness interventions be made available, in the words of one mental health charity 'for everyone who wants it' (Skidelsky, 2011), is framed in the language of inclusivity and equality. 'Another risk is that it becomes the privilege of the stressed middle classes who can afford the courses', warns Bunting (2014). While interest in the practice tends to be dominated by the middle classes, many single out work with disadvantaged groups as the most promising. 'Some of the most inspiring work is being done by people like Gary Heads in County Durham who is working with unemployed people', she continues. Of a mindfulness school programme, one article describes, 'It is an unlikely place, perhaps, to find a thriving mindfulness teaching programme. But English Martyrs is one of a growing number of schools in deprived parts of Britain that are embracing meditation techniques to help vulnerable children cope' (Walker, 2018).

In addition to policymakers, who both claim themselves and are claimed to need mindfulness training in order to affect their own self-management, 'business leaders', managers and professionals make up the next most frequent group discussed. Echoing the draw towards 'sin' of the capitalist forever torn between accumulation and enjoyment, mindfulness is claimed to be useful for CEOs seeking to get in touch with what 'really matters', but also to help improve the productivity of their workforce. Arianna Huffington's (2014) book *Thrive*, in which she advocates mindfulness meditation, begins with an anecdote of a fall she suffers due to exhaustion from overwork. 'In terms of the traditional measures of success, which focus on money and power, I was very successful. But I was not living a successful life by any sane definition [...]' (p. 3). Later she warns readers that studies have failed to find a consistent connection between money and happiness and exhorts them to move beyond the 'relentless competition to work harder, stay later, pull more all-nighters' (p. 77). Yet on her blog she writes,

There's nothing touchy-feely about increased profits. This is a tough economy, and it's going to be that way for a long time. Stress-reduction and mindfulness don't just make us happier and healthier, they're a proven competitive advantage for any business that wants one.

(Huffington, 2013)

The connection between high pressure, long working hours and profit appears to elude her. The desire for a bit of freedom and happiness turns in on itself and becomes another competitive advantage. Once again, the escape from calculation and competition itself becomes a business,[10] and in so doing duplicates the evils it was meant to relieve.

Reflecting on the penchant for mindfulness among CEOs, one journalist writes, 'We all get that we're supposed to be doing this mindfulness thing [...]. None more so than the CEOs, who deem it their new secret weapon, granting them more potency, better relationships and a clearer vision' (Gelles, 2015b). He concludes tongue in cheek, 'Practise enough mindful meditation, you see, and you can alter your neural pathways to lengthen your attention span and block out distractions. It's the ultimate in mind control.' Yet there is something to this observation that the need to control one's mind – and for managers and 'business leaders' to take an interest in this on behalf of their staff – should be foregrounded so prominently by claims-makers in spite of its potentially dystopian connotations. The words 'mind' and 'control' appear in 60 per cent of the articles sampled and occur within five words of each other in over 1,600 articles mentioning mindfulness in the Nexis database. Because a tendency towards poor decision-making is perceived as a default state, the notion that 'mind control' is needed and desirable does not appear unsettling, but rather as common sense.

Finally, subjectivity is posited as something that requires constant surveillance and vigilance to avoid things going wrong. Maintaining the innocence for dystopian phrasing, mindfulness apps are described as 'a Fitbit for the mind' by Google's 'head of mindfulness' (Confino, 2014). Looking forward to 'devices that will be able to show how meditation impacts brain waves' he foresees the 'potential for creating a whole industry of professional trainers'. 'Just imagine setting a goal like "a year from now, I want to be able to calm my mind in 40 per cent of the time it takes me now" and my personal trainer is accountable to that target'. Similarly, the CEO of Headspace, a mindfulness app, asks audiences to think of mindfulness as a 'gym membership for your mind' (Furnham, 2014). Indeed, the discourse is replete with physical fitness metaphors, appearing in 20 per cent of articles sampled. Like physical fitness, mental health and wellness are no longer presumed to be a default state but rather as requiring constant supervision and maintenance.

What mindfulness does is less important than the story it tells about human subjectivity. Subjects are positioned not as autonomous but as heteronomous, requiring careful and continuous self-attention with recourse to external guidance to avoid the wrong choice-making that leads to personal and social problems. In this way, a large part of claims-making was not only about conceptual entrepreneurship across a range of social problems, but also about constructing the subject itself as a problem for which mindfulness conceptual entrepreneurs possessed the answer.

Rhetorical warrants

Warrants rhetorically answer the question of why audiences should act. They make connections between a problem's grounds and proposed solutions, usually drawing on cultural values. Why should audiences care about mindfulness? In short, because like other therapeutic fad waves, it makes 'intuitive sense' but is also confirmed by science and ancient wisdom. It promises myriad savings for low initial costs and represents a novel opportunity to affect a revolutionary break with the status quo.

Science, intuition and ancient wisdom

As touched on above, the marriage of science, intuition and ancient wisdom was central to Kabat-Zinn's conceptual entrepreneurship. Explicitly seeking to pare mindfulness of its religious connotations, he emphasized its scientific, medical and secular nature. However, at the same time his claims-making maintained an aura of enchantment and intuition. This is taken forward by others as the discourse spreads. The science drawn upon is a naturalized one, confirming key features of human nature, rather than science in the sense of technological creation. Indeed, science in its latter meaning is positioned as part of the problem. Technology (16 per cent of the sample) and the pace of modern life (22 per cent) are posited as key disorienting features.[11] 55 per cent of articles sampled explicitly stressed the scientific nature of claims, but 40 per cent also blended this with philosophy, history and/or religion. The authority of claims is mostly drawn from medicine, psychology and psychiatry but also from religious leaders, practitioners and personal experiences. In this way, while mindfulness was thoroughly scientized, it was not completely shorn of its association with 'ancient wisdom' and religious connotations. Many articles begin by emphasizing the ancient origins of mindfulness discourses, before relating new scientific discoveries about the practice which confirm its truth and connectedness with human nature.

Like self-esteem and happiness entrepreneurs, Kabat-Zinn describes a quasi-religious origin story. While meditating, he claims that what eventually became MBSR appeared to him in a vision:

> I saw in a flash not only a model that could be put in place, but also the long-term implications of what might happen if the basic idea was sound and could be implemented in one test environment – namely that it would spark new fields of scientific and clinical investigation, and would spread to hospitals and medical centres and clinics across the country and around the world, and provide right livelihood for thousands of practitioners. Because it was so weird, I hardly ever mentioned this experience to others.
>
> (Kabat-Zinn, 2011, p. 286)

As a practice drawn from religion, it is perhaps unsurprising that mindfulness should foreground a sense of magic and enchantment more than other therapeutic fads. Kabat-Zinn recognizes, however, that the sense of mysticism, while potentially offering a certain novelty and mystique, also presents a drawback (to which he alludes by using the word 'weird' above, not fully committing to the spirituality implied by a meditative vision).

> [F]rom the beginning of MBSR, I bent over backward to structure it and find ways to speak about it that avoided as much as possible the risk of it being seen as Buddhist, 'New Age,' 'Eastern Mysticism' or just plain 'flakey.' To my mind this was a constant and serious risk that would have undermined our attempts to present it as commonsensical, evidence-based, and ordinary, and ultimately a legitimate element of mainstream medical care.
>
> (Kabat-Zinn, 2011, p. 282)

The practice must seem 'commonsensical' in the terms with which people are culturally familiar. It must have the aura of rationality but maintain its potential for enchantment. Echoing self-esteem conceptual entrepreneurs' penchant for the use of the word 'intuitive', Kabat-Zinn uses the word 'commonsensical' five times across this fifteen-page reflection. It is common sense in the same way that it was 'intuitive' that self-esteem played a causal role in social issues. Claims-makers take for granted that problems start at the individual level, in a tendency to be ruled by disordered emotions, and spiral out from there.

Financial costs and benefits

As is common not only of therapeutic fad waves but also social problem claims-making more generally, claims-makers promised financial benefits if their solutions were adopted and warned of dire costs if they weren't. Businesses are promised higher productivity and profits as well as savings on absenteeism. Mindfulness is presented as offering 'a "glimmer of hope" for tackling the spiralling cost of healthcare on the NHS' (Jenkin, 2014) and of police absenteeism (Pugh, 2016). Meeting with UK policymakers, Kabat-Zinn is described as having a 'compelling proposition: mindfulness has unlimited applicability to almost every healthcare issue we now face – and it's cheap' (Bunting, 2013). The Mindful Nation UK report recommended that secular meditation courses be made more widely available at an initial cost of £10m, training new meditation teachers, and for mindfulness to be taught in schools. In one year, the Mindfulness in Schools Project had trained 2,000 teachers at a cost of £2,500/each, with much of the growth coming 'from schools with higher than average proportions of vulnerable children' (Walker, 2018). However, these high upfront costs are justified on the basis of tackling more expensive future problems by inducing a range of benefits from well-being to behavioural control.

Conceptual entrepreneurs promise that large investments in their wares are trivial in relation to future benefits and savings. Governments, businesses and society as a whole lose out with underinvestment in such a simple, cost-effective practice.

Emotion revolutions

Despite its apparent simplicity, mindfulness claims are presented as a radical, revolutionary break from current ways of doing things. Vying for the scarce resource of media and public attention, claims-makers augment their claims' importance, using phrases like 'seismic changes', 'transformational', and alleging we are in a 'historical moment'. Its Buddhist roots are described as 'revolutionary' in their 'emphasis on compassion and non-harm' and 'profoundly counter-cultural' in their 'ascetism' (Bunting, 2014). A chapter in *The Mindfulness Revolution* promises the 'mindful consumer can help change the world' and offers tips on tracking the 'karmic virtues' of various consumer products (Goleman, 2011, p. 245). Mindfulness in schools could change the entire education system (Smellie, 2015); the UK could become 'mindful nation' (Booth, 2014a). Mindfulness-based technology requires a 'rethinking of the very ways that the industry and its money is structured, changing the entire assumptions that power the biggest companies in the world' (Griffin, 2018). Kabat-Zinn claims that mindfulness 'may actually be the only promise the species and the planet have for making it through the next couple hundred years' (quoted in Purser, 2019, p. 7).

The tendency, however, to 'sacralize the present', to use Purser's terms (2019, p. 93), alludes to its existence as a form of presentist romanticism. Like the related happiness discourse (Frawley, 2015, pp. 178–9), claims promise a revolutionary change which is oriented less towards a transformative future than towards a rediscovery of allegedly lost values and virtues that will somehow open individuals up to the problems of the present. One claims-maker argues, 'the challenge now is to secularize Buddhist ethics and philosophy so that they can address the conditions of our world by articulating a way in which we can flourish together on this earth' (Batchelor, 2016).

As mindfulness becomes more and more adopted by powerful corporations and tech companies, claims-makers begin to worry that the revolution may be stalled. 'Delinked from Buddhist ethics, mindfulness could become a form of performance enhancement – some of the enthusiasm coming from the corporate sectors and military leads it dangerously in this direction. That is a real risk', observes Bunting (2014). Kabat-Zinn (somewhat surprisingly given his history of unabashed instrumentalism) warns of a superficial

'McMindfulness' taking over, which ignores its ethical foundations and 'divorces it from its profoundly transformative potential' (Sherwood, 2015). One journalist observes,

> Yet mindfulness experts, aware that the technique could be used to turn us into placid worker drones, are taking rearguard action. Mark Williams, the founder of the Oxford Mindfulness Centre, said that seeing more clearly what is happening in their lives could make employees more subversive and critical. In other words, businesses may be cultivating an army of mindful rebels.
>
> (Little, 2018)

Yet, this journalist is suspicious: 'he said that three years ago – so where's the revolution?' (Little, 2018).

As mindfulness becomes bound up with performance indicators and enhancement, the emotional escape from a world of sterile quantification becomes itself an aspect of sterile quantification. Both the corporate and the radical uses of mindfulness appear also to share the central formulation that first we must promote *x* [internal modification of subjects] before *y* [insoluble problem] can ever be approached. There is a strong sense of impasse which is deflected onto the subject who requires a new ethics, new emotional outlook or new more mindfully approached behaviours. Political avenues having long been closed off, liberation is positioned as the result of the reform of subjectivity and nonspecific projects in awareness raising within vague chains of cause and effect. Claims evoke a rhetoric of radicalism, but the bridge between *is* and *ought* seems to curve backward, to rediscovering lost values and truths that will somehow offer answers to the predicaments of the present.

Rhetorical conclusions

As a conclusion in search of grounds, most claims-making focuses on how mindfulness acts as a solution to personal and social problems. Articles sampled called for or described interventions falling into the following broad domains (Figure 5.2).

Most interventions were commercial in nature; articles described mindfulness coaching and retreats, apps and consultancies. Individuals were also advised on myriad ways mindfulness could be used in daily life. Governments were exhorted to fund mindfulness training and to expand its influence into new policy domains. Children, it was argued, should be taught mindfulness in schools, while parents should learn mindful parenting practices and workplaces should implement it to combat stress and burnout.

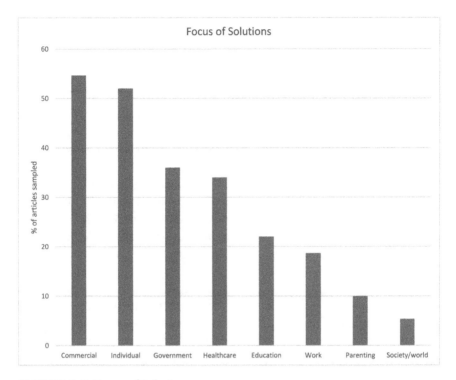

FIGURE 5.2 *Focus of Solutions.*

By attending first to the arena of emotion across these domains, it was argued that personal and social problems could be stemmed.

A 'deceptively simple' solution

While I have necessarily touched upon some of the ways in which mindfulness functions as a solution to social problems thus far, two further facets of mindfulness as a solution to social problems are characteristic of therapeutic fads and worth detailing further: its positioning as a 'deceptively simple' solution and as a magic bullet/social vaccine. Like other movements to promote positive emotions, mindfulness was always vulnerable to charges of 'flakiness', as Kabat-Zinn's reflections above illustrate. This puts claims-makers in the position of needing to augment seriousness and difficulty without deterring adoption. Positioning their concept as 'deceptively simple' highlights low barriers to entry while implying a high pay off for those successful. It's 'deceptively simple' but 'not easy to do' (Woods, 2013).

It may sound deceptively airy-fairy, but make no mistake, this isn't about chanting and there's no crosslegged spirituality involved. The US military (hardly a bastion of hippiedom) offers marines mindfulness training before they are deployed, in recognition that it is an effective form of mental discipline.'

(Woods, 2013)

The same number of articles claimed that mindfulness is 'easy' as claimed it was 'difficult'. Many articles claimed it was both easy and difficult. 'Mindfulness is both astonishingly simple and, for most of us who live in our heads, very difficult' (Bunting, 2014).

Claims-makers also positioned mindfulness as a magic bullet, with broad applications and few drawbacks. They promised risk-free benefits from better sex to lower anxiety and the prevention and treatment of depression. As one advocate asserts: 'You have nothing to lose but your stress' (Woods, 2013). Anthony Seldon, by then Vice Chancellor of the University of Buckingham, declares:

I'm absolutely convinced that for students, postgraduates, academic staff and support staff [mindfulness] is a natural, healthy, risk-free way of finding greater concentration and ensuring better mental health, and the ability to resist the problems of depression and anxiety and phobias and addictions.

(Swain, 2016)

The Mindful Nation UK report attempts to head off claims that mindfulness is a panacea (MAPPG, 2015, p. 6), but nonetheless argues there are 'benefit[s] in a wide range of contexts' while identifying few drawbacks besides the difficulty of spreading the practice as far as deemed necessary. Mindfulness is often counterposed to antidepressants and positioned as an opportunity to avoid their side effects. This is not only the case for the treatment of diagnosed illnesses, but also when proposing universal interventions. As head of Wellington College, Seldon advocated the teaching of mindfulness arguing that it can be 'more effective than pills in reducing vulnerability to depression, and without the side-effects of antidepressants' (Seldon, 2014). At the same time, counterclaims appear in newspaper discourses in 2014, warning that mindfulness can have side effects including 'depersonalization', 'impaired relationships' (Booth, 2014b) or even 'emotional distress, hallucinations' and 'ending up in a psychiatric ward' (Stella, 2015). However, in spite of the extreme nature of some of these claims, they have relatively little impact on broader claims-making and the Mindful Nation UK report mentions no negative side effects at all in spite of claims of such events going back to the 1970s.

Where self-esteem was a 'social vaccine' and promoting happiness would 'immunize' against future problems, mindfulness is compared to 'fluoride in the water' (Booth, 2015a). Like these movements, mindfulness is positioned as preventing problems before they start. 'It's a preventative treatment – that's what makes it different,' says a clinical psychologist (Derbyshire, 2014). In contrast to other therapies, mindfulness teaches 'people skills to stay well' (Derbyshire, 2014). In early claims-making, this preventative action is mainly described in relation to physical health conditions, but as time goes on, this expands to encompass problems from mental ill-health to criminal behaviour and even healthcare scandals. As to the latter, Kabat-Zinn is described as arguing:

[M]indfulness is relevant to the debate about how to instil compassion and attentive care in healthcare workers to avoid a repeat of the Mid Staffordshire scandal. Mindfulness training inspires compassion [...]. Just the act of being in the moment and paying attention to that moment allows the innate compassion within us all to emerge.

(Bunting, 2013)

At the same time, many claims-makers anticipate criticism that mindfulness is a panacea, 'quick fix' or magic bullet and are quick to head off such claims. A police constable and 'practising Buddhist' is 'clear that mindfulness is not a magic bullet,' but rather a 'strengthener' (Pugh, 2016). 'Mindfulness is not a quick fix,' warns a mindfulness children's book author (McMahon, 2014). 'It's not in itself the solution to your problems, but it is the necessary first step' says a clinical psychologist (Blair, 2015). 'MBCT is not a cure but it does teach people how to understand, manage and cope with their depression or difficulties and "points the way to health and happiness"' argues Ruby Wax (Crewe, 2013).

This speaks to a key characteristic of mindfulness as a solution, or perhaps non-solution, to social problems. In public claims-making, mindfulness's ameliorative potential lies in shoring up individuals to find peace 'in a frantic world' as the title of one mindfulness book puts it (Williams & Penman, 2011). As the authors describe:

Negative feelings persist when the mind's problem-solving Doing mode volunteers to help, but instead ends up compounding the very difficulties you were seeking to overcome. But there *is* an alternative. Our minds also have a different way of relating to the world – it's called the Being mode.

(Williams & Penman, 2011, p. 34)

In the latter,

you find that you can change your *internal landscape* (the *mindscape*, if you will) irrespective of what's happening around you. You are no longer dependent on external circumstances for your happiness, contentment and poise. You are back in control of your life. If Doing mode is a trap, then Being mode is freedom.

(p. 35)

Real freedom and happiness come from within, the more detached from the external world, the more authentic. The result, however, is not to become resigned to fate, but rather to 'deal with problems in the most effective way possible and at the most appropriate moment' (Williams & Penman, 2011, p. 40). There is a sense that the choices are readily available – or as they write, the 'wellsprings of peace and contentment' are 'living inside us all' – if only the subject can be released from the 'cage that our frantic and relentless way of life has crafted for them' (p. 2). Unfortunately, 'many of us in the Western world have largely forgotten how to live a good and joyful existence' (p. 2). Mindfulness provides solutions by putting human beings back in touch with what was 'well understood in the ancient world' (p. 2).

The starting point is the individual who must find some solid ground, some breathing space to think clearly, within a bewildering and ever-moving world. According to Kabat-Zinn, it can help us answer how to be 'at home in our own skin within the maelstrom' (2005, p. xxix). In this way, the argument that it is not a panacea is sincere in a much deeper sense. The vagueness about how the problems that mindfulness advocates have 'discovered' are actually to be solved reflects an intuition that most problems ultimately arise from a veil of irrationality separating the subject from the world of choices. At the same time, it speaks to a deeper sense that there might not be solutions. In the face of this, subjects are invited to make a home within the maelstrom when it appears impossible to see beyond it – to live calmly in a dangerous world.

6

Mindfulness from Adoption to Exhaustion

Every day audiences are confronted with myriad competing claims about the problematic nature of reality and what should be done to remedy it. Many of these will be short-lived. Those that are successful are inflected with this rhetorical struggle for acceptance. The success of mindfulness claims in terms of their widespread institutionalization gives insight into the cultural resonance of the narrative whose 'discovery' I detailed in the previous chapter. In this chapter, I discuss the widespread adoption of these claims and the way that claims-makers adapted and adjusted their rhetoric to suit more expansive needs. Over time, as claims were stretched beyond their breaking point and their novelty begins to fade, the discourse shows signs of exhaustion. However, the cultural impact remains.

Adoption

In a culture long accustomed to situating subjectivity at the heart of social problems, there is considerable receptivity to claims problematizing emotion. They have a narrative fidelity with the stories, myths and folk tales of the surrounding culture while also contributing to them. This, combined with experiential commensurability and their rhetorical flexibility, makes the scope for their adoption potentially much broader than other fads.[1] Recall that in contrast to owners who discover the problem, adopters jump on the bandwagon, implementing and further spreading the message once it has already become available in the public sphere.

The Mindful Nation UK report argues, 'Mindfulness could play [the] role as a popular, effective way for people to keep their mind healthy. Kabat-Zinn believes that mindfulness is on an even steeper adoption trajectory than jogging' (MAPPG, 2015, p. 6). And adoption has indeed been both steep and widespread. In the 150-article news media sample, 129 individuals and groups appear making claims about or are described as having adopted or institutionalized mindfulness. It is adopted across a breadth of institutions, the most commonly discussed being schools (19 per cent of articles sampled), the NHS (15 per cent), the US military (10 per cent) and the criminal justice system (9 per cent). News media articles report on the widespread uptake, functioning themselves as claims to significance:

> Mindfulness is selling millions of books and apps, it appears on the front cover of Time magazine, pops up in the Financial Times and is used by all kinds of people from corporate executives and nurses to sportsmen and primary school children. Once a poorly understood New Age fad, it has moved from the margins to the mainstream. Nothing demonstrates that better than the launch of an all-party parliamentary group on mindfulness on Wednesday.

> (Bunting, 2014)

Another advocate describes, 'Whereas for years meditation's public image was stuck in the 1960s, tainted with hippie self-indulgence or new-age flakiness, now it's being taken seriously by everyone from top academics to US congressman and government departments' (Halliwell, 2010b).

Celebrities including Goldie Hawn, Emma Watson and Oprah Winfrey extol the benefits of mindfulness in their personal lives and advocate its spread. On the cover of Winfrey's O Magazine in 2009, she poses next to an image of her former self baring a toned midsection. A caption runs across the image, 'How did I let this happen again?' Inside the magazine she describes a plan to tackle recent weight gain involving 'self-awareness, mindfulness, and guts' (Winfrey, 2009, p. 25). Actress Goldie Hawn's Hawn Foundation promotes mindfulness programmes in schools (MindUP, 2022), while other celebrities hire on-set personal mindfulness coaches and Gwyneth Paltrow and Emma Watson are described as 'rav[ing]' about the mindfulness app Headspace (Vernon, 2014).

Spreading rapidly in the mid-2010s, a growing number of employers began to introduce mindfulness to their employees to increase 'emotional intelligence' and reduce 'stress-related absenteeism' including the US Marines, the NHS, Google, General Mills and Transport for London according to a briefing paper on its benefits from the Institute for Employment Studies (L. Hall, 2015, p. 2). Arianna Huffington's wellness company Thrive Global advises its clients to promote mindfulness and even build nap rooms for employees (Greenfield Bloomberg, 2016). An article in the Huffington Post in 2014 advises:

Whether you are planning a live customer conference or an internal team meeting, create moments to unplug. Build a nap room (a practice which has gained popularity at *The Huffington Post*, General Mills, and Google offices), a place for people to meditate, or practice yoga. Your constituents will initially be skeptical. Eventually, they will appreciate, if not love, the gesture.

(Nirell, 2014)

The head of diversity and inclusion at accountancy firm PwC describes how they 'have introduced a holistic mental health and physical approach, including mindfulness training' to combat stress and depression (Matthews, 2014). So ubiquitous had mindfulness become by 2014 that one journalist commented, 'Last week I even got a press release from an office furniture manufacturer that claimed its products boosted "mindfulness"' (Sanghera, 2014).

American institutions and policymakers showed particularly early interest, with pilot programmes running in American prisons as early as 1992 and driven by an interest in its potential to '"rewire" or alter the brain in ways that literally change the mind and lead to more prosocial behaviors' (J. M. Dunn, 2010, p. 3). American universities including Harvard offer mindfulness training to students to help 'deepen self-reflection, help you manage stress and enrich your life' (President and Fellows of Harvard College, 2022). The National Center for Health Statistics National Health Interview Survey (Black et al., 2018) showed that use of meditation among American children aged 4–17 increased rapidly from 2012 to 2017. Mindfulness training among US marines is said to enable them to 'cut through the confusion of battle to distinguish between civilians and fighters' (Chynoweth, 2013). The training has also been given to officers in the British Army, Royal Navy and Royal Air Force with military forces in other countries following suit and NATO holding symposia on how to extend its use (Richtel, 2019).

This is in addition to the burgeoning mindfulness industry. Since the early 2000s, mindfulness courses have proliferated worldwide along with thousands of mindfulness apps, online courses, retreats, holidays, colouring books (for adults and children), children's books and an entire mindfulness self-help genre. As discussed in the previous chapter, estimates put the value of the mindfulness industry in the billions.

This adoption was affected swiftly. Recall that mindfulness had spread to hundreds of hospitals across the United States at a time when the evidence base was admittedly 'tentative'. In 2013, mindfulness is described as the latest 'buzzword' floating around UK parliament, with its application being discussed in relation to nearly everything from unemployment to depression (Woods, 2013). Cross-party groups in the UK House of Commons and Lords began attending mindfulness training and produced the above-described Mindful Nation UK report in 2015. Commentators speculated that the popularity of mindfulness across such sweeping areas of political and social life spoke to a demand or need on the part of the population. 'The public is calling for practical action. It's now time to hold the incoming government to commit to significant steps', claimed a mental health charity campaigner (Owen, 2015). While others surmised that its popularity was down to a societal 'awakening' (Stevens, 2019), mindfulness was initially adopted by those in 'elite' positions (Kucinskas, 2018, 2021), diffusing from the top down much like happiness and self-esteem before it. Adoption by individuals with access to both financial and political resources, with easy access to the media and policymakers and otherwise in positions where implementation is more direct, greatly aided its trickle down through institutions. But also important was its positive valence; movements framed as promoting positive emotional outlooks foster bipartisan support and thus swift institutionalization. Claims-makers have more to gain by framing their claims in the new discourse's terms. This in turn encourages more individuals and groups to draw on its language to make sense of their problems and missions, causing the wave to crest.

In 2017, politicians from fifteen countries met in the UK to 'meditate together' and discuss how mindfulness can be used in international and domestic policy (Booth, 2017). The event, which an article in *The Guardian* refers to as a 'world first', was organized by senior Conservative and Labour MPs (Booth, 2017). British politicians have influenced other national legislatures to adopt mindfulness courses including the Dutch and French (Bristow, 2019). 'Throughout this process of inquiry, and through visits to programmes in their local constituencies, some MPs have become passionate advocates of mindfulness-based approaches within government policy' writes Bristow (2019, p. 89). With such enthusiastic adoption and evangelical attitude towards its further spread, it is easy to mistake that, as this supportive review puts it, 'political advocates do recognise that innovation and research is still on-going to determine just how, when and where it's most appropriate for individuals to intentionally cultivate this capacity through training' (p. 89).

Indeed, in many ways mindfulness functioned not only as a solution in search of problems, but a policy in search of evidence. Once faith in mindfulness as a cure-all became widespread, policymakers expressed their disappointment that not enough evidence had yet been brought to bear on the solution in which they had already placed their confidence. As the Mindfulness UK report states, 'Also disappointing has been the inadequate investment in the high quality research needed to strengthen the evidence' (MAPPG, 2015, p. 24). That is, evidence is needed not to ascertain whether the proposed solution actually works, but rather to give a decided course of action a firmer foundation. This is not uncommon with interventions seeking to identify deficiencies within the population or some section thereof, wherein the presumption of efficacy is already established and pre-empts calls for evidence (see e.g. Edwards et al., 2017 with regard to ACEs [adverse childhood experiences]). As with these efforts, claims to the scientific foundations of mindfulness tend to underplay their shakiness, with much research suffering from issues of poor construct validity, a tendency for evaluative studies to be carried out by vested interests rather than disinterested observers, lacking replication, and suffering problems that plague reliance on self-reports (P. Grossman, 2019; Van Dam et al., 2018).

Yet such deficiencies do not slow the spread of the solution. Recall that solutions in search of problems find their most enthusiastic adopters in institutions generally prone to fads, for instance, in education and medicine which have high expectations for progress or management which is highly competitive (Best, 2006a). Indeed, mindfulness appears to have proliferated with the greatest speed within these spheres, in spite of weak or at least initially tentative evidence bases. Skilled conceptual entrepreneurs exploit existing spaces in institutions created by previous fads. When those waves have rolled through, there are management experts, educationalists and an entire psychotherapeutic industry on the lookout for the next novel intervention. For instance, one supportive review notes that 'organizational mindfulness research is still developing a comprehensive case for the wide scale application of mindfulness' (J. Passmore, 2019). However, mindfulness had been adopted in organizations at a wide scale for at least a decade prior to this publication and the author of the review remains enthusiastic about its further spread.

Similarly, education has been particularly receptive to therapeutic fads. Mindfulness has appeared in UK classrooms since at least the early 2000s, being incorporated as a method of teaching emotional literacy and in the broader Philosophy for Children movement (Jeffries, 2002; Topping et al., 2019) and later piggybacking on policy interest in 'character education' (e.g. Marks, 2015) and the ascendance of happiness and well-being education as a tool for their facilitation. For instance, the Mindfulness in Schools Project (MiSP) was justified in 2014 by a spokeswoman who claimed: 'Teaching mindfulness in the classroom reduces children's behaviour problems, improves general feelings of wellbeing and improves their ability to pay attention' (McMahon, 2014). Through initiatives like MiSP's 'Stop, Breathe and Be!', mindfulness was incorporated into schools' personal, social, health and economic education (PHSE) or well-being programmes (Marks, 2015) while, under Anthony Seldon, Wellington college promoted mindfulness as part of its well-publicized happiness and well-being classes (Seldon, 2007).

The NHS was another particularly early adopter, with the National Institute for Health and Clinical Excellence (NICE) recommending MBCT for the prevention of recurrent depression in 2004 (National Institute for Clinical

Excellence, 2004). Yet Van Dam et al. (2018) argue that this adoption in the UK as well as by American counterparts was the result of 'high profile' and 'select results' when 'much more research will be needed before we know for what mental and physical disorders, in which individuals, MBIs [mindfulness-based interventions] are definitively helpful' (p. 46).

Whether or not mindfulness interventions can be said to 'work',[2] what is more interesting is the way that the story it tells about the relationship between individuals, social problems and social change was found to be so compelling, so 'common sense', across so many institutions in public life.

Expansion

Once the solution becomes accepted, nearly all problems fall into its scope, accounting for the large number of problems appearing in the newspaper sample. Asserting a preventative power not only means that a broad range of problems can full under its purview, but also justifies expansive universal interventions with their focus on the entirety of the population. The same is true for economic costs discussed under warrants in Chapter 4. The effect is to say that mindfulness is for everyone and is everyone's concern. Given this expansive purview, many observers begin to refer to the discourse as a panacea. Yet as I have shown in the previous chapter, claims-makers are keen to head off such claims, perhaps aware that they signal the fad reaching a saturation point. Still there remains a desire to hold on to the benefits that expansion brings while remaining alert to its drawbacks. One claims-maker demonstrates the careful rhetorical navigation this entails:

> 'Mindfulness is everywhere, and we hear that it can sort out just about anything – anxiety, depression, insomnia, even heart disease. Why, then, do a growing number of my patients, having tried mindfulness, tell me how disappointed they feel? [...] The fault, I'm afraid, lies with us – with therapists. When a new and promising technique is introduced, we tend to get over-excited about what it can offer and we start promising too much. We also have a tendency to package up the technique, to create one set of easy instructions so anyone can do it. That, I'm afraid, is what's happening with mindfulness. By suggesting that this technique is the answer to all distress, we set it up to disappoint. And by suggesting there's only one "right" way to do it, we're in danger of sabotaging its true value.

The claims-maker concedes that the practice has been too simply packaged yet warns readers that there is no one 'right' way to do it, thus maintaining a certain degree of permissiveness that drives its uptake. However, as the exhaustion section details, this leads to the inevitable criticism that if there is no wrong way to do it, what is it that people are doing that is said to be associated with so many benefits?

Yet, as the discourse spreads, this flexible syntax is regarded as an asset. As Wilson (2014) and Kucinskas (2021) note, adoption leads to adaptation. The authors of a chapter in a *Clinical Handbook of Mindfulness* observe,

> As mindfulness is adopted by Western psychotherapy and migrates away from its ancient roots, its meaning is expanding. Most notably, mental qualities beyond sati (awareness, attention, and remembering) are being included in "mindfulness" as we adapt it to alleviate clinical conditions. These qualities include nonjudgment, acceptance, and compassion.
>
> (Siegel et al., 2009, p. 19)

In this way, as practices diffuse, they are innovated by those who adopt and transmit them. For instance, as less influential advocates sought to institutionalize mindfulness claims, they 'deliberately adapted contemplative practice to resonate in their professional contexts to avoid coming across as esoteric, too New Age, or dogmatic' (Kucinskas, 2018, pp. 11, 15). In other contexts where such factors were beneficial, advocates changed tack and emphasized the practice's inherent spirituality or religiosity, a practice which critics have termed 'code-switching' (C. G. Brown, 2016) or turning the 'Buddhist switch' on and off (Purser, 2019, p. 87). Mindfulness, like self-esteem, becomes a 'word for all seasons'.

Expansion is thus fostered by this flexibility and permissiveness. Claims-makers emphasize different aspects of the more expansive meanings attributed to mindfulness depending upon their focus. For instance, advocates focusing on education highlight its ability to promote attentiveness and impulse control. One teacher describes thoughts as 'buses' passing a stop. 'You can choose to get on the bus and get carried away with your thought or you can chose to let it pass' (Booth, 2015a). 'All you are doing', she continues, 'is giving [students] a tool to exercise some level of control over what their thoughts are and how distracting they are on a day to day basis'. Another explains mindfulness practice with children thus:

> Sit with your child in a quiet place and introduce the exercise as follows: "A frog is a remarkable creature. It is aware of everything that is happening around it but the frog tends not to react right away. The frog sits still and breathes, preserving its energy instead of getting carried away by all the ideas that keep popping into its head. The frog sits still while it breathes. Its frog tummy rises and falls. Anything a frog can do, you can do too."
>
> (McMahon, 2014)

Claims-makers for mindfulness at work are similar, emphasizing its purported ability to heighten attention and focus. 'What is it all about? Essentially, to be actively attentive and aware' (Furnham, 2014). Others emphasize its origins in stress reduction and ability to promote relaxation. One practitioner and author argues that secular mindfulness 'holds the key to saving us from the purgatory of constant stress' via 'breathing techniques' that enable people to be 'in the present movement – right here, right now, without wanting it to be somehow different' (Hawksley, 2014).

Yet a more significant area of expansion occurs in the variety of practices and interventions developed and made available. Barriers to entry become more porous, with the time required to master the practice gradually dwindling, reaching out to more and more people who might initially be put off by long periods of dedication. According to one observer, mindfulness is absent of 'the kind of snobbery that whispers that you will not really cut it unless you have spent four years in an ashram' (Cavendish, 2014). Over time, accounts of mindfulness practice move from long retreats to descriptions of how audiences can glean its benefits in hours or minutes per day. One article assures readers, referring to Chade-Meng Tan, then Google's head of mindfulness training and 'Jolly Good Fellow':

> For those who worry that mindfulness takes years to have any impact, Tan insists that it can create a measurable change in 100 minutes. For those who want a more fundamental impact that can change their lives, this can be achieved in 52 hours [...].'

> (Confino, 2014)

Another advocate claims, 'People fear that it will take ages, that they will have to meditate for 30 minutes a day, but if I tried doing that I would just end up creating a shopping list' (Chynoweth, 2013). A headline in 2004 declares that mindfulness can be achieved by taking '20 minutes to eat two raisins' (Kleeman, 2004). By 2017, even this was a five-minute endeavour (e.g. Kidd, 2017).

In an early claim from 2001, Kabat-Zinn's approach to stress reduction in the United States is described as requiring an hour of '"concentration" meditation, sitting still and focusing on the breath, in order to develop the mental discipline necessary for mindfulness' (Woodham, 2001). However, a UK claims-maker follows this with a keenness to stress the fluidity of the practice:

> It's different strokes for different people. Some people love chanting; others can't stand it. Some love to sit still for 15 or 20 minutes, others fidget. Meditation is an intensified version of what granny used to do when

she stroked the cat – a mindful awareness often accompanied by gentle repetitive activity. There are all kinds of unsung forms of meditation in our culture, from knitting to swimming 30 lengths in the local baths.

(Woodham, 2001)

Indeed, mindfulness is said not to require anything that laypeople might recognize as 'meditation' at all. Observing the proliferating array of mindfulness books and commodities on offer, one bemused commentator observes, 'You can move mindfully, travel mindfully, even go to the loo mindfully' (Norton, 2015). Claims-makers allege that mindfulness need not 'necessarily conflict with a busy existence' (Burkeman, 2016). Rohan Gunatillake, author of a book promising to 'redesign' mindfulness, alleges that people can 'use any activity we happen to be engaged in as the basis for our development of awareness, calm or kindness'; as the reporting journalist describes:

Try focusing on the physical sensations in your hands, or any other body part, while riding the bus or shopping for dinner, and you're "doing mindfulness" no less authentically than you would on a Himalayan retreat.

(Burkeman, 2016)

Similarly, Ruby Wax's six-week programme promises that:

you don't have to perch on a gluten-free cushion, you can do the exercises anywhere, anytime; in the gym while pumping the pecs, or while eating a chocolate-chip cookie (or both at the same time). Even if you don't like the "M-word", the practice gives you the skill of focusing your attention where you want it focused.

(Wax, 2017)

Separated from meditation, mindfulness is described as 'the specific practice of peaking your awareness of your surroundings, actions and physicality' (Agate, 2018).

This expansion underscores that the widespread agreement uniting these claims is less about a specific practice than the underlying narrative they take up and disseminate. Human beings have a tendency to act automatically and unthinkingly; interventions promising to somehow 'raise awareness' are the key first step in ameliorating, or at least living with, personal and social problems.

Finally, adoption in one institution or area leads to claims that it should be expanded into others. The most prominent example is the adoption of MBCT by the NHS in relation to recurrent depression in 2004. This represented a 'seal of approval' for many claims-makers to argue that the practice should be spread elsewhere. One article opens with '"Mindfulness" is the buzzword of the moment – but it's a lot more than a passing trend. It's an NHS-approved approach to helping deal with anxiety, and it's also proven to help you sleep better and sharpen your focus' (Agate, 2018). Applications were not confined to specific mental health applications; its approval by NICE was mentioned in 19 per cent of articles, giving credence to the introduction of interventions from apps and cancer recovery (e.g. Jenkin, 2014) to schools (e.g. Cavendish, 2014).

Once mindfulness made headway in some schools, advocates used this as a basis to claim for its inclusion as an 'integrated feature of the curriculum' and for it to be extended beyond this to 'the establishment by government of a task force charged with overseeing the "implementation of mindfulness"' across even more areas of public life (Fay, 2017). Policymakers' initial interest as evidenced by Mindful Nation UK became a stepping stone for 'taking mindfulness to their constituents', 'in policy – health, educations, prisons, the workplace – because there is a massive need for it' (Booth, 2017). The author of a supportive review looks on hopefully:

> The popularity of mindfulness practice is often miscast as a symptom of navel-gazing individualism. In a short gestation period however, transformative benefits for politicians gave rise to an extensive policy inquiry with far-reaching results. Now we are witnessing a crucial further development: consideration of mindfulness as helpful to the whole: the whole body politic, the whole of society.
>
> (Bristow, 2019, p. 90)

Exhaustion

At least insofar as the number of articles mentioning mindfulness in the news media in 2022 (Figure 5.1), interest in mindfulness may be showing signs of decline, but has not dissipated. However, already by 2015 as the fad wave began to crest, the words 'hype', 'trend' or 'fad' begin to appear with increasing frequency, showing up seventeen times across the twenty-seven articles sampled that year. Its expansiveness, so important to its spread, becomes a drawback that claims-makers are less and less able to ignore. While criticism had appeared throughout the discourse, particularly objections that mindfulness had 'watered down' and/or commodified ancient, sacred or otherwise complex practices, they become more prominent and associated with clear claims-makers who begin to take ownership of opposition. Observers begin to refer to a 'mindfulness backlash':

You hear a lot about mindfulness these days. It seems to have spawned an industry based around people trumpeting its benefits in various unlikely areas of modern life, such as weight loss, parenting, business leadership, horticulture (probably) and so on. This has also prompted a backlash, with many describing the popularity of mindfulness as a "fad".

(D. Burnett, 2015)

Several prominent critical or semi-critical books including the *Buddha Pill* (Farias & Wikholm, 2015) and *McMindfulness* (Purser, 2019) emerged and began to make an impact on public discourse. Claims about side-effects initially brushed aside as 'rare' by claims-makers along with other negative consequences of intervention begin to assume a position of prominence. One report released in 2017 warned that those advocating expansion 'do not adequately, if at all, consider the costs or potential negative effects' which are 'gaining more attention', including 'difficult or challenging experiences' and the worsening of symptoms (Woolcock, 2017). While positive and evangelical claims-making campaigns are still in full-swing, reports begin to turn their attention to 'a new strain of critical thinking about mindfulness meditation amid an avalanche of hype' (Booth, 2014b). The movement begins to appear passé, referred to in past tense, its criticisms appearing obvious:

"Mindfulness" – the mental health fad focusing on awareness of the present moment – appears to be following a similar pattern. As a miracle cure to our attention-deficited world, mindfulness could effectively re-wire our brains, we were told, making us happier, healthier and cleverer, better parents and better lovers. Business leaders, Gwyneth and the NHS embraced the technique. Adults went on mindfulness retreats. Kids were given "mindfulness" classes (although why you would teach a three-year-old to marvel at the shape, texture and taste of an apple, when three-year-olds naturally marvel at the shape, texture and taste of apples never made much sense).

(Walden, 2016)

The flexible syntax, so powerful in driving adoption, is also a risk factor for exhaustion. One observer reflects that 'Mindfulness has become a secular religion, a warm and fuzzy buzzword on the tip of every trendy tongue' (Fay, 2017). He adds, 'the practice behind the patter is as vague as it is voguish. [...] To be mindful is to be focused, yet the definition of what constitutes mindful behaviour is so broad as to be virtually meaningless.' Critics like Grossman (2019, p. 103) referred to mindfulness as having 'porosity' while Van Dam et al. (2018, p. 41) refer to its 'semantic ambiguity' to describe the difficulty of ascertaining precisely what is being measured and to what studies are attributing benefits. Such critique signals that the discourse is passing the point at which expansiveness can be counted as an asset. Claims-makers must draw boundaries.

Yet a strong part of this exhaustion is a loss of novelty or news value, while the emergence of critique was itself newsworthy. However, it takes time for long-term studies to come to fruition, and they often do so after the discourse has already begun to wane. These discourses thrive on novelty. When their novelty wanes and problems persist, they begin to recede into the background. Exhaustion is often and will likely be in this case protracted as mindfulness entrepreneurs remain invested in the discourse.

Indeed, like self-esteem and happiness, many critics are adherents to or advocates of Buddhism and/or meditation who lament a revolution betrayed. Where in 2011 authors could unabashedly publish a book called the *Mindfulness Revolution* (Boyce, 2011), Purser begins his *McMindfulness* (2019) with a chapter entitled, 'What Mindfulness Revolution?' Leggett (2022) writes that the popularity and institutionalization of mindfulness has led to backlash, but nonetheless attempts to hold on to the 'political potential' of mindfulness in its ability to '[cultivate] a more engaged and critical outlook' than is implied by its commodified forms (p. 262). For Leggett, more 'resonant insights are offered by analyses of how meditation can cultivate critical awareness' as well as the ability to focus on means rather than ends and waking people up from 'autopilot' (p. 272).

These critics hope that by bringing out its foundations in Buddhist ethics (e.g. Hyland, 2017), or a 'deep commitment to personal practice by secular mindfulness trainers' (Dawson, 2021, p. 134) or encouraging 'pro-social behaviours' (Purser, 2015, p. 42), the radical kernel of mindfulness can be seized from the commodified shell. Similarly, Scherer and Waistell (2018) highlight the appropriation of mindfulness by contemporary capitalism, setting out an alternative framework relying on Buddhist critiques of consumerism. Yet this problematization of consumerism hints at a deeper issue even within these otherwise illuminating critiques: the main problems of capitalism remain rooted in behaviours and choices – change these, and it remains possible to change the world. As with conceptual entrepreneurship more generally, it is assumed that the problems are already well-known. All that is required is that the subject be sufficiently awakened to solutions already within their grasp – or selves. In other words, subjectivity remains implicitly the barrier to social change; change this and larger changes will follow.

Cultural diffusion

As was also the case for self-esteem and happiness, in the face of criticism claims-makers fall back on intuition and anecdote. In response to emergent evidence that mindfulness in schools had not met expectations and may even have caused harm, Seldon claims, 'My own experience is that it is generally helpful for schoolchildren, but much more reliably helpful for their teachers, who create a calmer, more purposeful school culture when they practise it' (Woolcock, 2017). Similarly, a major review carried out by key conceptual entrepreneurs for mindfulness and published in July 2022 showed that mindfulness had not improved mental health nor prevented mental ill-health in secondary school students (MYRIAD Project, 2022). The study, named My Resilience in Adolescence (MYRIAD), followed a mindfulness intervention over eight years with 28,000 adolescents between 11–14, 650 teachers and 100 schools participating. It produced results that were undoubtedly disappointing. Media reports highlighted that not only had it not prevented mental ill-health, a majority of students rated the programme negatively, found it 'boring', and that positive effects where observed, for instance on teacher stress, were short-lived (Kirby, 2022; Weale, 2022b). Yet echoing the response of claims-makers to the review of Social and Emotional Aspects of Learning (SEAL) a decade before, advocates defended the concept, pointing to the need for better teacher training, a more thorough application across the whole institution as well as a more targeted interventions (MYRIAD Project, 2022). While upfront about the lack of effectiveness of the intervention tested, one project member concludes:

> The findings from MYRIAD show that the idea of mindfulness doesn't help – it's the practice that matters. If today's young people are to be enthused enough to practice mindfulness, then updating training to suit different needs and giving them a say in the approach they prefer are the vital next steps.
>
> (MYRIAD Project, 2022)

Mindfulness is declared to be associated with mental health, but a different approach to teaching students these 'skills' is seen as necessary. These relationships and the necessity of mindfulness 'skills' do not need further proof because they are simply common sense. Notwithstanding long-standing questions regarding the quality of the evidence-base, mindfulness lobby groups protested that a wealth of evidence already existed to prove the importance of mindfulness in education (Weare & Ormston, 2022). But such proof is not really needed. The ethnopsychology already takes for granted that calibration of the internal emotional world of children and young people is a necessary prerequisite to learning and 'resilience'. The only question is how best to go about it.

Mindfulness programmes may not help students be more mindful, resilient or promote their mental health. But what they may do, as Purser (2020, p. 166) describes, is

teach students a neurological vocabulary, where a student will conceptualize their emotions in neurological terms. Now, a student will say "my amygdala hijacked me," with the implication to be more mindful. The importation of "folk neurology" into public and educational discourse illustrates not only how such institutional knowledge is being internalized, but also how such discourses are framing youth's cognitive and affective life as being confined to, and locatable within, the brain.

In this way, while mindfulness may eventually lose its ability to garner significant funding and ability to act as a label for a convincing and novel range of interventions and commodities, it will not have simply done nothing. Mindfulness emerged from the pre-existing saturation of Americanized Buddhism into Western cultural beliefs and practices. It is likely that when the discourse is no longer capable of galvanizing new rounds of media coverage, attracting research funding or inspiring new commodities, it will recede back into this cultural backdrop, available for making sense of personal and social problems but no longer a banner for novel interventions. Critique in the exhaustion phase has largely not touched the underlying ethos that drives the claim – that it is ultimately a failure of human subjectivity that drives social issues. The gap between is and ought to be is a void within humanity. The difficulty of mindfulness is a difficulty within the subject. They are simply unable to sit quietly in one room.

7

A Prehistory of Mental Health in Higher Education

Over the past decade, claims about a 'mental health crisis' in universities have taken off in the UK. While this was not the first-time campaign groups and advocates had attempted to problematize the emotional life of students in Higher Education (HE)[1], the late 2010s saw unprecedented media attention focused on the issue of student mental health. Newspapers reported daily about a seemingly ever-proliferating range of student experiences said to be damaging to student mental health, ranging from access to drugs and alcohol (S. Griffiths, 2013) to climate change (Sarner, 2017)[2] and 'anxiety about the future' (Marsh, 2017a). In the late 2010s, newspaper headlines began to declare that UK universities were amid a 'mental health crisis' which must be a 'top priority' (Vaughan, 2018). A headline in *The Guardian* warned that 'the way universities are run is making us ill' (Shackle, 2019). Universities were exhorted to 'do more to tackle [the] growing mental health crisis', and that once common experiences like 'exam stress' could be 'the straw that broke the camel's back' (Busby, 2018a). Seemingly overnight, advocacy groups like Student Minds emerged offering 'practical guidance' to 'students, parents and staff' on getting 'the help they need' (B. Thomas & Sahota, 2018).

Policymakers have been swift in endorsing such claims. In 2018, Sam Gyimah, then Conservative Minister for Universities, Science, Research and Innovation, affirmed that mental health was the biggest issue facing students, trumping even tuition fees (Zeffman, 2018). Gyimah even went as far as advocating the return of 'in loco parentis', or the institutional assumption of a quasi-parental responsibility for student welfare, and warned audiences that the 'prime purpose' of universities was no longer the 'training of the mind', but rather the provision of a range of pastoral and emotional supports (C. Turner, 2018a). Writing to university Vice Chancellors in England, he instructed them that 'Collectively, we must prioritise the wellbeing and mental health of our students – there is no negotiation on this' (Gov.uk, 2018). This governmental mandate oversaw the expansion of a number of research and development programmes including an Office for Students (OfS) £14.5 million mental health research programme and the creation of The Student Mental Health Research Network (SMaRteN) (Ecclestone, 2020), funded as part of an £8 million governmental spend on mental health research (Economic and Social Research Council, 2018). In December 2019, Student Minds issued the University Mental Health Charter (UMHC). Backed by government, the OfS, and Universities UK (UUK), the Charter calls for 'support services, accommodation, teaching and university bureaucracy to be geared towards students' mental well-being and to '"enable them to thrive"' (Ecclestone, 2020). Backed by policy affirmations, the UMHC exerts considerable influence on the mental health agenda in universities. These claims – that 'thriving' must be 'enabled', that universities are experiencing a mental health crisis that must be prioritized even above the once highly contentious debate about tuition fees – have been scarcely contested. How did this happen?

Part of a broader discourse continually expanding the purview of 'mental health' (Cosgrove & Karter, 2018; J. Davies, 2021; C. Mills, 2014) and suffusing this narrative with an 'apocalyptic' sense of crisis (Ecclestone, 2017), it seems that the 'crisis' already endemic in schools (Ecclestone & Hayes, 2019; Matthiesen, 2018; cf. Weare, 2010) has only belatedly reached universities. Indeed, the claim was that universities were simply worsening the situation. *The Telegraph* ran headlines quoting a 'leading psychiatrist' that 'Universities may be fuelling the mental health crisis' (C. Turner, 2018b). This represents a marked shift in the framing of the university experience, at least in public discussions of universities as set out in mainstream media discourses. Taking off in the mid-2000s, going to university came to be conceptualized not as the end of problems nor a sign of success in itself, but rather as an aggravator – or even source – of mental ill-health as a society-wide problem. What is more, the emergence of claims-making for student mental health as a dire social problem predates the evidence used to underpin such claims.

In this chapter, I consider in detail the rising significance of 'mental health' as a social problem from its recent prehistory to its emergence as public problem, using the rise of the issue in the context of Higher Education (HE) in the UK between 2005 and 2019 as a case study. This 'prehistory' explores key factors laying the groundwork for receptivity to claims about a crisis of student mental health before moving in the next chapter to examining early claims-making problematizing self-reliance and strongly encouraging help-seeking, a subsequent rise in which became fuel for increasingly shrill claims about a mental health crisis as more and more students appeared to heed the call to seek out specialized interventions. As the concluding portions of this section of the book will show, mental health follows the trajectory taken by mindfulness discussed in the previous chapter. That is, what Cabanas and Illouz (2019) see as an inversion of Maslow's hierarchy of human needs appears here not simply in inverted form, but with its new top entirely severed. Often, meeting material needs and attending to material problems appear in HE mental health discourses as significant only insofar as their existence and implied insolubility leads to mental health concerns. Material problems slip seamlessly into individualized health problems so that mental health subsumes nearly every social issue. Once again, audiences are asked not to imagine bridging the gap between what is and what might be, but rather to locate myriad 'supports' in the personal project of attenuating oneself to external circumstances too complex and everchanging for the subject to grasp. Evident in these discourses is a vision of subjectivity that is no longer so much the cause of social problems, but which rather has become *the* social problem.

Across the ensuing chapters, I reconstruct a trajectory of discovery, adoption and expansion to make sense of these developments. However, there is little sign, at least at the time of writing, that these trends are exhausting. While in earlier developments of the arguments laid out in this book (Frawley, 2020b), I referred to the problematization of positive emotions as being affected in 'cycles', this case study shows most clearly that this is not simply a cyclic repetition. That is, history is not simply repeating itself. In each emotion problem wave, claims-makers criticize some of what has come before, but they also subsume and expand upon existing claims. Claims-makers' intertextual engagement with the social memory of previous problematizations means that, for example, claims that experienced opposition in previous problem formulations have fallen away while others are adapted and taken for granted. Most importantly, in the case of mental health, emotions no longer appear so significant. Rather, and as Nikolas Rose has also observed, emotions come to be 're-coded' as mental health issues (2020, p. 30), for which a range of supports can and must be identified. Yet in all of these formulations, the fundamental certainty about the centrality of human subjectivity to social problems is only compounded. The repetition of 'positive' emotions as social problems seems therefore to represent the central thesis of this book. These are not cycles but rather expressions of underlying cultural and political tensions regarding the relationship between the individual and social problems that society has not yet been able to resolve.

This chapter takes as its starting point a detailed analysis of a 126 article sample of news media discourses on mental health in HE appearing between 2005 and 2019 (see Methods Appendix for further details). While, like the previous consideration of mindfulness, this sample does not encapsulate all public discourse of mental health in HE, it gives insight into some of the most oft-repeated public claims about the state of student mental health since the mid-2000s and the most prominent sources of those claims. Most importantly, it gives a sense of how these claims and claims-makers have changed over time, which claims appear salient and are thus repeated and which fall away in the highly competitive arena of news media claims-making (Hilgartner & Bosk, 1988). The overall purpose is not to give an extensive nor definitive history of student mental health as a social problem. Rather, and in line with the aims of the present monograph, it is to give insight into the way that one discourse of problematized emotional life makes way for, and potentially gives way to, the next. More significantly, it highlights the underlying visions of the subject and the relationship of that subject to broader social issues that emerge – visions discernible by how often they are taken for granted and repeated as the truth about the current state of student subjectivity.

Prehistory

The 'crisis' of student mental health is only the most recent iteration of earlier problematizations of the state of student emotion and of young people in general. Its renewed uptake by new groups and in relation to new issues in the 2000s only ensured that it did not become exhausted. The expansion of one problem often sets the stage for the emergence of the next. Problems also draw on prevailing ideas about the causes of and solutions to social problems and the ethnopsychology of the time. While what follows is not an exhaustive accounting of the pre-existing cultural themes and opportunities that fed into an almost feverish focus on student mental health over the past decade, a number of phenomena stand out as particularly significant. These include broader ethnopsychological beliefs about the centrality of individual psychology and especially of early experiences to broader social problems, the extension of trends and interventions already happening in schools, an institutional context of uncertainty about the meaning and purpose of HE, and the pre-existence of organized bodies of university counselling services who acted as conceptual entrepreneurs in earlier cycles of problematized student mental health. I attend to each of these in turn.

As to the first, claims about a mental health crisis in universities entered into and drew upon a cultural landscape already saturated with claims about the fragility of the human psyche and pervasive ethnopsychological beliefs about the centrality of that fragility to broader social problems. With change to broader economic structures of society increasingly closed off, claims-makers have become inclined to seek out simple solutions to complex problems. In addition to and complementing themes discussed in Chapters 2 and 3, as an outlook on social problems, mental health discourses in universities largely follow a growing narrative framing that I have elsewhere termed (drawing on

Rubington & Weinberg, 2011) a 'pathological civilization' approach (Frawley, 2015c). This is a perspective on social issues that inverts the older 'social pathology' paradigm which had seen society as a healthy body infected by sick individuals who bear responsibility for creating social malaise. Instead, society itself is seen as 'sick', infecting the bodies and minds of vulnerable individuals.[3] In this way, and like the older social pathology paradigm, a strong emphasis remains on change at the individual level. Social engineering to affect individual change becomes the main means by which social problems are ameliorated. This often takes the form of educational interventions with the aim of 'preventing' problems in the future for which the present appears to offer few solutions.

The intense focus on flawed subjectivity as the source of problems leads advocates to search ever deeper within childhood and even 'pre-birth' 'in the search for interventions that "work"' (Edwards et al., 2017, p. 1). As Hennum (2014, p. 444) has observed, children's apparently 'iconic status' can be attributed to (among other reasons) a 'general state of fear pervading contemporary Western societies, triggering the need to exercise overt control of children symbolizing the future, and in so doing, control the future itself'. Infancy, childhood, the womb and even the pre-pregnancy activities of mothers come to be viewed deterministically, as decisive factors in the future course of events individually and for society (Furedi, 2001; Lee et al., 2014; Macvarish et al., 2014). This constant focus on childhood as the ultimate source of social ills produces a widespread sense of childhood in 'crisis' (Kehily, 2010), with the beginning of the twenty-first century saturated by a series of 'relentlessly repetitive problematizations' of children's and young people's experiences (Isin, 2004 in Ecclestone, 2018, p. 227). Here, as other sociologists have noted, life experiences are assumed to leave lifelong scars, and childhood itself becomes increasingly bound up with discourses of risk, trauma and metaphors of toxicity (Gilligan, 2009; see e.g. House & Loewenthal, 2018). As Tsaliki and Chronaki (2020, p. 8), drawing on the work of Michel Foucault, write,

> It is due to such "risk talk" – driving policy-making at national, cross-national and global level for some time now – that the "discursive formations" [...] of children and teens in (pre- and) post-millennial times construct under 18s as always "at risk" of being harmed (from almost everything – too much food, too much fun, too much sex, too much popular culture).

Assertions about the dire state of student mental health in universities represent the expansion of this pervasive sense of crisis about the state of childhood and of childhood mental health into higher education. This expansion of pre-existing concerns targeted at children is particularly clear when one considers the way that claims-makers involved in earlier interventions in schools have extended these projects onto university campuses. For example, Sir Anthony Seldon, who as Headmaster of Wellington College introduced well-being classes in 2006, slips seamlessly between claims about a 'mental health crisis' in children to the failures of schools, parents and finally, universities. 'British children are facing a mental health crisis' (Thomson, 2015), he claimed in 2015 while still in his post as head of the prestigious school. 'Parents, teachers *and universities*', he continues, are a 'disgrace in their lack of regard for the wellbeing and mental health of students' (Thomson, 2015 emphasis added). Not long later, it was announced that Seldon would be taking over as Vice Chancellor of the University of Buckingham with plans to introduce the same positive psychology inspired well-being education he had pioneered for schoolchildren (R. Bennett, 2015b), later championing the University as 'Europe's first "positive university"' (Lydall, 2017).

Yet Seldon's well-being classes were only the most visible of a rash of therapeutic interventions introduced in schools since the late 1980s (Ecclestone & Hayes, 2019). It was then that self-esteem, discussed in previous chapters, was 'catapulted into educational policy thinking' in the US (Beane, 1991) and spread across the English-speaking world. However, by the mid to late 1990s, the significance and faith in the efficacy of promoting self-esteem in schools began to wane (Baumeister, 1996; Baumeister et al., 2003). But the discourse did not simply disappear. It was replaced by similar discourses which also affirmed the centrality of emotional life to educational achievement and social problems. For instance, along with counterparts in the United States and Australia, England rolled out the Social and Emotional Aspects of Learning (SEAL) programme in 2005. SEAL and its American and Australian equivalents utilized 'experience-based learning tools' including board games and 'circle time' with the intention of reducing bullying, increasing resilience (Hromek & Roffey, 2009, p. 627) and promoting a range of 'positive behaviours' (DCSF, 2007 cited in Humphrey et al., 2010, p. 1). Following reviews apparently showing that SEAL had done little in the way of meeting its stated objectives (e.g. Humphrey et al., 2010), the programme was quietly abandoned in the UK in 2011. Yet its 'DNA' remained evident in later iterations of 'character education', teaching 'resilience' and 'grit' (Humphrey et al., 2016, p. 272).

In short, in spite of criticism and belated revelations that such interventions lacked efficacy and may even do harm, the core belief in the centrality of subjectivity to both educational and wider social problems remained (Ecclestone, 2013). As one journalist complained in 2012, 'wellbeing has been cast into Ofsted's dustbin at a time of soaring youth unemployment, when teenagers routinely hear themselves described as a "lost generation"' (Northen, 2012). Yet how 'wellbeing' will solve these problems remains unclear. It is simply taken for granted that such issues must be attended to in the realm of emotions. And indeed, that emotions are one of the few places towards which meaningful action can be directed.

By the time students come to university, they are primed to focus intensely on their feelings and to see the provision of a range of supports as both progressive and intrinsic to their experience. In this way, the dramatic rise of discussions of mental health in relation to universities at least partially represents an expansion of trends already prominent in schools, not only reflecting a general cultural sense that psychology is foundational to social problems, but also extending beliefs about the fragility of childhood into early adulthood.

Yet this expansion of claims would not have been successful had they not found fertile ground in the institutional context of HE suffering an ongoing loss of certainty regarding its meaning and purpose and thus open to claims problematizing, in Gyimah's words, 'the training of the mind' and even a therapeutic recasting of its mission. Of course, universities have served many purposes over time and debates about their significance to society and who should attend recur throughout their history. However, there has been a perceptible and general shift away from more liberal ideals of HE as a broadly public good (whether or not such ideals were ever realized in practice) towards more personalized and commercialized benefits accorded primarily to individual students (e.g. for skills-building and job prospects) (Chan, 2016; J. Williams, 2013). While the provision of broadly social benefits remains a central concern, these tend to be construed in terms extrinsic to subject knowledge, such as increasing national economic competitiveness or reducing broader social inequalities (Chan, 2016). Facing attacks that universities are 'ivory tower' elitist institutions responsible for a range of ongoing inequalities, universities have perhaps understandably gone on the offensive.

Researchers in numerous countries, not only in the primarily English-speaking world, have noted that this shift towards more individualized and commercialized goals has fostered the movement of therapeutic ideals into the heart of HE. For instance, Finnish researcher Kristiina Brunila describes a 'therapeutic ethos permeating the entire higher education system in Finland' as well as across the EU, which has been intensified by the rise of 'project-based' education and the marketization of the public sector (Brunila, 2012, p. 452). This creeping process of 'therapization' refers to the rise of a 'psycho-culture' across a range of institutions which attaches heightened significance to phenomena like positive psychology, diagnosing and the provision of mentoring and a range of counselling interventions to support mental health and 'emotional well-being' (Brunila, 2012, p. 451). A loss of meaning and purpose tied to university marketization thus paved the way for a therapeutic recasting of its institutional role.

Finally, after successful campaigns beginning in the first half of the twentieth century, universities became home to counselling services who were also connected to and represented by broader professional organizations in possession of resources to launch and/or contribute to campaigns to expand their services. These early campaigns are particularly interesting because they demonstrate the underlying logic of contemporary therapeutic discourse in the naked albeit inverted form of early attempts to understand social problems through a social pathology lens. That is, towards the end of the nineteenth century and beginning of the early twentieth, many social thinkers had seen the problems of society as outgrowths of sick or otherwise malfunctioning individuals, analogous to a diseased outgrowth of an otherwise healthy organism. It was the job of the social thinker to diagnose and treat such pathologies. This outlook spawned the mental hygiene movement, which, as Rose (1999, p. 21) has described, '... stress[ed] the importance of such "functional" nerve disorders and their role in social problems from crime to industrial inefficiency, and [sought] to promote mental health and welfare by early intervention, out patient treatment and prophylactic measures.'

It is little surprising then that one of the earliest claims-makers for therapeutic supports in universities was the American mental hygienist and psychiatrist Stewart Paton. Paton, who bore an eclectic though not uncommon range of views for his time, was an outspoken eugenicist and believed that mental pathologies ultimately underlay a range of social issues from assassinations of public figures (Paton, 1912) to opposition to the first world war (Paton, 1915). Paton was an early conceptual entrepreneur for mental hygiene research and treatment centres housed in university settings and was the founder of the first recorded mental healthcare service in a college setting in 1910 (Kay & Schwartz, 2011). The subsequent growth of mental hygiene clinics in the post-war period can at least partially be attributed to a concern that unchecked mental health issues could weaken a nation's military strength, but later extended well beyond this to encompass a broadening range of social objectives. While obviously shedding the darker eugenicist aspects of social pathology, the central claim to be able to deal uniquely with student problems and thus the broader problems of society is something that more and more organizations fought over in the decades that followed. In other words, many groups in society competed to become early 'owners' of the newly discovered problem of student mental 'hygiene', and later 'health'. By the 1930s, 'the psychologist, the physician, the psychiatrist, the mental hygienist, the sociologist, for that matter the butcher, the baker and the candlestick maker, each took his turn at claiming ... that he was the one and only individual to deal with student problems' (Brotemarkle cited in Kay & Schwartz, 2011, p. 22).

Towards the present, there has been a considerable expansion of therapeutic supports as well as representative bodies in position of receptivity to push for and take up new claims regarding student mental fragility as well as its role in wider social problems. For instance, as 'wholesalers' of student mental health, counselling services became more and more common in UK universities in the 1990s and groups like the Association of Managers of Student Services in Higher Education (AMOSSHE), Heads of University Counselling Services (HUCS) and others lobbied heavily for their continued expansion. The range of services that counsellors offered also expanded, encompassing study methods and communication skills (*The Irish Times*, 1996). Spurred by the Disability Discrimination Act 1995 which put an onus on institutions to accommodate disabilities, the Higher Education Funding Council for England (HEFCE) published a guidance document in 1999 that included mental health problems in its definition of disability, stipulating a number of responses and requirements for flexibility and adjustment (Manthorpe & Stanley, 2002). Crucially, this document noted that the needs of students with mental health difficulties may require much broader forms of intervention, 'since behaviour affects all aspects of an institution' (HEFCE 1999 para.37(d) cited in Manthorpe & Stanley, 2002, p. 16). Statements such as these opened up the possibility that such students not only represented a potential market previously left out of insufficiently inclusive institutions,[4] but also that student behaviour represented a potential risk that both needed to be and could be managed with appropriate investments. In this way, counselling professionals' support for student mental health was presented as a solution to universities' desire to both seize new opportunities, but also to avoid exposure to the risks that these opportunities allegedly entailed.

Indeed, this period saw a number of documents produced by representatives of student services and counselling bodies pressing universities to accept a legal, moral and ethical 'duty of care' to students which included commitments to the ongoing funding and expansion of mental health and counselling services (e.g. AMOSSHE, 2001; Rana et al., 1999). Universities UK (UUK), a representative body of university management which was then called the Committee of Vice-Chancellors and Principals, were swift adopters, producing a report in 2000 entitled *Guidelines on Student Mental Health Policies and Procedures for Higher Education*. This document affirmed the centrality of student mental health to HE and the need for a range of supports/awareness among relevant staff in terms of identifying and referring affected students, placing a strong emphasis on institutions' legal liabilities should they fail to fulfil their 'duty of care' (Manthorpe & Stanley, 2002, p. 16). These responsibilities were institutionalized in the Special Educational Needs and Disabilities Act 2001, which saw higher education institutions deploying and expanding a range of new and existing services to meet its requirements in the early 2000s.

In 2003, the University Mental Health Advisers Network (UMHAN) was launched to represent the interests of mental health advisers in HE. Like these earlier groups, this network has pressed for the expansion of mental health into a 'whole institution' approach, as well as the expansion of their mandate to include a variety of other social issues (UMHAN, 2021). A conglomeration of these professional groups was formed as a working group to concentrate on the issue of 'mental well-being' in universities in 2003, called the Universities UK/GuildHE Working Group for the Promotion of Mental Well-Being in Higher Education (Royal College of Psychiatrists, 2011, p. 92), a wording which hints at an expanding boundary of concerns beyond mental ill-health to more diffuse notions of 'wellbeing'. These developments exist alongside the enormous rise in the training of therapeutic professionals who also have vested interests in the expansion of their services as well as other special interest groups that emerged in the early 2010s mentioned towards the outset of this chapter and detailed in the chapters that follow.

Communities of fate

Taken together, the rise of mental health as a social problem and even 'crisis' in the 2010s cannot be understood outside of these organized lobbying bodies and the institutional spaces and receptiveness that were already firmly established by the early 2000s. However, the existence of these organized bodies as institutional niches and sites for the reception and diffusion of claims would not be possible without conditions of institutional and cultural receptiveness.

In terms of the former, in addition to the ongoing reorientation of the purpose of universities discussed above, institutional responsiveness on the part of university managers was likely fostered by the existence of universities as what Stinchcombe (1965, p. 181) has called 'communities of fate'. These are collectivities in which damage to the whole affects damage to individuals (and so too for success). Individual institutions become increasingly conscious of industry-wide risks, responding with coordinated risk management (Braithwaite, 2011). Larger players within the industry may also push for greater regulations knowing that weaker rivals will struggle to compete within increasingly strict regulatory frameworks. Waggoner and Goldman (2005, p. 88) have argued that universities represent clear examples of such communities of fate, in which the retention of students is linked to organizational success. Their study of American university student retention rhetoric also showed that an ethos of 'care' and 'caring' formed an increasingly defining focus of institutional ideology. Towards the present, this 'care' appears to have become increasingly therapeutized. Many of the reports discussed above singled out the risk of suicide, but also the risk of litigation that could potentially be brought forth by students who felt that universities had breached their 'duty of care'. Thus, early claims adeptly focused on institutional opportunities and risks including student recruitment and retention and the risk of legal action and even suicide should institutions fail to heed the call for expanded investment in therapeutic services.

Conclusions

At a cultural level, the centralization of human subjectivity to the life course of social problems, vital to social pathology, but inverted in the pathological civilization narrative, which sees an ever more complex society threatening the fragile psyche of the population, feeds a broader receptivity to claims that radically recast the role of the university in individual and public life. The university moves from playing a more liberal role in the sense of 'freeing' toward a more protective role in the sense of 'safety'. Without a much deeper disorientation regarding the role and ability of human beings to understand and change the material world discussed in Chapters 2 and 3, these ideas are likely to fall on deaf ears or even be outright rejected by students, administrators and the public at large. Indeed, an early and short-lived claims-making campaign led by the National Union of Students (NUS) and a schizophrenia special interest group which argued that serious mental illness was widespread in universities was downplayed by 'university doctors' in the early 1990s (Chateau, 1993). By contrast, they maintained that serious mental health issues were rare, and that mental distress associated with university was situational and transient. Now even this transience is seen as a cause of the broader social problem of student mental health.

Only in a world of profound disempowerment regarding the ability of the human subject to overcome or make sense of distress contextually, and much less to understand and control external problems thrown up by the material world, can statements like Gyimah's privileging of mental health over fees discussed at the outset of this chapter be received as unproblematic. As the ensuing chapters detail, the site of interest and control is displaced ever deeper inside of subjectivity. As the problem formulation progresses and spreads, even the notion that 'the only thing you can control is yourself' is cast into doubt.

8

The Discovery of a Problem

Constructing a crisis

While student mental health had been problematized in the past and had been the subject of extensive lobbying by university counselling service representatives by the 1990s, the idea that HE presents a uniquely problematic emotional experience and even as experiencing a mental health 'crisis' does not appear as widespread in newspaper articles before 2010 as is the case in the decade that followed. As this chapter details, it is with the take-up of student mental health by various organized student groups that the 'discovery' of a student mental health 'crisis' begins.

In the early 2000s, though increasingly rarely as time progresses, going to university is sometimes depicted as a sign of success and of problems coming to an end. For instance, a *Guardian* article from 2004 describes applying for a place at university as a successful outcome for an individual who had been struggling with mental health issues (Mayhew, 2004). Another article in *The Independent* from the same year describes how one young person overcame 'cannabis-triggered trauma' to be, 'back at university and, with a bit of luck, [sitting] his finals this summer' (Arnold, 2004). Such claims did co-exist with attempts to problematize student mental health, but these were not nearly as widely repeated as is the case beginning in the early 2010s. The sampling strategy of including only those articles in which mental health formed the main focus produced few results until 2013, with fewer than ten of the first 100 most relevant listings being solely focused on the topic (Figure 8.1).[1]

The dramatic take-off of claims about student mental health as a social problem and 'crisis' is inseparable from the emergence of student groups who took ownership of the extant and rising mental health agenda on UK campuses. Many of these groups were closely connected to the counselling bodies discussed in the previous chapter, with UMHAN, AMOSSHE and

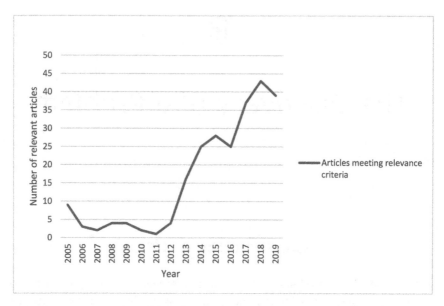

FIGURE 8.1 *Mental Health and Higher Education in UK Broadsheets.*

HUCS acting as advisers and trustees.[2] An early significant example of this phenomenon is Mental Wealth UK, founded in 2009 (officially launched in 2010) at the University of Leeds by Leeds student Ed Pinkney. However, the name 'mental wealth' appears to originate in a pre-existing social enterprise initiative in Leeds to set up 'social firms' providing employment to people with mental health problems and backed by Social Firms UK (Mental Wealth, 2008). According to media reports, Pinkney had been the President of the Enterprise Society (Yorkshire Post, 2009), a student group devoted to encouraging entrepreneurship at the University which was supported by UnLtd (a foundation for social entrepreneurs) (Young, 2014). Mental Wealth UK (initially titled the Mental Wealth Project) received support and sponsorship from UnLtd as well as a number of student mental health trusts, HEFCE and the University of Leeds (Mental Wealth UK, 2011). Its explicit goal was to promote mental health and well-being and the take up of the mental health agenda by student groups across university campuses, creating links between students and 'wider stakeholders' (The Mental Wealth Project, 2010). One of the organization's major (and successful) campaigns, entitled 25by2012, aimed to instigate at least twenty-five student mental health societies across the UK by the end of 2012.

The creation of nodes, often led by young people with 'leadership qualities', is a common claims-making activity, also observed in the construction of 'happiness' as a social problem, wherein claims-makers consciously seek to create sites through which new ideas can be disseminated and lobbied for across institutions (Frawley, 2015c). Moreover, there had been some concern that mental health policy in institutions was too 'top down' and a desire for students to take more control of the agenda. For instance, in a report prepared for HEFCE by the Institute for Economic Affairs and Researching Equity, Access and Partnership (M. Williams et al., 2015), the authors note that policies in the area had tended to be formulated at the top levels of institutions, which, although ensuring that there was 'buy-in at the highest level' and enabling 'support services to lever sufficient funds to implement their policies and approaches', might cause institutions to overlook 'challenges "on the ground"' and the role that students could play in implementing agendas and 'shar[ing] responsibility' (M. Williams et al., 2015, p. 52). Leeds' mental health student groups, including the Mental Wealth Project, are listed in the document as key examples of 'good practice' in this regard. It is notable too that there is a sense in this document that HE institutions viewed greater inclusion of students and staff at various levels as potentially diffusing risk (see e.g. M. Williams et al., 2015, pp. 50–2). If the primary solution to mental health issues is for universities to provide high-quality, well-trained counselling staff and demand gets 'out of hand' (p. 50), universities face the risk of failing in their 'duty of care'. In other words, spreading out this risk and encouraging other parties to take ownership of the issue represents an opportunity on the part of institutions to diffuse risk across its staff and student body.

Mental Wealth UK later merged with Student Run Self-Help (SRSH) in 2013 to become Student Minds (Student Minds, 2022). SRSH began as a peer support group at Oxford University in 2009 by then DPhil student Nicola Byrom, but had evolved to include significant campaigning for the spread of student mental health campaign groups similar to Mental Wealth UK. Members and former members of Mental Wealth UK and what would become Student Minds had worked with the NUS, for instance providing training and campaigning, with Pinkney leading an NUS mental health project in Northern Ireland in 2013 (HuffPost UK, 2022). In 2014, Student Minds announced a closer partnership with the NUS, after having already linked with the organization for several years, to ensure that 'student mental health is high on the agenda of all universities and the wider mental health sector' (NUS Connect, 2014).

It is not surprising then that a key moment in the construction of a 'crisis' came in 2013 in association with claims-making by the NUS. The first of these claims came in the form of a Student Distress Survey (Kerr, 2013), with data being both collected and press released in May of that year and timed to coincide with Mental Health Awareness Week. The associated press release, which included supportive quotes from the mental health charities Together UK and Mind, headlined the claim that '20 per cent of students consider themselves to have a mental health problem' (Disabled Students, 2013). According to the fuller presentation of the research findings (Kerr, 2013), this figure was created by bringing together the proportion of students who believed they might have a diagnosable mental health condition (8 per cent), those actively seeking diagnosis (2 per cent) and those with a diagnosed condition (10 per cent). Other claims highlighted for the press were that 13 per cent of students experienced suicidal thoughts and that 92 per cent had a 'feeling of mental distress' including 'feeling down' (which, according to the survey, referred to the entire time 'spent at your current place of study' (Kerr, 2013)) (Disabled Students, 2013). The press release also highlighted course work and financial difficulties as sources of distress. In accompanying quotations, claims-makers highlighted that their 'primary concern' was that students did not seek help for their problems (Disabled Students, 2013). This was also the case in the presentation of survey results, which drew particular attention to the figure that 64 per cent did not seek help from formal services for their 'mental distress' (Kerr, 2013).

In the weeks that followed the issue of the press release, seven articles in the UK press reported the results with a further article appearing that September which mentioned the survey as part of a broader claim urging students starting university to seek out mental health supports. Five out of these eight articles highlighted the 20 per cent figure (or '1 in 5') in the headline or opening paragraph. Four of the articles also highlighted the prevalence of suicidal thoughts in their opening lines, and a further three foregrounded that students did not seek help from formal services as the 'primary' issue. In two of the eight articles, claims from the press release were incorporated into further claims-making; for instance, on students turning to gambling to deal with financial issues (Denham, 2013b) and the need for new students to seek professional supports (Ashton, 2013). Yet none of this coverage reported the above-described breakdown of the 20 per cent figure and only one report mentioned any survey limitations. This latter article noted that 'NUS researchers admit that their survey was self-selecting and may exaggerate the prevalence of mental health problems among students', but goes on to stress that the 'primary concern' is student's lack of help seeking (Ratcliffe, 2013). It was also the only article to point out that the 20 per cent figure was 'in line with' that of the general population.

Two articles highlighted the claim that 92 per cent of students (or '9 out of 10') suffered from 'mental distress', described as including 'feeling down, stressed and demotivated' (Dowling, 2013; Marshall, 2013). While the NUS had reported these as 'symptoms of mental distress' (Kerr, 2013) the original survey question had not described the available options as 'symptoms' nor as 'mental distress', but rather asked if respondents had 'ever experienced any of these' during their studies, followed by a list of available options. Options ranged from 'feeling unhappy/down' and 'irritability/anger' to 'suicidal thoughts' so that very slight to very severe negative feelings were captured within the '92%' figure. Stated this way, it is surprising that 7 per cent of respondents reported feeling no 'negative' emotions at all throughout their university experience (1 per cent selected 'prefer not to say'). Feeling that their issue is important, claims-makers have an incentive to try and capture all of its aspects. However, this can have the effect of inviting an inflated perception of the issue.

Indeed, the notion that student mental health was particularly at risk appeared to have been a foregone conclusion. One report quotes Poppy Jaman, chief executive of Mental Health First Aid England stating that the NUS findings are 'unsurprising'; 'The student community is considered high risk for mental ill health, with exams, intense studying and living away from home for the first time all contributing factors' (Ratcliffe, 2013). Yet, the findings of the survey showed that they were at no greater risk than the general population of the same age, and indeed may have experienced even self-reported mental health conditions at a slightly lower rate. News media reportage also demonstrated slippage between those experiencing 'mental health problems' and 'mental distress'. For instance, *The Guardian* reported 'Those who do experience mental health problems cite coursework deadlines [...] and exams [...] as triggers of distress' (Ratcliffe, 2013). However, this question had been asked of all respondents, not just those who thought they had a diagnosable condition. While the press release communicated deadlines and exams as causes of 'mental distress', the fuller presentation of survey results also frequently slipped between the language of 'symptoms' and 'feelings' (sometimes referred to as 'symptoms/feelings'), the latter becoming subsumed into the symptomology of mental (ill) health.

Self-reliance was also assumed to be de facto problematic and a result of 'stigma' but the survey did not appear to ask students why they chose not to seek help. 'Paul Farmer, chief executive of Mind, says this may be because of the stigma attached to mental illnesses. He adds that universities should do more to reach out to students', reports one article (Ratcliffe, 2013). Yet this too was a pre-determined conclusion. The press release included a demand for more funding for services and announced that the NUS had teamed up with mental health groups to advocate more strongly for student mental health (Disabled Students, 2013). However, the survey itself had only been carried out three weeks prior to this announcement (Kerr, 2013), after these partnerships were likely well underway. This is a common practice, but it operates in the reverse of what might be expected of social problem 'discovery' in which a condition becomes so pressing that people are no longer able to ignore it. Instead, the search for data succeeds the take-up of the agenda, and acts as a post-hoc justification.

As was the case with mindfulness discussed in Chapters 5 and 6, it was the rate at which a given population sought, or failed to seek, specified professional supports that was initially singled out as problematic by claims-makers. In this case, relying on oneself or informal support systems such as friends and family was depicted as risky. While students were already seeking support in larger numbers since the mid to early 2000s despite there being 'no empirical evidence to confirm that students are more likely to suffer diagnosable mental disorder or illness than the age matched non-student population' (Royal College of Psychiatrists, 2003, p. 7), that many students still preferred to rely on informal support mechanisms was explicitly problematized. 'Opening up to friends and family can help those feeling stressed or anxious, but anyone experiencing suicidal thoughts, or consistently feeling down, may have an enduring mental health problem, so it's best they visit their GP' (Marshall, 2013). This article continues by quoting a spokesman for Universities Scotland adding,

> The health and wellbeing of their students is of the upmost importance to all of Scotland's universities. All universities take their duty of care very seriously and have in place a range of student support services including a dedicated, confidential counselling service for students to provide help and advice on a range of issues whether personal or academic. Any student who feels they have mental health issues are [sic] encouraged to seek help from their institution and should do so without the fear of being stigmatised.

It is notable that there is some ambivalence visible at this relatively early stage regarding what exactly the university's 'duty of care' entails. The injunction in the press release is for those experiencing more severe forms of distress to see a GP, not university services. University services are positioned as needing expansion to attend to more diffuse 'symptoms' of 'mental distress'. Mental health is forwarded as something overseen and surveilled by university services, but actually providing a service for those experiencing severe problems was positioned as the domain of the NHS. On the other hand, the statement from Universities Scotland implies that those experiencing mental health issues should seek help from the university. This becomes more significant in later stages of the problem as precisely who provides services and who provides more diffuse forms of guidance and support becomes increasingly unclear.[3]

Two years later, the more restrictive language of diagnoses recedes in a new NUS survey which asked students, 'Do you believe that you have experienced problems with your mental health in the last year, regardless of whether you have been formally diagnosed?' (National Union of Students, 2015). Instead of diagnosable conditions, the survey opted for the much more expansive 'problems with your mental health' and did not ask students to define further what this meant instead asking about 'feelings' experienced in the past year including stress and feeling 'unhappy/down'. The release of the poll results was timed to coincide with a parliamentary meeting of MPs and peers to discuss student mental health with NUS spokespeople highlighting cuts to maintenance grants and disability allowances (Gil, 2015). While the 2013 survey summary had mentioned the limitation that self-report surveys can produce inflated estimates of prevalence, no such caveat is listed in the results for the second survey which invited students to self-report on a much more expansive construct. This tendency to slip between terms like 'mental health' (as opposed to formal diagnosis), 'feelings', 'wellbeing' and 'distress' has also been observed in claims-making more broadly (H. J. Jackson & Haslam, 2022, p. 3) and come under increasing scrutiny of late for inflating the prevalence of mental ill-health and medicalizing everyday forms of emotional upset (Haslam, 2016; Horwitz & Wakefield, 2007; H. J. Jackson & Haslam, 2022; Paris, 2015). While the results of such processes may not all be negative, there is the potential for a 'discourse that prioritizes vaguely defined, undifferentiated concepts' to incorrectly imply that 'all conditions within a broad category are the same, need the same treatment and require the same level of expertise to treat' (H. J. Jackson & Haslam, 2022, p. 2).

The 2015 NUS poll is thus a case in point, producing the headline-grabbing statistic that 78 per cent of university students suffered from 'mental health problems'. Ten articles appeared in the mainstream print news media in the six months following its release in December 2015. Of these, five mentioned this statistic in the headline and/or first two paragraphs, with some stating it as 'eight out of ten' or rounding up to 80 per cent (e.g. Gil, 2015; J. Smith, 2016). The release summarizing the survey results was less careful about detailing survey limitations (National Union of Students, 2015) than had been its predecessor and none of the ten articles reporting on the poll mentioned any.

In an otherwise supportive foreword for a book on 'mental health and wellbeing' in the context of HE, Simon Wessely notes that by the time he became President of the Royal College of Psychiatrists in 2014, it had become common practice for local students unions to conduct mental health surveys, 'which often reported high rates of mental health problems, usually in the 70 to 80 per cent range, well above what more formal studies using standardised interviews found' (Wessely, 2019, p. xvii). He notes that the problems students described, including loneliness and academic pressures, 'are not normally constructed as "mental disorders"', which, he adds, 'probably explains some of the difference in prevalence' (Wessely, 2019, p. xvii). Nonetheless, this awareness raising and identification of negative emotions and experiences as mental ill-health is seen as requiring a robust, 'whole institution' response including not just mental health professionals but staff and 'students themselves' (Wessely, 2019, p. xvii).

However, while these more expansive claims for whole institutional approaches became commonplace later, the discovery of large numbers of students experiencing mental ill-health represented by these two surveys was positioned as specifically requiring more professionalized and formalized types of help-seeking. Again, news reports problematized that many students did not seek out formal supports. An article in *The Independent* begins, 'A recent study by the National Union of Students (NUS) has revealed the majority of students experience mental health issues (78 per cent), while 54 per cent of students do not seek help, begging the question: Why don't students seek help from their universities – and how can this be reversed?' (Hearing, 2016). The author goes on to suggest that expectations for university mental health provision should be raised and more students should be encouraged to become aware of and draw upon the supports available, 'Because mental health issues are far more common than people think' (Hearing, 2016). Students are warned that if they do not seek out help, even seemingly normal experiences can lead to severe problems. 'It's important to bear these steps in mind because ultimately, if high stress situations go unmanaged, they can sometimes develop and even lead to mental illness' (Heritage, 2017). Another claims-maker argues, 'Those who are unable to cope may drop out. Left unrecognized and untreated, their problems may become more severe. They may start to self-medicate with drink or drugs, self-harm, or even take their own lives' (J. Smith, 2016).

In the sample analysed, solutions to the problem of mental health that involved encouraging students to disclose problems and seek out supports were one of the most coded themes across the sample, appearing in 38 per cent of articles sampled, peaking in 2015 where eight of fourteen articles sampled contained this claim. One article informs students that 'the help is there, and making the most of it can make a positive difference to your life' adding a quote from a spokesperson from Mind stating, 'We know that stigma can prevent people from seeking help but early intervention is vital – people can recover from a mental health problem but this is more likely if they seek help sooner rather than later' (Page, 2014).

No problem was too small to be brought forward. One claims-maker opines that 'Too often "minor" issues' are 'brushed away', and that universities must 'reverse this psychology [and] provide a bridge between the student and support services' (Denham, 2013b). Another argues in a *Guardian* blog that 'Support should not come as the last resort when students are at breaking point. Problems need to be tackled as early as possible, no matter how small the students – or their peers – believe them to be' ('Anonymous Blogger', 2016). Still another urges students to seek out university mental health and well-being services, 'even if your problems don't seem "serious"' (Tobin, 2016). 'It's not just for people with mental health disorders,' offers a representative from the Royal College of Psychiatrists. 'It is really for everybody, and there are all kinds of things available' (*The Times*, 2017). No problem is too small to bring to specialized supports; left unchecked such issues can easily fester and spiral out of control.

Yet increases in disclosure and help-seeking were also seen as indicators of the scale of the problem and a sign of a mental health 'crisis' in universities. One headline promised an inside scoop on the 'counsellors on the frontline of the student mental health crisis', with evidence given including increasing numbers of students disclosing mental health problems and seeking mental health supports (Sarner, 2017). As is common in the sample, statistical claims in this article were also related without the context of substantial overall increases in student numbers[4] nor the strong injunction for students to seek help and disclose problems, 'no matter how small'. 'A growing number of undergraduates are reporting mental health problems,' says a report on the 'crisis' (Marsh, 2017a). Another points out that 'Mental health is now considered one of the biggest challenges facing the sector, with 94 per cent of institutions reporting an increased demand for the services in recent years' (C. Turner, 2018a). Conscious campaigns to raise awareness of mental ill-health, which elided negative feelings with mental health problems and that positioned early and frequent help-seeking were seemingly forgotten.

In all, these claims represent key moments in the 'discovery' of the problem: it had passed from wholesalers to retailers. Beginning with claims-makers associated with providing mental health supports in universities described in the previous chapter, student mental health was taken up by student groups alongside other mental health special interest groups and charities. Many of the students involved in these initiatives discussed their own struggles with mental health as instigators for their involvement. For these 'professional exes' (J. D. Brown, 1991), taking up the mental health cause may have been a way of imputing meaning to their experience, developing a sense of mission and an exit from a potentially 'deviant' career onto a more 'legitimate' career path. This 'career' is sometimes literal as they translate their mental health struggles into employment opportunities and CV-building. I will return to this point in the discussion of typifying examples below.

For the NUS, receptiveness to the mental health agenda was likely driven both by the increased cultural receptivity to framing social problems in psychological terms, but also more pragmatically, it may have offered a new opportunity to reframe student grievances, especially around fees, in the seemingly uncontroversial idiom of health and illness. Like happiness and well-being, the language of mental health has a positive valence, but has the added benefit of a clearer 'health' framing, allowing it to connect to broad audiences already familiar with 'health' as a widely accepted cultural 'good'. Critics thus risk downplaying the importance of something obviously positive. This is particularly clear in relation to fees, the debate about which had been much more contentious. Raising the cap on tuition fees at UK HE institutions to £9,000 had been highly controversial at the turn of the decade. The NUS had led a series of student protests in November 2010 which were unsuccessful in convincing the then coalition Government of Liberal Democrats and Conservatives not to vote in favour of the legislation and fees were raised by nearly all UK HE institutions to £9,000 per year in 2012. However, as was the case with attention to work stress, in which campaigns intending to draw attention to material grievances and the structure of work were resolved into 'minimal and therapeutic responses' (Wainwright, 2008b, p. 88), very few of the solutions proffered by claims-makers in the articles sampled actually focused on grants or lowering fees. Indeed, fees have subsequently been raised in line with inflation, but the amount of funds that universities should spend on mental health support, including mental health problems that were alleged to have been caused by fees and financial distress, has continued to increase.

This is how Gyimah's 2018 statement that mental health was a much more serious concern than tuition fees was able to be received with little commentary. While scrapping or lowering tuition fees no longer appears so high on the agenda, their effect on mental health is. For instance, one article quotes a claims-maker stating that there is 'a vicious cycle whereby financial difficulties exacerbate mental health problems, and these mental health difficulties can then make managing a budget harder still' (Gani, 2016). This is followed by a statement from a representative of UUK boasting of increased investment in counselling services on UK campuses – most likely funded in part by rises in tuition fees. Some claims-makers warned against lowering fees precisely on the grounds that it would affect mental health provision. 'If the Augar review of higher education funding, due to report next month, concludes as expected that tuition fees should fall to £6,000, students with mental health issues may suffer as the fee helps to finance pastoral services' (Watts et al., 2018), warned staff from *The Times*. This is also the case with key documents produced by central claims-making organizations like UUK and Student Minds, which scarcely mention fees, except as, in the words of the latter organization, they 'may impact on mental health and wellbeing' (Hughes & Spanner, 2019, p. 32). Indeed, while the latter document, Student Minds' University Mental Health Charter (UMHC), mentions 'finance' here as one of many issues that may impact on student mental health, it is not mentioned again in the text that follows which focuses primarily on the quality of mental health supports that universities should make available.

Indeed, none of the solutions identified in the sample involve removing or lowering fees. Rather, the most commonly appearing 'conclusions' (Best, 1990, 2021), or solutions offered by claims-makers, were not that fees should be scrapped but that students should seek mental health supports. In the next section I examine the major claims that appeared in the articles sampled in greater detail utilizing Best's (1990, 2021) framework of grounds, warrants and conclusions.

Rhetorical grounds

Using Best's (Best, 1990, 2021) framework for analysing the common rhetorical forms that claims about social problems tend to take, each article was analysed sentence by sentence and claims were coded in a phrase that best encapsulated each claim and subsequent similar claims coded within it. These were then grouped into larger themes and sorted according to whether they represented claims about the nature of the problem (grounds), rationales for action (warrants) or proposed solutions (conclusions). Table 8.1 represents the most common ten types of grounds identified in the sample.

Table 8.1 Ten most common types of grounds identified in sample

Ground type	% of articles in sample containing ground type (n=126)
Descriptions of mental health problems in HE and their scale	83
Causal stories	66
Increases in disclosure, help-seeking, counselling demand	34
Typifying examples	34
Inadequacy of current mental health approaches, interventions, services	34
Groups at risk or in need of support	26
Cuts to or insufficient spending on mental health services	25
Problematic nature of university for mental health	22
Insufficient disclosure and help-seeking	20
Student mental health is worsening, in crisis; 'epidemic' of mental ill-health	17

Rhetorical recipes

In a common 'rhetorical recipe' followed by claims-makers for many social problems, social problem claims often begin with a 'typifying example', or a story that is intended to illustrate, in a relatable and personalized way, the severity and experience of the alleged condition (Best, 2021, p. 32). This is often accompanied by giving the problem a name, in this case subsuming these stories under the umbrella of 'mental health' difficulties or issues, and finally statistics or numbers that 'suggest the scope of the problem' (Best, 2021, p. 33). The implication is that the typifying story is represented by the statistics, which is often not the case as the latter may reflect a range of severity from quite serious to very mild, as discussed above. Indeed, the stories selected to illustrate social problem claims are often atypical, selected because they are particularly severe and eye-catching.

The construction of student mental health as a social problem follows a similar rhetorical recipe, with 34 per cent of articles sampled beginning with or containing at least one typifying example of a student experiencing distress while at university. Many of these stories concern student suicides while others refer to students experiencing severe forms of mental ill-health. For example, one article relates the story of a student with 'bipolar disorder, anxiety and severe depression' before reporting a claim that one in four people has a mental health problem which is then equated to thousands of students at a single university (Sarner, 2017). The implication is that these students are experiencing the same or similar issues when the range of issues that might be included in the '1 in 4' statistic is not stated.

On the other hand, some typifying examples report more minor experiences such as struggling to fit in, encouraging a redefinition of these problems as not banal, but as indicators of problems that require attention and support. 'I hadn't realised how disorientated I would feel away from my friends and my family,' one report quotes a student describing (Lantin, 2005). 'I was permanently exhausted – partly because of stress – and didn't feel I belonged,' she continues. While the student goes on to report that things turned around once she made friends and settled in, the article goes on to quote a Royal College of Psychiatrists report claiming that 'as many as 60 per cent of first-year students report homesickness, and of all university students they are at the greatest risk of developing mental health problems' (Lantin, 2005). The apparently common experience of homesickness and difficulties making new friends becomes a risk factor for mental illness should students fail to recognize it as such and seek out the proper supports.

Interestingly, the typifying examples identified include few 'success stories' of students entirely. Overcoming their difficulties on the other hand, there were many stories of young people who turned their mental ill-health into a positive aspect of their identity and even career or potential career path. As touched upon in the discovery section, many of the typifying examples represent 'professional exes', or individuals whose exit from deviance involves the transformation of a 'deviant' career into a legitimate one (e.g. formerly incarcerated individuals who become mentors, counsellors, life coaches, etc.) (J. D. Brown, 1991; LeBel et al., 2015), or 'wounded healers' – those whose own experiences leave 'lingering effects' that serve in ministering to others (S. W. Jackson, 2001, p. 2). While in the present case study, the objective of many of these missions is precisely to remove the notion of mental ill-health as a 'deviant' position, the exit from deviance nonetheless persists in these narratives in the form of recognition of one's struggles as involving 'mental health' and the adoption of effective coping strategies, sometimes involving mentoring and/or campaigning roles. For example, in one article a student describes how, 'his moods were becoming darker, his motivation disappeared and he started missing lectures' (K. Thomas, 2018). He sought and received a medical diagnosis and was able to carry on his education with help from a variety of services and his department. This student would later go on to take up campaigning for mental health as part of his university's Students Union. Another details the difficulties experienced by a student transitioning to university: 'I had feelings of stress about going to lectures, and felt really depressed about continuing university. [...] If I had a bad day I might miss lectures and then afterwards I worried about falling behind. I felt isolated very quickly' (Fazackerley, 2018). It goes on to describe how the student founded a campaign group with the support of her university entitled, 'My Mind Matters too', dedicated to improving support for students (Fazackerley, 2018). This initiative would later grow into MindMapperUK, an organization offering mental health workshops and coaching sessions to young people with the student quoted in the aforementioned article now acting as its CEO (MindMapperUK, 2022). This example is not exceptional; many of the students quoted describing their mental health difficulties are also described as going on to find meaning and purpose in working and campaigning in the field of mental health.

The relative paucity of stories of overcoming one's mental health issues is likely explained by the fact that maintaining aspects of one's identity as a sufferer of mental ill-health is not an obstacle to the professional ex- or wounded healer position, but rather strengthens it. As Brown (1991) describes, aspects of the former role are carried over, as the professional ex must remain constantly vigilant over 'potentially recurring symptoms' and enact rituals of self-care as a key aspect of providing care and support to others (p. 223). Their 'recognition of the need for constant vigilance is internalized as their moral mission from which their spiritual duty (a counselling career) follows as a natural step' (p. 223). It is their identification with their past role that undergirds the present one and differentiates them from other professional colleagues.

Returning to the theme of communities of fate discussed in the previous chapter, with professional exes in other fields, like formerly incarcerated individuals, the role also transforms the individual from a liability to be supervised to an asset to be utilized (LeBel et al., 2015). For HE institutions, struggling students no longer represent individuals whose behaviours (e.g. failing to complete course requirements thus affecting completion rates, becoming a danger to themselves or others, etc.) represent a putative risk to the institution. Instead, they become assets and repositories within which risk and responsibility can be diffused. A Student Minds document on co-producing mental health strategies with students puts this explicitly, 'When students are fully engaged in the context of strategy development, they are treated as partners in making decisions that will ultimately affect them or their peers. Students are regarded as assets with a great capacity for change, rather than "problems" that require fixing' (Piper & Emmanuel, 2019, p. 41).

Following typifying examples, the vast majority of articles contained claims describing the nature and severity of the problem, making up 83 per cent of articles sampled and comprising nearly 100 claims, the ten most common of which are given in Table 8.2 below. However, most of these were repeated very few times and a large chasm separates the most common claims from the remainder.

These articles often included statistical claims. Yet many of these statistics referred to the general population of young people rather than HE students alone. Absolute rises were often communicated without the context of a general rise in student numbers and the low numbers of students initially affected (thus inflating per cent increases). These phenomena are particularly evident in claims about student suicides, which are the most common indicators of a serious issue in universities cited by claims-makers. For instance, one article blends a variety of figures, not all relevant to HE, to create an image of generalized decline. It begins by stating that three suicides took place in a year at a single university, gives statistics regarding increases in university counselling website hits and ends with a statistic from a youth suicide prevention charity stating that 'between 600 and 800 people under the age of 24 kill themselves each year' (Kozma, 2010). Claims were made that student suicide was an 'epidemic' and a serious and growing issue. One article begins,

'University suicide epidemic; student mental health crisis – these terms are rarely far from the headlines. And the evidence that backs them up is concerning. An Institute for Public Policy Research report last year showed that five times as many students as 10 years ago are reporting mental health conditions to their universities, while student suicides have risen from 75 in 2007 to 134 in 2015.

(R. Hall, 2018)

However, the figures cited actually included all individuals classified as 'full-time students' over the age of eighteen, including those in Further Education (ONS, 2016) and also do not account for the general growth in student numbers. According to ONS estimates released in 2018, the number of HE students who committed suicide in 2014/2015 was ninety-three (ONS, 2018). More significantly, the rate at which university students commit suicide appears to be half that of the general population of the same age (ONS, 2018).

Yet when these latter statistics were released, the story in the news media remained highly pessimistic. A *MailOnline* headline proclaimed that the '[n]umber of university students committing suicide nearly double[d] since 2000' (Ferguson, 2018). 'SUICIDE UNI SHOCK' ran a headline in *The Sun* (Birchall, 2018), while another declared, 'Nearly 100 university students killed

Table 8.2 Ten most common claims describing the nature of the problem

Indicators of the problem of student mental health and its severity	% of articles in sample containing ground type (n=126)
Suicide	38
Anxiety, anxiousness	29
Depression	24
Increasing numbers of students experiencing mental health problems	21
Stress	18
Loneliness, isolation	14
Mental health 'crisis' claims	11
1 in 5 or 20% have mental health problems (NUS survey)	7
Eating disorders	6
Students failing to complete course requirements[5]	6

themselves last year – as numbers seeking counselling soar' (Rodger, 2018). The *i* ran a cover story demanding: 'Mental health crisis among students "must be top priority"', citing the ONS figures as showing, 'student suicide rates had risen by more than a fifth over the past 10 years, with 95 deaths in 2017, up from 77 in 2006–07' (Vaughan, 2018). This is in spite of the release's express warning that such conclusions should not be drawn from the overall low numbers involved. Indeed, a number of conclusions could be drawn from the data depending upon which year one chooses to emphasize; for instance, that the student suicide rate per 100,000 had fallen since 2004/5 or that, overall, going to university appears to cut suicide risk by half. Unsurprisingly, these more optimistic conclusions failed to make headlines. Instead, the statistics became fuel for a plethora of claims about the need to make mental health and well-being a priority.

Again, the theme of risk is significant; it is likely that suicide appears with such frequency because, in spite of overall low numbers, it is one of the most eye-catching and thus powerful of industry-wide risks – the ultimate failure in the 'duty of care' and a threat to universities who do not heed claims-makers' calls.

The next most common claims indicating the nature and severity of student mental ill-health in universities are anxiety and depression. Students were said to be anxious due to financial difficulties, coursework and the uncertainties of the graduate job market with surveys diagnosing signs of 'clinical' anxiety (e.g. Haidrani, 2013). Yet the evidence for these claims was either left unstated or came from symptom surveys, which tend to inflate estimates of the prevalence of anxiety disorders in the general population (Baxter et al., 2014). Moreover, what is considered a 'clinical' level of anxiety has also expanded over the past several decades, capturing more and more of everyday worries under the umbrella of illness (Horwitz, 2013; Horwitz et al., 2012). Advocates routinely referred to student worries about their lives as mental health problems. 'When I asked students around the country about their experiences of mental health, they talked about stressful deadlines, difficulties forming new relationships, balancing a job with studies, financial worries and social pressures' said one (Sarner, 2017). They also often referred to students as 'especially vulnerable' to 'suicide and depression' (e.g. Kozma, 2010) without offering evidence or by using estimates that vary widely. For instance, articles variously claimed that students suffering from depression number 1 in 10 (Haidrani, 2013), 1 in 4 (Dyckhoff, 2013) or 1 in 3 (Coldwell, 2012). The latter of these included students reporting 'feelings of sadness or depression'. This elision is common, with many articles eliding not only sadness with depression, but other phenomena like unhappiness and 'emotional strains' with mental health issues. For example, one claims-maker states that 'We know that most university campuses have completely inadequate student support services which has contributed to a snowballing of student mental issues in recent years,' continuing, 'It's really no wonder that students are more unhappy than ever' (Busby, 2018a). Thus there is considerable 'concept creep', or semantic inflation of harm-related concepts including but not limited to psychological and psychiatric categories (Haslam, 2016; Haslam et al., 2021).

Taken together, the rhetorical recipe of providing typifying examples, naming phenomena of wide-ranging severity problems of 'mental health', and offering expansive statistics, has the effect of constructing student mental health as both a common problem and a serious problem.

Causal stories

In addition to this rhetorical recipe, grounds included 'causal stories' or stories about what underlies the issue. As Stone (1989, p. 283) describes, '[...] causal stories move situations intellectually from the realm of fate to the realm of human agency.' They transform situations into something soluble, usually by the tools that claims-makers have at their disposal. The ten most common of these are shown in Table 8.3.

Table 8.3 Most common causes of student mental health problems alleged by claims-makers

Cause	% of articles in sample containing cause (n=126)
Academic pressures	39
Transitions	38
Financial causes	26
University social life	25
Unrealistic or unmet expectations	17
Broader social problems and uncertainties	16
Causes outside of university or exacerbated by university	12
Isolation or impersonal nature of university experience	6
Insufficient support from university and or other services	6
Academic staff	5

Causal stories also apportion blame. In stories about student mental health, blame tends to be apportioned as what Stone calls 'unintended consequences of willed human action' (p. 285). That is, the problem is said to be caused by people who 'do not understand' the consequences of their actions (p. 286). Students do not realize how difficult things will be and how important it is to seek help. They may not recognize their problems as issues of 'mental health' for which supports are available. In turn, HE institutions (and sometimes academic staff) also do not realize the risks and thus provide insufficient supports. However, in terms of the latter, HE institutions risk veering into a kind of inadvertent causation that Stone describes as 'carelessness or recklessness' (p. 286) which leaves those who do not heed claims-makers' calls for more supports vulnerable to charges of greater culpability, pursuing 'cost-cutting' in spite of risks. One headline puts it thus, 'When higher education cares more about recruiting students than whether they actually want to be here, is it any surprise so many are miserable?' (Swindells, 2019).

But in all causal stories, claims-makers set up the issue in a way that invites their brand of solutions. As Stone describes,

> Just as different causal stories place the burden of reform on some people rather than others, they also empower people who have the tools or skills or resources to solve the problem in the particular causal framework. People choose causal stories not only to shift the blame but to enable themselves to appear to be able to remedy the problem.

> (1989, p. 297)

As will be shown in the conclusions (i.e. alleged solutions), the solutions coalesce around the provision of therapeutic knowledge and supports, however diffuse these end up being. Any broader social issues said to be a cause of mental ill-health remain in the realm of 'fate'.

What is striking is the extent to which once normal pressures and challenges at university have become the causes of problems needing intervention or 'treatment'. Indeed, recall that university 'doctors' in the 1990s (Chateau, 1993) had noted that student problems tended to be short-lived and transient. Now even this transience is depicted as a problem. An advocate from Student Minds argues that 'Students are particularly vulnerable to mental health issues. The transient nature of student life can create problems and things like moving away from home for the first time, being independent and coping with the academic pressures of university, make it hard' (Young-Powell, 2014). Therefore, she continues, students need to 'know what help is available, like counselling and peer support groups'.

I will return to these themes in relation to the expansion of the problem and the blurring of causation in Chapter 9. However, it is worth noting here that many of the broader social problems identified by claims-makers as causing mental ill-health might be considered worthy of pursuing in themselves – like fees and poor job prospects. Instead, these are considered just some of so many causes of mental ill-health. Material problems slip into health problems. Indeed, as noted previously, the NUS had once campaigned heavily against the introduction of fees. It is possible that this problem has ultimately come to be seen as all but insoluble. On the other hand, through effective causal stories linking together causation, risk and therapeutic solutions, the problems identified by claims-makers were successfully moved from the realm of fate or normal aspects and difficulties of life to the realm of human (and institutional) responsibility and control. However, at the same time, while specific and sometimes serious mental health problems are singled out by claims-makers, the range of causes of mental ill-health stipulates that even the most seemingly mundane and banal discomfort is a potential source of illness.

Rhetorical warrants

Warrants offer a rationale for acting on claims, frequently invoking cultural values that, at least claims-makers hope, their audiences will hold dear or otherwise find compelling (Best, 1990, 2021). The ten most common warrants identified in the sample are detailed in Table 8.4 (overleaf).

Suicide and liminality

Suicide was not only singled out as indicative of the scale of the problem of student mental health, but also positioned as a rationale for action. If steps are not taken, claims-makers warned, student mental health problems would worsen and many more young people would take their own lives. Some articles gave details of such tragedies. It is notable however that, while still overall low in number, students aged over thirty had a considerably higher rate of suicide (6.4 deaths per 100,000 students) than those under 20 (2.8 per 100,000 students) according to ONS estimates (ONS, 2018). Yet of the five articles in the sample that focused on detailed cases of student suicide, all were students under twenty years old.

This brings forth a theme implicit across the heightened concern for student mental health, that of liminality. Liminality refers to the 'betwixt-and-between' or transitional space occupied by individuals leaving one social role

Table 8.4 Ten most common warrants identified in sampled articles

Warrant type	% of articles in sample containing ground type (n=126)
Student suicide (prevention, etc.)	19
Benefits to universities or university staff	17
Mental health as warrant	15
Student retention	13
Will improve future individuals, employees, citizens, generations, etc.	11
Improved academic outcomes	10
Universities shape next generation's well-being	10
Progressiveness or radicalism	7
University responsibilities	6
Prevention of mental ill-health and other problems	6

or status but not yet having entered into another (V. Turner, 1967, 1974). It is a common motif in widely spread urban legends, like the ubiquitous 'vanishing hitchhiker' tales, which often feature liminal characters meeting with tragedy – the bride-to-be, the girl on the cusp of adulthood, the father headed home to his new born child (G. Bennett, 1998). These are the quintessential 'innocent victims': young and often female with everything to hope for, but not yet realized. Audiences tend to connect with the image of a young person on the brink of life, which may become particularly compelling in the context of HE so often promoted as the main passage to individual and societal advancement (e.g. Weale, 2022a).

Many spaces within the university (dormitories, boundaries between campus and the surrounding community) and even the experience itself are characterized by liminality (E. Tucker, 2007). In the university experience, young people leave behind their previous social status to reach, ostensibly, a higher one. Liminal spaces, while often entailing great difficulties, are also often ludic – fun, where normal social rules are suspended. But this suspension of rules and codes of behaviour of the surrounding community and world of childhood/adulthood as well as the threat of non re-integration means that they are often discursively positioned as potentially dangerous spaces too. These features of the university as a liminal, ludic/dangerous space are often invoked by claims-makers in the frequently appearing motif that university is 'supposed to be the best time of your life', variations of which are repeated thirteen times across the sample.[6] The image put forward is of young men and women on the boundaries, on the cusp of life, supposed to be having the 'time of their lives' but potentially confronted by unknown dangers and a darker, crueller reality.

Thus many claims about university mental health risks appear to both point to and draw upon growing societal uncertainties regarding the university as a rite of passage. As Thomassen writes, 'In anthropological usage, the liminal state is always clearly defined, temporally and spatially: there is a way into liminality, and there is a way out of it. Members of a society are themselves aware of the liminal state: they know that they will leave it sooner or later [...]' (Thomassen, 2015, p. 52). But in situations of collapse,[7] the future becomes 'inherently unknown' and there is less certainty regarding the existence of a 'home society' awaiting the initiand's reintegration (p. 52). Thus, the frequent singling out of uncertain job prospects as the source of mental ill-health alludes to this growing ambivalence about university as a rite of passage and initiands' risk of being 'stuck' in a liminal state.

At least it appears clear that, like urban legends passing by word of mouth, such claims draw much of their rhetorical power from the ambivalences of universities and university students as liminal spaces and liminal subjects. In spite of the shaky foundations of the risks associated with student suicide, it becomes particularly compelling as a warrant within this wider context of liminality and its associated dangers and uncertainties.

Benefits and costs

As is common in claims-making about social problems, claims-makers referred to financial costs and benefits of action versus inaction. In doing so, they again drew on universities as communities of fate, arguing that the sector would benefit in terms of greater student recruitment and retention if they invested in greater mental health supports. 'Reputational concerns should never trump student welfare; ultimately, universities will receive more kudos if they are perceived as being ahead of the curve' argues one claims-maker (Clayton, 2017). Individual universities with greater buy-in would be more competitive than those who failed to invest appropriately, thus balancing costs and benefits. This claims-maker adds, 'The cost of mental ill health to the economy, NHS and society is estimated at £105bn per year and, put simply, the looming spectre of psychological anguish is making universities less wonderful places to be' (Clayton, 2017). In this way, universities' failure to act is positioned as a risk not only to individual institutions and the sector, but also to taxpayers and the economy as a whole. Like the emotion waves discussed in previous chapters, savings are also promised to come in the form of preventing future problems. For instance, the OfS offers policy affirmation for this claim in 2019 when it argues that the aim is 'both to improve support for students with existing mental health conditions and to encourage universities and colleges to identify early warning signs that individuals may be at risk, as well as improving the wellbeing of all students' (Office for Students, 2019, p. 3).

This may explain why university Vice Chancellors (VCs) and other representatives of university management were often quick to affirm the mental health agenda and new technologies of mental health monitoring and even appeared as the sources of many claims. For instance, one VC was quoted early on affirming universities' responsibilities in relation to student mental health, adding, 'We know that if we aren't proactive the most terrible tragedies can happen' (Curtis, 2005). A representative of UUK expressed 'delight' at a digital mental health monitoring platform as reaffirming, 'that the UK sector is taking a leading approach to mental health in higher education' (Busby, 2018a). Mental health promotion sometimes featured in the efforts of VCs to promote their own universities, as in the case of one VC who advocated building characteristics like 'self-belief' into the curriculum as part of a plan to improve the university's failing reputation (Bowditch, 2006).

Of course, the effect is often the opposite. As more spending is introduced, more tends to be demanded, leading to an upward spiral in demand (Summerfield, 2012). Conversely, any reductions after initial spends are criticized as 'cuts'. This appears true of university mental health spending, increasing substantially over the past two decades with claims-makers continuing to demand more. By 2018, universities began to claim that, even after some institutions had doubled their mental health-related budgets, they could 'no longer cope' (Watts et al., 2018). However, as the expansion section shows, the institutionalization of these claims via 'whole institution' approaches saw the diffusion of responsibilities across institutions as one means of dispersing risk and controlling costs. As Brewster and Cox (2022, p. 5) write, 'Responsibility for student mental health becomes a nebulous aim, positioned as part of the everyday work of teaching and learning and everyone's responsibility. This integration into expected activity also seemingly justifies the lack of resources allocated to the problem' (Brewster & Cox, 2022, p. 5). However, it appears that with the domain of mental health expanding so rapidly, no amount of resources would be enough.

Mental health (and well-being) as warrant

Of course, mental health itself acted as a warrant. The issue of mental health in universities is an iteration of the pre-existing construction of mental health as a social problem but expanded into universities. The growing purchase of mental health in the broader ethnopsychology of the culture as a result of previous claims-making campaigns more generally was drawn upon by claims-makers who often took it for granted that the value of mental health was self-evident. For instance, it was used as a warrant in claims about other areas in need of attention. One claims-maker wishing to highlight students' allegedly poor diets claimed, 'Most people are familiar with the physical consequences of a poor diet, but the mental health implications are largely ignored,' before concluding, 'It is vital university students understand the mental health benefits and risks associated with poor diet' (Qureshi, 2009). Complaints about a survey with allegedly offensive wording were justified on the basis of harm to the mental health of students (Ali, 2015). The university was also positioned as the root of both individuals' and society's long-term mental health. '75 per cent of all mental health conditions begin by the age of 24, so the years in university dorms are crucial for shaping the next generation's mental wellbeing,' writes one commentator (Clayton, 2017).

Mental health as a warrant gains from the authoritativeness of a quasi-medical framing, but in avoiding the language of 'mental illness' it at least attempts to eschew the professionalized connotations of the latter. Thus, mental health can be positioned as both the responsibility of professionals but also institutions that are not formally tasked with attending to illness. Claims-makers appear to make great effort to avoid the term 'mental illness'; it appears only forty-six times in the sample compared to 1,173 appearances of 'mental health' and 201 for 'wellbeing' or 'well-being'. As will be discussed in greater detail in Chapter 9, mental health also has the benefit of inclusiveness. It is something that focuses not just on a few individuals, but everyone. As the student mental health campaign group Student Minds reminds audiences, 'We all have mental health' (Student Minds, 2018). But this mental health is always at risk and can potentially create further risks. Student Minds continues, '[…] our mental wellbeing can fluctuate day-to-day. When you're not feeling great, it can feel harder to take action to benefit your wellbeing' (Student Minds, 2018). This implies that everyone possesses a vulnerability about which they must be vigilant, that they must be aware of and constantly work to protect. Nicola Byrom, also of Student Minds, tells audiences of a student newspaper, 'We all have mental health and we all need to look after it' (A. Fitzpatrick, 2017). At the same time, while many groups appear to jostle for ownership of student mental health, student mental illness is positioned as particularly risky, and as the responsibility of other parties, as the next section on conclusions (proposals for action) shows.

As everyone needs to protect and guard their mental health, the term becomes gradually more pathologized so that it comes to stand for its opposite. Some articles speak of a 'mental health epidemic', when what is meant is presumably an epidemic of mental ill-health. Indeed, this shift towards signifying its opposite or negative meaning is largely how I have used the term throughout this book following these tendencies in the phenomena being described. Discourses of mental health have traversed a similar path to health more generally, in which the latter gradually came to be positioned not as the absence of illness but rather something which requires constant attention and care (M. Fitzpatrick, 2002; Lupton, 1995). Individuals become 'patients-in-waiting', tasked with constant self-surveillance for signs of mental 'distress'. This constant attention and surveillance with reference to authorities in the care of the self are positioned not as a form of discipline, but rather as a right and 'fundamental good' about which individuals should obviously be concerned (Lupton, 2012, p. 34) and even demand.

This shift also occurs in relation to other emotional signifiers discussed throughout this book. As Furedi observed, the concern for self-esteem was its low level (Furedi, 2004). The concern for happiness was that people were not happy enough (Frawley, 2015c). Mindfulness came to imply mindlessness. And mental health has come to mean 'mental ill-health'. As this signifier gets bound up in a new emotion problem cycle, it comes to be defined by its lack. It is self-evidently problematic. One does not necessarily need to say 'low self-esteem', 'unhappiness' or 'poor mental health'. Their widespread lack and problematic nature come to be taken for granted.

This signification of absence explains the clumsy phraseology that sometimes appears in public and social media discourses in which individuals and advocates will speak of 'suffering with' or 'from' 'mental health'. For instance, the headline of an article in *Psychology Today* assures readers that 'Suffering With Mental Health Doesn't Make You Ungrateful' (Strauss Cohen, 2021). *CBS News* reports on an app that can help veterans 'suffering with mental health' (Herridge, 2021). While walking through the foyer of my own university, a student handed me a flyer informing me that '1 in 4 people will be affected by mental health', a phrasing repeated by the Department of Health on their Twitter account: '[...] 1 in 4 of us are affected by mental health and the damage this can do, every day of the year, is very real' (Department of Health and Social Care [@DHSCgovuk], 2019). This avoidance of the language of mental illness is particularly evident in the appearance of other awkward terminologies like 'mental health illness'. For instance, the American Psychiatric Association recommends that rather than stating in media coverage that someone 'suffers from mental illness', one should instead state that the individual 'has a mental health illness' (American Psychiatric Association, 2022). As 'mental health' comes to signify its absence or at least a kind of pervasive mental vulnerability, new terms like this are sometimes needed to signify not 'mad', as 'mental illness' can be interpreted to signify (Nairn, 2007), but nonetheless beyond the experience of everyday 'negative' emotions now subsumed under the banner of mental health. If everyone has (at risk) mental health, this leaves behaviours and experiences outside the range of 'normal' struggling for signification within the broader and ever-widening discourse of 'mental health'.

Instead of illness, the more comfortable dwelling ground for claims-makers is the realm of morality and behaviour, recast in the language of mental health and well-being. Since the 1990s, sociologists have identified a rising tide of 'health moralism' where risk analysis functions to moralize a wide range of behaviour (Ericson & Doyle, 2003). As Mary Douglas (1992, p. 26) has put it,

> If Western industrial democracy were ever to build a homogeneous culture using a uniform vocabulary for moralizing and politicizing the dangers around, it could not use the vocabulary of religion. The neutral vocabulary of risk is all we have for making a bridge between the known facts of existence and the construction of a moral community. But this is why the public discourse about modern risks has fallen into an antique mode. Risk, danger, and sin are used around the world to legitimate policy or to discredit it, to protect individuals from predatory institutions or to protect institutions from predatory individuals.

Mental health becomes a moral shorthand for desirable behaviours and warrant for claims whose outright moralism might otherwise fall on deaf ears. For example, alcohol and raucous behaviour are reframed not as threats to public morality or even straightforwardly as an institutional risk, but rather as a threat to the mental health of individuals which in turn creates institutional risks. In a manner that sums up this outlook, Anthony Seldon is cited as claiming that 'Universities are being negligent about the mental health of their students and turning a blind eye to "ultra-cheap alcohol" for sale on campus' (Sanderson, 2015).

In these ways, mental health is a powerful warrant in a range of claims, not just of course in relation to universities (see e.g. Lee, 2003). The expansiveness of mental health can connote a sense of 'holism' so that there is little to no limit on the reach of demands. For instance, the UMHC mentions 'holism' and 'holistic' and 'whole' (university, sector, community, etc.) no less than eighty-eight times across the document's ninety-two pages. The term 'mental health' appears 516 times, whereas 'mental illness' appears thirty-nine times. Moreover, the document (consistent with the gradual expansion of mental health to encompass mental illness) expressly defines 'mental health' as encompassing 'a full spectrum of experience' from mental health to mental illness (Hughes & Spanner, 2019, p. 9) as does UUK's #StepChange framework (UUK, 2020). It is implied but not stated that if everyone has mental health, then everyone has mental illness too.

However, its medical connotations in this domain act as both a benefit and a drawback. Even with the avoidance of the language of illness, the quasi-medical framing that the language of 'health' invites can inhibit the holistic focus on institutions and behaviours so desired by these claims-makers, and particularly university management. In Brewster and Cox's (2022) study of the interpretation of this agenda within HE institutions, and specifically by university libraries, they point out that library staff often shifted from mental health to well-being. They argue that

> […] including wellbeing in practice is a direct response to a recognition of the boundaries of expertise by those being given responsibility for mental health such as librarians. As noted above, activity did not focus on risk and regulation – areas more traditionally associated with trained mental health specialists – but instead was positioned as preventative. While a whole-university approach may make all accountable for student mental health, this indicates some push back against being given this accountability.
>
> (p. 12)

The authors describe how activities undertaken and interpreted as contributing to the institutional mental health agenda were frequently quite broad, indicating that 'non-specialists were unwilling to claim mental health expertise or to take on activities outside their scope' (p. 12). The more 'nebulous' language of 'well-being' therefore allowed ownership and involvement in activities 'that could be constructed as beneficial to mental health without directly addressing symptoms of mental health issues' (p. 12). Unsurprisingly, the UMHC, while avoiding the language of mental illness, uses the word well-being 224 times, facilitating the smoothness of this switch for institutions wishing to put the Charter into practice.

Claims-makers therefore dance back and forth between well-being and mental health as the focus of their demands and activities shifts. Well-being more easily facilitates a 'holistic' outlook, seems less specialist and is something seemingly anyone can promote. Mental health, while connoting medical authority and seriousness, can sometimes seem too professionalized and medicalized. While mental health may have expanded to include the full 'spectrum' of human experience, well-being is sometimes preferable as a 'floating signifier', a symbol or concept 'loose enough to mean many things to many people, yet specific enough to galvanize action in a particular direction' (Smucker et al., 2012, p. 234). It is capable of extending to a broader range of obviously non-health-related phenomena while also avoiding connotations of (and responsibility for) 'mental illness'.

Success of individuals and society

Finally, many of the warrants listed in Table 8.4 fall under the general heading of promising success to individuals and other institutions in society. Mental health promotion and spending were promised to improve educational outcomes, create better employees and even shape the future well-being of society as a whole – yet these claims were not always as optimistic as they may seem.

Good mental health via student support was positioned as, in the words of one claims-maker and AMOSSHE representative, 'inextricably linked' to educational purpose (Slack, 2012). Mindfulness interventions in universities were said to be able to 'build resilience' and allow students to 'study more effectively' based on 'very hard data' (Swain, 2016). Echoing arguments made in schools, Anthony Seldon, by then VC of the University of Buckingham, argued that 'Some vice-chancellors still think [mental health care] is not the business of universities and it's just about development of the mind, but developing minds means nothing unless you also help people learn how to become settled down and ready to learn' (Marsh, 2017a). According to Steve West, chair of UUK's mental health advisory group and also a university VC, 'With 50 per cent of school leavers now entering higher education, our mentally healthy universities will play a leading role in supporting a generation of young adults to thrive and succeed' (Busby, 2018b). Moreover, mental health is not simply necessary for educational outcomes, but the two are claimed to be indistinguishable. As a chief executive of a mental health charity claims, 'Educational outcomes are dependent upon student wellbeing so separating the two is a totally foolish distinction' (Denham, 2013a).

Warrants thus tended to adopt the same strategy of flipping Maslow's hierarchy of needs observed in other emotional idioms discussed in previous chapters, where it is alleged that if individuals and institutions first promote x [*emotional outlook*], then y [*e.g. success or solution to wider societal problem*] will follow. It is claimed that by promoting mental health in the present, future mental health problems will be prevented. Universities will create better citizens and students themselves will be more successful in their studies. In this way, these aspects of the self-esteem, happiness and mindfulness problems are maintained. Yet there is also a sense of the top of the hierarchy being stripped away, where mental health becomes not a path to material outcomes, but rather *the* outcome. As one claims-maker argues, 'The higher education sector has a duty to redesign its offering to bring emotional and social education to its heart, making these as foundational to the university experience as academic education' (R. Hall, 2019). As it becomes the foundation, it becomes increasingly unclear what, if anything, lies beyond it. While it is often promised that promoting mental health will lead to educational attainment (e.g. by improving study skills and reducing dropout rates), the future success that is discussed is not one of material achievement, but rather good mental health or, more frequently, the prevention of poor mental health.

Thus, there is a sense that the mental health agenda in HE is not about optimization and achievement so much as avoiding an allegedly impending disaster. As Brewster and Cox (2022, p. 5) also observe, particularly in institutional guidance like the UUK #StepChange framework, 'the concern is less around negative effects on students themselves, but instead success emphasizes the potential risk of not delivering on promised outcomes.' This is the case in news media claims-making as well. According to Seldon, 'The pressure within the academic system to demonstrate quantifiable results, rather than turning out well-rounded, properly equipped graduates, is creating an anxious, ill-equipped and emotionally fragile generation of workers' (R. Hall, 2019). It is not that mental health promotion necessarily creates optimal workers. Rather, not acting creates a generation of 'fragile' and 'ill-equipped' workers. It is the fragility of subjectivity that presents a problem – an in-built tendency that requires active intervention to thwart.

It is claimed that entire generations will be failed and put at risk by the sector's failure to act. 'Students' mental health must be treated as seriously as academic studies or authorities risk failing a generation,' Sam Gyimah is quoted as saying (R. Bennett, 2018). A VC claims, 'Health services aren't properly designed to help students as they move from home to university. This is too important to ignore and we must not fail a generation by not doing what is required' (Weale, 2018). If these issues are dealt with appropriately, they are 'less likely to get passed on to the next generation' says a child and adolescent psychotherapist (Sarner, 2017). Indeed, references to generational impacts, 'generations' and 'generational' appear seventy times in the 126 article news media sample.

In this way, it is not about promoting an optimal state of being but rather avoiding a natural sense of destructiveness that exists when individuals are left unchecked. Rather than being seen as situational and transient, difficulties now coded as student mental ill-health would worsen without support and impact upon other institutions and even future generations. Without action, society as a whole would be failed.[8]

Rhetorical conclusions

What is perhaps most interesting about the structure that the rhetorical problematization of student mental health took is the way that conclusions (i.e. solutions to the putative problem) and even their institutionalization into policy appeared to precede grounds. As discussed in the grounds section, the existence of a problem and the need for mental health support in universities appeared to be a foregone conclusion evidence for which was sought post hoc. Therefore, it is not surprising that the majority of conclusions identified in the sample referred to interventions that were already underway. Table 8.5 shows the most commonly appearing conclusions identified in the sample.

Table 8.5 Ten most common conclusions identified in sampled articles

Conclusion type	% of articles in sample containing conclusion type (n=126)
Reports of existing interventions, solutions and university responses	57
Demands for actions to be taken by universities	42
Increase disclosure/help-seeking, widen access to services and early intervention	38
Demands for expansion of or increased funding for mental health supports	27
Actions to be taken by students (besides disclosure and help-seeking)	24
Cross-sector collaboration	22
More people/groups require support, intervention, treatment, prevention, etc.	17
Recognize and seek to find signs of mental ill-health in student populations	11
Demands for actions to be taken by non-specialist university staff	10
Development of or changes to government policies	7

Reports of existing interventions

In this way, some claims-making appears as post hoc justifications for and expansion of an agenda that had already been taken up, even before evidence of a serious problem within HE was constructed. Indeed, across most of the years sampled, there are more reports of existing or ongoing interventions than demands for further intervention. The sample contained a total of 130 interventions and responses described as being ongoing in universities. These ranged from mobile apps to hypnotherapy, from free yoga to craft classes. However, the most commonly appearing were descriptions and announcements of increased institutional spending on mental health and the hiring of additional mental health support staff.

The assumption that a problem must exist, without evidence or even in the face of evidence to the contrary, has been described elsewhere as a 'problem in search of grounds' (Lee, 2017, p. 28). In this case, there is not only a problem in search of grounds, but also to a certain extent conclusions in search of grounds. Some conclusions identified were pre-existing interventions which had been extended into HE institutions like hypnotherapy and mindfulness apps. The interest in mindfulness also appears to have crept from schools to universities, as one headline reads, 'Mindfulness: the craze sweeping through schools is now at a university near you' (Swain, 2016). Anthony Seldon's extension of the well-being agenda into universities as a solution to its ostensible problems has also been an earlier case in point. Of course, the existence of campus counselling services meant that changes to HE, including widening access, were taken *de facto* to mean that existing services would require a radical expansion. As a Royal College of Psychiatrists' report from 2003 stated, 'Widening participation, with its welcome emphasis on hitherto disadvantaged groups, implies an increase in the number of students likely to require additional support, both educationally and emotionally' (Royal College of Psychiatrists, 2003, p. 43). As with the happiness movement, at least initially, the existence of solutions preceded the construction of a dire problem to which these interventions could be directed (Frawley, 2015c). Or, recalling Hewitt's observations regarding self-esteem, once there is hammer, everything looks like a nail.

Demands for actions to be taken by universities

Nonetheless, the second most common demand concerns additional actions to be taken by universities. Among these claims, the most common was that universities should emphasize the importance of mental health. This predominantly comes in the form of advocating for mental health awareness days, raising awareness more generally within the student population and making mental health central to their mission. 'It's time for universities to put student mental health first', proclaimed a headline in *The Guardian* (Wakeford, 2017). The chief executive of a mental health charity argues that 'Universities have the knowledge and skills to deal with student mental health but they need to make it a priority' (Denham, 2013a). Another claims-maker asserts that mental health support should be 'central to a university's obligations to its students' (Marsh, 2017a). What is more, failure to heed such calls has dire consequences: 'Students' futures are blighted, there is a knock-on effect to the NHS, and universities will inevitably suffer an impact to their reputation' this claims-maker continues (Marsh, 2017a). As time goes on, these claims become more strident and tied to an alleged 'crisis' situation. Willem Kuyken, of the Oxford Mindfulness Centre, is described as alleging universities need to address the 'mental health crisis at its roots', and is quoted arguing that 'The higher education sector has a duty to redesign its offering to bring emotional and social education to its heart, making these as foundational to the university experience as academic education' (R. Hall, 2019).

These claims culminate in the demand that universities must adopt 'whole institution' or 'whole university' approaches. As Brewster and Cox (2022, p. 2) describe, a whole university approach stipulates that 'mental health support should not just be a stand-alone service provided by a specialist team' but instead be 'integrated into all aspects of university life – from design of curricula and assessments to the built environment.' The 2017 UUK #Stepchange framework on mental health was described by a *Guardian* writer as highlighting 'the need for student mental health to be a strategic priority, embedded across all university activities' (Wakeford, 2017). Yet, once again, the demand for a whole university approach within news media articles appears to grow only after it had already been institutionalized into frameworks such as that of UUK (recall, an organization which represents university management). Approaches described as 'whole institution' or 'whole university' begin to appear in the articles sampled in 2016 (one article) and 2017 (five articles). A search of the Nexis database in UK broadsheets for the terms ('whole institution' OR 'whole university') AND ('higher education' OR 'university' OR 'universities') AND 'mental health' shows a take-off of such keywords between 2018 and 2020.

However, the idea of a 'whole institution' approach to mental health and health more generally has a longer history. Calls for the university campus to be designed in 'therapeutic' and 'preventative' ways can be heard as far back as the 1970s (Western Interstate Commission for Higher Education, 1973), though they would go on to be more influential in primary rather than further and higher education. It was only later that these claims were institutionalized in HE. As Dooris and Doherty observe (2010, p. 7), 'Within the UK, most health-related interventions and other activities within higher education settings [...] [target] the "traditional" 18–24 year old population – taking the opportunity to extend school-based and college-based programmes to a setting that is characterized by many young people as an important life transition stage.'

Thus, extending school approaches into HE seemed a natural next step, even if the evidence was not necessarily forthcoming. Advocates claimed in the news media that such an approach would end suicide and prevent mental health problems before they start. However, little evidence is brought to support such claims and indeed, the broader literature is short on evaluations of whole institution approaches to health promotion, particularly in higher education settings (Sweeting et al., 2021). It appears to be another hammer in search of a nail.

Who is responsible for mental illness?

Additional conclusions such as the injunction to seek out supports have been discussed in earlier sections. However, it is worth considering a key overarching theme implicit within conclusions, namely, responsibility for mental illness. Gyimah's strong statement on the need for universities to take action seems to imply that responsibility lies with HE institutions. Yet, across news media claims-making and associated documents produced by a variety of stakeholders, the responsibility for mental illness remains ambiguous. Statistics for mental illness are frequently given in the news media and stakeholder documents, but treatment for such issues is peripheral to the conclusions for what should be done. For instance, in a Royal College of Psychiatrists report from 2011, the authors state that 'There is a perception that student counselling services are facing demands from students who would formerly have been offered NHS care. Doubts have been expressed about whether it is the role of counselling services to compensate for what seem to be shortfalls in NHS provision' (Royal College of Psychiatrists, 2011, p. 19). The report also notes that most people with serious issues are treated by GPs and NHS. However, they then recommend that universities invest in hiring more people to help ambiguously termed, 'mentally troubled students'.

NHS cuts are criticized for placing undue stress on universities. Ruth Caleb, then head of counselling at Brunel university, is cited as arguing that 'a reduction in specialist services in the NHS, as well as longer waiting lists for psychiatric assessment and therapy, have put more pressure on universities as students wait for diagnosis and treatment' (*The Guardian*, 2014a). As early as 2005, VCs were lamenting that NHS focus on other groups would leave universities having to pick up the bill (e.g. Curtis, 2005). On the other hand, student seeking help on the NHS is positioned as a failure on the part of universities. A representative from the Royal College of GPs is quoted saying, 'This should be central to a university's obligations to its students. If you fail to provide adequate support, everyone loses. Students' futures are blighted, there is a knock-on effect to the NHS, and universities will inevitably suffer an impact to their reputation' (Marsh, 2017b). One article that begins, 'There is a mental health crisis on college campuses, and it's getting worse', argues:

> This is a tragedy. 75 per cent of all mental health conditions begin by the age of 24, so the years in university dorms are crucial for shaping the next generation's mental wellbeing. The cost of mental ill health to the economy, NHS and society is estimated at £105bn per year [...].
>
> (Clayton, 2017)

Another claims-maker argues that universities positioning themselves as responsible for 'well-being' is simply a mask for cuts to student services: 'If [...] students have to get counselling from an external provider not embedded into the university, that is a cut. If students have to get counselling from the already overstretched and underfunded NHS services, that is a cut' (Lightfoot, 2018).

This uncertainty regarding responsibility for mental health is fed by a tendency towards fluidity with language when attempting to refer to precisely what the problem is. For instance, a document produced by the OfS in 2019 refers to 'mental health conditions' and discusses 'mental ill health' as a 'longstanding concern' in FE and HE, giving details of the support on offer when 'mental ill health arises' (Office for Students, 2019, p. 1). Yet it goes on to say that

> The Office for Students (OfS) takes a wide-ranging approach to encouraging, considering and sharing innovative and effective practice to improve the mental health and wellbeing of the wider student population. Our overall focus is on incentivising and promoting change across the whole higher education sector and student population'.
>
> (p. 2)

A document produced by the Higher Education Policy Institute (P. Brown, 2016) is similar. Here, responsibility for serious issues is pointed towards the government and the NHS while universities are responsible for 'poor wellbeing' or 'what might be described as mental health problems' (p. 53). Yet earlier in the document it is suggested that treatment within universities might be preferable to treatment on the NHS, with rates of improvement within HE approvingly cited (p. 13).

The ideal response to what is positioned as a mental health crisis in the grounds of claims resolves into a broadly targeted and diffuse 'whole university approach' focused on the promotion of 'mental health and wellbeing'. Responsibility lies with everyone in the university community, including and even especially non-counselling staff including academics and those working within halls of residence (Hughes & Spanner, 2019). Mental health and well-being promotion are more open and ambiguous terms, while mental illness appears both professionalized and fraught with risk. Indeed, the UMHC refers to risk as a major overarching theme across the document. Mental health promotion has the potential to diffuse risk across the institution, while treatment of mental illness is positioned as the responsibility of other institutions.

The eye-catching severity of claims regarding suicide risk and severe mental health problems means that they are frequently cited as a rationale for the need for adopting new interventions, increasing funding, and, as time goes on, adopting a 'whole university approach'. Yet treatment of mental illness does not figure in conclusions, which instead focus on promotion and prevention. While there is a lot of rhetoric of crisis, there is a clear sense that universities are not responsible for 'serious issues'. One news media report hints at this tension and confusion when describing how Bristol University's lawyer, Keith Feeney, argued that the institution was 'not a healthcare provider' but rather a public body for 'research and education' (Agnew, 2019). On the other hand, as the author points out, the university's mental health and well-being strategy, published the month before, says, 'Placing student mental health and wellbeing at the forefront of university decisions and working alongside our student body to shape policies is crucial to creating a representative Bristol community', while its VC the year before had urged, 'all vice-chancellors to make [mental health] a priority of their institutions'.

While 'serious' mental health issues appear in the grounds as justifications for a wide range of interventions, in conclusions, serious mental health issues are positioned as the responsibility of other parties. While it seems that while there is no shortage of interventions aimed at 'minor issues', few are willing to take responsibility for more 'serious' concerns. As Brewster and Cox (2022, p. 6) also observe, while mental health is forwarded as a problem, it is unclear 'why a whole-university approach is a solution' (Brewster & Cox, 2022, p. 6) except perhaps as a means of dealing with and diffusing risks.

Conclusion

The idea of being at the cusp of one's life coupled with the uncertain gains that follow makes HE a fertile site for stoking social concern. The ludic mix of danger and fun, set away from the prying eyes and safe rules of broader society, means that claims accentuating its risks are particularly likely to take root. In this respect, student suicide became a powerful claim as a potent industry wide risk. Those in charge could hardly afford, sometimes literally, not to take notice. Claims-makers were able to position suicide as the ultimate failure in the duty of care and a threat to universities who do not heed advocates' calls.

Yet in the dominant solutions I identified, claims reverted to more diffuse forms of mental health and well-being promotion. There was a coalescing with the earlier agenda of well-being promotion and a more holistic focus on individuals and behaviours. And it is into such promotion that the issue ultimately resolved itself. The overall problem discovered therefore appears as follows: Students suffer greatly and in serious ways, yet common, everyday once normal and typical university experiences are also a source of suffering and deserve attention. Indeed, the commonality of experiences alludes to the commonality of mental ill-health and is part of a drive to destigmatize mental illness and 'coming forward' for help, and to offer inclusive approaches. A huge range of support is needed to deal with every aspect of life, no matter how seemingly banal. Failure to act on claims-makers' demands constitutes not only a risk to institutions, but also a failure in terms of the institution's responsibility to society as a whole. If students attempt to deal with problems on their own, they are likely to fester. Failure to heed the claims of advocates can result in situations spiralling out of control and ultimately, student suicides. The 'ideal' solution may be the proffering of expensive professional supports. However, a whole university approach to mental health and well-being promotion which subsumes the entire university community under its purview is positioned as being able to prevent problems before they begin. Early intervention and a focus on the entire university community should be the main focus, while responsibility for mental illness and the putative risk that this entails is ambiguous or belongs to other institutions.

9

Adopting, Expanding, but not Exhausting

Like previous therapeutic fads, mental health discourses in HE are permeated with a rhetoric of progressiveness and radicalism. 'There couldn't be a more forward-thinking time for mental health' (News media, 2017). Society is said to be at last opening its eyes to the realities of mental health and breaking down barriers and stigmas. 'At long last, the subject matter has caught the attention of so many, with help from well-known individuals doing their bit in removing its stigma, and in turn, inspiring people to come forward to avoid suffering alone' (Castle, 2017). Norman Lamb, then chair of the House of Commons Science and Technology Select Committee, told the news media,

> Every university has a duty to provide decent support to its students. Any that fails to do so must be challenged. It can no longer be tolerated. Moving to university can be a particularly challenging and stressful time for many young people, with some struggling to adapt to moving away often from home, family and other support networks.
>
> (Buchan, 2018)

Student groups are reported as demanding more attention to mental health (e.g. Busby, 2018b). However, as described in previous chapters, this was after the agenda had been set. Indeed, enlisting students in co-production and implementation of institutional mental health policies as well as in the uptake of advocacy of student mental health have been key goals identified by UUK (2020) and Student Minds (2019), respectively. For all intents and purposes, students are being asked to push at an open door.

Adoption by university management

The most frequently appearing claims-making organization in the sample was UUK, the representative group of university managers. The organization and its representatives appeared in 20 per cent of articles sampled. They were also one of the earliest appearing claims-makers. Indeed, the category of university management and their representatives in general (including VCs) appeared in 35 per cent of the articles sampled, the most common grouping of claims-makers followed by mental health charities and related mental health special interest groups (33 per cent). In 2017, UUK launched the Stepchange framework giving guidance to HE institutions on making mental health a priority across sweeping domains of university life. In 2020, it was remodelled to become *UUK Mentally Healthy Universities* (UUK, 2020), though I will continue to refer to it as the Stepchange framework hereafter. The warrants described in Chapter 8 were broadly institutionalized in this framework, with its motivation for action framed in terms of student and staff attainment, risk and legal responsibility, and the impact and severity of the issue (UUK, 2020, pp. 10–11). UUK was also involved in the creation of the University Mental Health Charter (UMHC) (Hughes & Spanner, 2019), which codifies the institutionalization of a whole university approach through an award scheme for HE institutions going furthest to implement it.

Indeed, the enthusiastic embrace arguably takes it beyond uptake in schools (Ecclestone & Hayes, 2019). The Stepchange framework and UMHC, key documents in the demand for mental health to be institutionalized across institutions and the sector as a whole, argue that mental health must be embedded in everything that universities do. There are a number of reasons for this swift affirmation and adoption by governing bodies of the HE sector. As discussed in earlier chapters, education in general tends to be prone to fads because of high expectations for progress and its role in creating future citizens (Best, 2006b). Adoption of therapeutic ideals in HE shows a 'therapization' of notions of progress whose focus is more rooted in the mind than the outside world (Ecclestone & Brunila, 2015). As discussed in Chapters 2 and 3, it expresses a strong cultural conviction that what goes right and wrong in society is reducible to something going right and wrong within the human mind (see also Frawley, 2022). This coincides with universities' ongoing uncertainty regarding their purpose and role in society. As a rhetorical framework, mental health also offers to individualize and medicalize risks and difficult problems, like the inevitable rise of student withdrawals as more and more students of varying levels of interest and preparedness enter universities. Among staff, complaints of rising pressures and workloads can be recast as issues requiring 'wellbeing support' rather than decreasing workloads and/or hiring more academic staff. Higher student numbers also come with expectations of greater inclusivity, leading to a strong desire to be seen to be shedding their ivory tower and elitist imagery but also to avoid perceived risks that come with a larger and more diverse student population.

Indeed, the most powerful rationale for adoption is risk avoidance. The UMHC mentions 'risk' no fewer than seventy-three times across its ninety-two pages. Contributing to the creation and widespread adoption of regulatory frameworks has been a key path for the sector to attempt to see its way out of this risk. For particular HE institutions this also leads to regulatory competition as they compete to be seen to be making the most headway on an overarching agenda. This explains the early buy in of university VCs and pro VCs who compete to show awareness of and action towards the cause. The VC of the University of Bristol affirmed in 2018, 'Certainly for me, [student wellbeing] is a top priority for our institution. I think there is a real appetite among UK universities to take the lead in this area' (Busby, 2018b). Institutions with larger endowments make promises knowing that their weaker competitors may not be able to compete. Cambridge and Oxford frequently appear in the news media advertising their dedication to student mental health; they also spend the most on mental health among UK universities according to Freedom of Information requests produced by student news site *The Tab* (TheTabOfficial, 2016). On the other hand, the University of Southampton's VC complains of rising costs. 'There are a number of challenges – there's no funding from government' he told the press (Watts et al., 2018).

However, as discussed in the previous chapter, while mental health is widely affirmed, the risks that acted as a warrant for this adoption are not taken on quite so straightforwardly. Instead, they are diffused throughout the institution or sent elsewhere through 'collaborative approaches'. The UMHC (Hughes & Spanner, 2019) offers detailed guidelines for collaboration with outside agencies. It also recommends mental health training for a variety of non-counselling staff including accommodation staff and academics. A report from the Higher Education Policy Institute (HEPI) is similar in recommending training for, 'All staff, whether permanent, contract or agency staff' to have 'the confidence to recognize potential issues and know how to respond to them' (P. Brown, 2016, p. 43). In the news media, non-counselling staff are offered as part of the solution, or even, when appearing detached or lacking adequate knowledge, as part of the problem. 'Most university lecturers don't even know the names of their students,' laments one claims-maker (S. Griffiths, 2013). Another warns that while a 'serious mental health issue' is 'for the professionals', all staff should have a heightened awareness of mental health issues brewing (Security Leak, 2018). 'Keep your eyes open for emails received in the small hours, or that read like there might be hidden emotions behind them' this claims-maker advises. It is argued that 'Careers offices should interface with mental health services' and universities should 'offer staff a variety of training courses that help them learn how to develop their and students' resilience' (Vailes, 2017). Anthony Seldon claims that 'university tutors needed to learn from state and independent schools about how to look after young people and to equip them with the skills necessary to cope with trauma such as the breakdown of relationships' (Sanderson, 2015).

Unsurprisingly, this surrogate adoption of risk is received with scepticism by academic staff, who are often the first points of contact with students, which the UMHC acknowledges:

> [I]t should be noted that many staff are wary of receiving extra training [...]. Much of this stems from a concern that, if they receive additional training, they will be expected to have greater expertise and responsibility. As such, many fear they may miss something, get something wrong or make an ill individual worse.
>
> (Hughes & Spanner, 2019, p. 47)

However, the response to these concerns is to suggest somewhat vague lines of support wherein staff are supported in increasing their 'confidence and ability to respond to instances of poor mental health', which is itself to be supported by 'other inclusivity training' as well as training for managers to support staff to support students (Hughes & Spanner, 2019, p. 48). The solution is to further spread the risk through seemingly endless chains of training and support.

Adoption by the media

In terms of the media, a key moment for the broader appearance of the problem onto the public agenda occurred with its adoption by mainstream media outlets. Almost half of the news media articles sampled were found in *The Guardian*, nearly twice as many as the next most common paper to cover the issue, *The Independent*. The news media tend to be fickle in their attention to social issues, often chasing novelty and abandoning 'old news'. While for these reasons they are not well-placed to take sole ownership of a problem and press for action without some other special interest group assuming 'ownership', adoption by a news media organization can be a significant boon and, in combination with other claims-makers, help keep the problem in the public eye (Best, 1999).

Between 2013 and 2014, *The Guardian* began a series dedicated to the 'university crisis' of mental health, with the strapline, 'Mental health issues have become a growing problem among students and academics. This series will uncover a hidden side to university life' (*The Guardian*, 2014b). Along with its 'Blogging students' section, many of the articles in this series are written by current or former students, aspiring writer/advocates who acted as what I have previously described as 'professional exes' or 'wounded healers'. One of the earliest articles to appear was headlined, 'How Cambridge University almost killed me' (Jones, 2014) while another from the same year is 'I couldn't stop crying, then counselling changed my life' (Gurkan, 2014). Articles in these sections detail the struggles of students, at the time currently enrolled in university, with what they identify as mental health issues. Many were engaged in student advocacy for mental health and/or would go on to work in mental health advocacy organizations (e.g. Baird, 2014). *The Independent* similarly dedicated space to 'aspiring' young journalists who contributed stories uncovering the problems of UK campus life (see e.g. *The Independent*, 2022).

News media also did not simply report on the claims of advocacy organizations but also engaged in their own news-making investigations. For instance, *The Times* and *The Independent* conducted their own probes regarding the demand for and availability of counselling services at HE institutions (Buchan, 2018; Pells, 2019). *The Times* even launched *Time to Mind* in collaboration with claims-makers and claims-making organizations dedicated to childhood and adolescent mental health in March of 2015 (R. Bennett, 2015a). This campaign calling for 'urgent improvements to funding, waiting times and training to ensure that all young people with mental health issues received support' extended to include drawing attention to the mental health of students entering HE (Hurst, 2017) and received sweeping endorsements from policymakers (R. Bennett, 2015a). These activities helped keep the issue in the public eye by refreshing claims and creating a space for dedicated advocates of a variety of backgrounds to communicate the issue to a broad and general audience.

Adoption by policymakers

Crucially, the issue was also adopted by policymakers. In John Kingdon's (2003) well-known discussion of agenda setting, he discusses how interest group pressure campaigns (especially those that lack organized opposition) can coincide with legislative turnover to ensure that some issues achieve agenda prominence over others. 'In particular,' he writes, 'turnover of key participants, such as a change of administration, has powerful effects on policy agendas' (p. 20). In January 2018, Sam Gyimah began serving as Conservative Minister for Universities, Science, Research and Innovation and almost immediately adopted mental health as a key issue. Some of his first statements in this position referred to the 'mental health and wellbeing of our students' and its relationship to 'the very broader purpose of universities' (Belfast Telegraph,

2018). In June of that year, he stepped up this advocacy, launching the UMHC with his support (Yorke, 2018). For Gyimah, it was an opportunity to appear to take a strong stand on a highly visible and apparently non-controversial issue. Hence the strong language of 'no negotiation' and universities' ostensible current focus on knowledge as 'no longer good enough'.

Mental health had also formed a central focus of earlier ministerial positions held by Gyimah. For instance, when taking on a position overseeing childcare in 2014, one of his first statements referred to children's mental health (McCardle, 2014). Indeed, mental health formed a key focus of the incoming Education Secretary, Nicky Morgan, who appointed Gyimah to oversee a mental health taskforce in 2014 (Department for Education & Morgan, 2014).

It is likely that mental health appealed as a problem on which to take an early stand because, in spite of the strong language, it is highly uncontroversial. Mental health is positively valanced, has bipartisan support and is unlikely to attract at least organized opposition. Like the happiness agenda, few would argue that people should feel bad. However, mental health in HE offered the added benefit of a well-developed 'crisis' framing and in general possesses fewer connotations of governments overstepping their bounds. Taking a stand on mental health therefore represents an unproblematic option for policymakers. Indeed, one of the few criticisms that the aforementioned adoption of the mental health agenda in 2014 received from the opposing party was that the same Government had acted in the past to cut funding (Cockerell, 2015).

Moreover, at least for governments, pressing the mental health agenda in universities appears as relatively low risk in terms of spending, since it ostensibly places responsibility for mental health on universities, lest 'universities' risk 'failing a generation of students', to use Gyimah's words (Yorke, 2018 emphasis added). While the Charter that Gyimah endorsed placed responsibility for mental illness ultimately on the NHS, it was implied that universities taking responsibility would reduce this burden. As Kingdon describes, policymakers have a high incentive to endorse programmes that are perceived as inexpensive, with the health of young people being a key example in this respect (2003, p. 108). He identifies three types of inexpensive programme: regulatory, money-saving and low cost – all of which the warrants of mental health discourses promised to offer.

Adoption by industry

As the issue initially gained a foothold, other groups began to affirm and adopt the agenda. Existing organizations began rallying around student mental health and tailoring their offerings to students. The mindfulness app Headspace for instance introduced special meditations for students, a Student Plan (special pricing for students) and partnerships with universities in the early 2020s. In 2021, the *Financial Times* reported a 'mental health tech boom', with companies like BetterUp, which provides electronic resources 'focusing on resilience, leadership and motivation rather than psychotherapeutic treatment for mental illness' reporting valuations in the billions (USD) (Jacobs, 2021). These tech companies began tailoring their information to students (e.g. Lyons, 2021) while social enterprises offered training programmes for those in contact with students (e.g. Maudsley Learning, 2022). The mental health charity Mind released an app called Emoodji, dedicated to helping students reduce stress and track their moods (Gil, 2016). Mental health charities also partnered with private enterprises on a variety of initiatives including fundraising and creating information materials distributed to students (e.g. Lloyds Banking Group, 2022). Many of those who adopted mental health as their main motivation, be it in the development of apps or social or commercial enterprises, are also professional exes. The origin stories of many initiatives are in the experiences of its founders while in higher education. For instance, one app recommended in the press for use by students was Koko, which offered a form of crowdsourced peer support. Its founder describes how his struggles with depression while learning to code in university led to his development of the app (Morris, 2022). It is worth mentioning that much of Koko's technology, which had been repurposed to monitor online interactions, was eventually acquired by Airbnb for an undisclosed amount (Sonnemaker, 2020).

However, looking more closely, many of these interventions contain disclaimers regarding their suitability as treatments and resources for mental health issues. For instance, Koko's founder told the press in 2016, 'Users are continually reminded that the app is not a formal mental health resource, and it doesn't claim to be' (Skenderi, 2016). Yet its website at the time described it as offering 'crowdsourced cognitive therapy' (ItsKoko.com, 2016). The 2022 relaunch of its therapeutic and peer support portions foregrounds its mission as making 'mental health accessible to everyone' (ItsKoko.com, 2016). Like universities, while denying responsibility for treatment of mental ill-health, it is nonetheless used to justify intervention. For instance, Koko's 'why this matters' webpage begins with the claim that 'two in five' suffer from 'mental illness' (Kokocares.org, 2022). It also continues to offer surveillance technologies to tech firms, framed in terms of risk management. Another mental health app with resources geared towards students, Being, frames its in-app subscription ask as 'with subscriptions you can help us offer affordable mental healthcare to even more people'. Yet despite the medicalized connotations of the term 'healthcare', the app carries the disclaimer that it is not intended as a form of treatment (House of Being, 2022). Its associated website also refers to it as offering a 'personalised mental healthcare experience' and justifies its existence on the basis of mental ill-health and a crisis in terms of a lack of support (Being, 2022).

Forms of digital surveillance in general are also often offered as a solution to the problem of student mental health in media discourses. Through, for instance, attendance and other forms of engagement monitoring, students with potential mental health issues can be identified and intervention affected early on. For instance, the University of Chester's use of such an app downloaded to student phones is described approvingly by a report by the Institute for Public Policy Research (Thorley, 2017, p. 59). Representatives of the university were keen to stress that such monitoring was 'supportive' and not 'disciplinary', but student attendance presents a number of risks to UK institutions beyond mental health, including repercussions on their ability to sponsor visas for lucrative overseas students. Therefore, digital monitoring offers potential for protection from risks on a number of levels, in spite of any privacy issues that might be meaningfully raised.

While justified on the grounds of allegedly severe and worsening mental illness, many adopters do not promise to provide a solution but rather diffuse forms of 'wellbeing support', often for profit and sometimes in automated form, as well as surveillance and risk management for a variety of stakeholders.

Opportunities for adoption

This widespread adoption of the student mental health agenda by a variety of parties means that the mental health promotion wave in HE is likely to be prolonged. Regardless of its merits, once discovered and widely adopted, the problem towards which such interventions are ostensibly directed is unlikely to fall out of the public eye. A growing number of individuals and groups now exist whose everyday workings include campaigning for attention to student mental health. Concern for mental health also offers a variety of stakeholders an opportunity to instigate, expand and refresh their claims, justifying ongoing funding and indeed, their own existence. This gives the appearance of the problem not going away and, to justify the ongoing attention and funds, steadily worsening.

At the same time, something else is happening. As Ahmed observes, 'If we have a duty to promote what causes happiness, then happiness itself becomes a duty' (Ahmed, 2010, p. 7). While the objective here is 'mental health', the point remains salient: the duty to promote a thing implies the duty to be that thing. UUK's Stepchange framework states that 'Good mental health is central to staff engagement, productivity and creativity' and goes on to offer the recommendation to universities that they 'Build mental health into performance regimes' (UUK, 2020, p. 17). This confluence between duty and surveillance is also evident in the mental health 'tech boom' more broadly. BetterUp, the controversial start-up endorsed by Prince Harry discussed in Chapter 4, offers an app which is advertised as providing, 'reading materials, leadership coaching, performance psychology or a parenting coach', yet more chillingly, it also 'provides anonymised data on employees' engagement, motivation and effectiveness' (Jacobs, 2021).

The duty to promote also implies that there is a deficit that needs to be filled, a chasm that individuals cannot bridge on their own or with each other outside of institutionalized, professionalized and other 'supports'. The message is that whatever is wrong is primarily individual and emotional; it is primarily about feelings. These feelings have been recast as 'mental ill-health' and amenable to be worked on directly via outside intervention. Adoption allows universities to transform many of the insoluble issues of society with which they have been tasked, like social mobility and propping up a fragile economy, into seemingly more soluble or at least isolable issues of promoting mental health and well-being. However, this entails a risk. It is risky to adopt fully a mental health agenda if doing so leaves an institution or even the sector as a whole culpable when 'serious' problems arise.

Careful adoption was likely calculated to be worth the risks, at least insofar as those risks could be mitigated by diffusing them across the institution and deferring responsibility for more serious problems to other actors. Adoption of mental health offered institutions the ability to transform much more difficult issues into those for which a diffuse range of emotional supports could be prescribed. Embedding supports into curriculum, digitized support and surveillance strategies, and proliferating forms of regulation offered to further disembody these supports. Risks and controversies can be translated into the broadly agreeable language of 'mental health'. Previous chapters have outlined one of the strongest examples of this in relation to tuition fees. While fees may still be mentioned in mental health discourses, students can be assured that 'support is available'. And what is meant is 'emotional support'.

Expansion

Expansive language

As more and more individuals and organizations adopt the discourse, it becomes more and more expansive. This is facilitated by an existing fluidity with language and the meanings attached to words and terminologies mobilized to make sense of the alleged problem. This fluidity allowed for nearly every student experience from 'suicide' to 'feeling down' to be considered part of a growing problem. While 'mental health' was the overarching banner of concern, within this claims-makers routinely utilized a wide range (over 100 keywords and phrases were identified in the news media sample) of broad and rarely defined keywords. These are listed in Table 9.1.

Table 9.1 Keywords and phrases appearing in news media sample

Blunted mood	Mental ailment	Mental stress
Declining well-being	Mental and physical health	Mental struggles
Diagnosed/able conditions	Mental breakdowns	Mental welfare
Digital well-being	Mental capacity	Mental well-being
Distress	Mental challenge	Mentally healthy
Emotional baggage	Mental demands	Mentally ill
Emotional breakdown	Mental difficulties	Mentally troubled
Emotional burnout	Mental disorder	Mentally unstable
Emotional challenges	Mental distress	Mentally unwell
Emotional damage	Mental equipment	Mood
Emotional development	Mental exhaustion	Negative behaviour
Emotional disorders	Mental fitness	Negative emotions/ feelings
Emotional distress	Mental (ill) health	Negative psychological effects
Emotional experience	Mental health challenges	Negative thoughts
Emotional fatigue	Mental health concerns	Poor mental health
Emotional health	Mental health conditions	Poor/low well-being
Emotional health difficulties	Mental health crisis/es	Psychiatric conditions
Emotional hurdles	Mental health diagnosis	Psychiatric illness/disease
Emotional intelligence	Mental health difficulties	Psychiatric disorder

Emotional needs	Mental health discrimination	Psychiatric disturbance
Emotional problems	Mental health disorder	Psychological anguish
Emotional resilience	Mental health epidemic	Psychological discomfort
Emotional strain	Mental health hardship	Psychological distress
Emotional stress	Mental health issues	Psychological disturbance
Emotional turmoil	Mental health literacy	Psychological harm
Emotional upheaval	Mental health needs	Psychological (ill) health
Emotional well-being	Mental health pressures	Psychological issues/problems
Emotional wounds	Mental health problem	Psychological state
Feeling(s)	Mental health sufferer/ing	Psychological triggers
General well-being	Mental health symptoms	Psychological well-being
Good mental health	Mental health troubles	Resilience
Happiness	Mental health vulnerabilities	Sadness
Harmful feelings	Mental health woes	Unhappiness
Harmful thoughts	Mental illness	Well-being
Holistic well-being	Mental issues	Well-being education
Less happy	Mental pain	Well-being needs
Low mood	Mental problem	Welfare
Low well-being	Mental state	

Much of this expansion appears to be a frustration of the early conviction that mental health in universities must be more at risk than in other populations. This is evident for instance in mental health claims-makers' comments that the 2013 NUS survey findings were 'unsurprising' since students' greater risk was well-known (Ratcliffe, 2013), in spite of the survey's findings to the contrary. Key early reports such as that produced by the Royal College of Psychiatrists in 2011 admit that evidence of the scale of the problem alleged to exist in universities is scant but go on to state many reasons to believe that, once these statistics become available, the problems will be severe. Expanding student populations and the prevalence of alcohol use are cited as key reasons to believe that students will be at risk of mental disorders (RCP, 2011). The realization that rates of mental disorder and even suicide appear to be the same or even much less than that of the general population of the same age range must have been disappointing. Without evidence, or in the face of evidence to the contrary, claims-makers expanded their purview. A report produced by the Higher Education Policy Institute (HEPI) (P. Brown, 2016) admits that 'mental disorders are fairly common in higher education but not as high as in the general population – 12 per cent compared to the estimated 25 per cent in the whole population,' but goes on to argue that, nonetheless, 'the number of students suffering from poor wellbeing is high' (p. 12). Another report by the Institute for Public Policy Research (IPPR) (Thorley, 2017) combines formally declared mental health conditions and subclinical 'mental distress' as indicators of a need to intervene:

> As well as a significant increase in the number of students who formally declare a mental health condition to their HEI, there is also a high level of self-reported mental distress among the student population. While not always meeting the threshold for a clinical diagnosis, this is likely to have a significant effect on individual students' ability to thrive both academically and personally, as well impacting on demand for a range of student services.
>
> (pp. 15–16)

Often two or more keywords are elided so that it is unclear how they differ. References to 'mental health and wellbeing' are the most common of these. An explicit conflation between mental health and well-being is evident in the naming of the Mental Wealth Project discussed in Chapter 8, which is portmanteau of mental well-being and mental health to create a new term alluding to the promotion of both. It also subtly reconceptualizes 'wealth' from a material basis into mental and emotional terms. The effect of such elisions is to signify expansiveness, to blur the boundaries between health and illness and to include in claims-makers' purview the largest possible swathes of human experience. As a phrase, 'mental health and wellbeing' may refer to medical problems and severe issues or to more diffuse forms of upset or even a 'holistic' concern for an individual's development. For instance, one claims-maker flips between several terminologies thus: 'Mental health and wellbeing are complex issues and there is no simple solution. There is already a lot of good work being done to support student welfare' (Busby, 2019). Shifting from 'mental health' to 'wellbeing' to 'welfare' in this way allows for diverse forms of student support to be justified as solving a larger problem. It encompasses diverse emotional states and justifies calling for expanded surveillance of and attention to students' personal lives. It also signifies that this is not a 'niche' interest requiring only the attention of specialists, but a huge range of quasi-authorities with varying levels of training. The focus is not only on (and, as I have attempted to show, sometimes not 'even' on) those with mental illnesses, but everyone.

Documents produced by think tanks and charities attempted to define many of these keywords but there remained a general lack of agreement regarding their meaning. While definitions are needed for objectives to be clarified, broad definitions are more rhetorically useful for claims-makers as they allow them to cast as broad a net as possible regarding those affected. Once operationalized in advocacy research, broad definitions provide large and eye-catching estimates of the problems' prevalence. Estimates that mental illness in universities is on par with or even slightly less than the general population may be hardly worthy of note. But claims that 80 per cent of students suffered from mental health problems or that 92 per cent suffered mental distress that includes 'suicidal thoughts' grabbed headlines.

Part of what drives this expansiveness is the need to gain a voice in the cacophony of claims. Every day, audiences – news media consumers, the general public, policymakers, etc. – are bombarded with claims about new social problems. There is only so much compassion, so many minutes in a newscast, space in a newspaper or points on a policy agenda; claims-makers must adopt effective rhetorical strategies in order to get noticed (Hilgartner & Bosk, 1988). For example, in July 2021 the news media reported on claims made by the Resolution Foundation that young people were worried about how their mental health would affect their job prospects (Partington & correspondent, 2021). It is notable that another press release put out at the same time by the Institute for Fiscal Studies noted that 'It is no surprise that young people report being more pessimistic about their immediate financial future than other age groups' (Cribb et al., 2021) given that employment changes due to the pandemic had caused many to return to living with their parents. However, when these claims were reported together, it was the former statements regarding the mental health impact of the pandemic and the effect that this would have on future employment that made headlines (Holden, 2021; e.g. *The Express*, 2021). While claims about the employment impacts of the pandemic might be met with counterclaims about the latter's transience, claims about the effects of these phenomena on mental health and its ongoing impact on future job prospects offered a novel and more dire framing for the problem.

The added effect is that once again, economic phenomena subtly slip into mental phenomena. Another example of this slippage occurs in the IPPR 2017 report:

'Finding a job after university' is the second highest cause of stress reported by students (YouGov, 2016). And these concerns are not unjustified – between 2004 and 2014, the proportion of younger workers who were graduates working in nonprofessional/managerial jobs doubled from 7 to 13 per cent, as the graduate jobs market has failed to keep up with the supply of new graduates (Thorley & Cook, 2017). Young graduates in jobs for which they're overqualified are more likely to experience mental health problems (ibid), but it is also true that the anticipation of entering a competitive jobs market could have an adverse effect on students' mental health and wellbeing.

(Thorley, 2017, p. 34)

However, none of the five recommendations foregrounded in the report deal with this broader economic context. Instead, government is called upon to increase funding for student mental health initiatives and improve the integration of services. Framing issues in terms of mental health effects appears more soluble than calling for changes and expanding opportunities within a struggling economy and service sector, now additionally grappling with the fallout of the Covid-19 pandemic. More deeply, these discourses feed into a broader and more generalized consensus that the inner world is the domain of change while the outside world, and especially its economic processes, is beyond democratic bounds.

In this way, expansive language allowed for a wide range of claims to be reconceptualized as mental health issues. That normal experiences require intervention lest they spiral out of control is a claim that appears early in the discourse, but over time, a huge range of problems comes to be considered under the broadening umbrella of 'mental health' or even 'negative emotions', together with other 'negative feelings' and 'symptoms' that require attention. Even transient issues – notably, that appear to improve on their own – are problems requiring attention. As the UMHC report describes, 'In some cases, student wellbeing has been found to reduce on entry to university and not to reset to their original, pre-university, baseline for many months' (Hughes & Spanner, 2019, p. 24). Having a difficult first few months is portrayed as a precariously forgotten problem, fumblingly dealt with by uninitiated students rather than carefully curated by professionals, as one article describes:

She was referring to the widely recognised malaise thought to strike students about five weeks into the first term. A month of relentless slog has bred exhaustion, and the four remaining weeks stretch far into the distance. Surviving till the holidays seems like an impossible feat. Fifth week blues are generally combated by activities such as group biscuit decorating and the email circulation of a "cute animal of the week", organised by whichever poor 19-year-old has misguidedly volunteered to take responsibility for student welfare.

(N. Tucker, 2018)

Experiences that might once have been viewed positively become fraught with risk. For instance, leaving one's parents and becoming independent for the first time is routinely singled out as an obvious cause of serious issues:

You've left home, your friends are scattered across the country like Pumpkin cafes, you're barely sleeping long enough to charge an iPhone, you're anxious about fitting in, you've no one to eat lunch with, you're probably going to break up with your first love, you can't keep up with the reading, you're skint, you've gone from full-time education to only seeing your tutor for an hour a week, you have no idea where the nearest Argos is, you're stressed, you're living with strangers, you're drinking every night, you're worried you've just spunked thousands of pounds up the wall to study a subject you don't even really like, you're living on potatoes and rolling tobacco, you miss your mum, you don't understand the buses, your tutor can't remember your name – and everyone keeps telling you that this is amazing fun. No wonder depression, anxiety, eating disorders and addiction are so rife.

(Frizzell, 2015)

In the foreword of the 2016 HEPI report, MP Norman Lamb singled out transitioning to university as a potentially 'overwhelming' experience, noting that while for most people 'these stresses and challenges of student life will not directly "cause" mental illness' they can 'certainly' affect 'emotional resilience and overall wellbeing', leaving students 'more vulnerable' to developing mental health problems like depression and anxiety (Lamb in P. Brown, 2016, pp. 3–4). Transitions form a particular focus for the Stepchange framework, which states that 'Universities cannot do this alone' and calls on universities to 'work with parents, schools, colleges and employers to mitigate the risks of transitions' (UUK, 2020, p. 12).

Over time, it becomes difficult to differentiate between what had initially been identified as a potential 'cause' of mental ill-health and what is a mental health problem itself. For instance, loneliness is often described as a potential cause of or contributor to mental ill-health. On the other hand, it is described as a symptom, 'mental health issue' and/or problem in itself.

'One of the biggest problems was loneliness' says one news report (Murphy, 2019). 'About 89% of the 3,340 student respondents to the survey had felt lonely at some stage. A fifth of students, sadly, did not know who to speak to about their mental-health issues,' it continues. The RCP exemplifies this tendency to blur causes and problems when it claimed that 'failure to act on climate change will become a growing mental health problem' among young people (Royal College of Psychiatrists, 2021). The President of the association is quoted as adding that 'The climate and ecological emergency is a mental health emergency'.

As causes and problems become blurred, so too does the direction of causation. Lower socioeconomic status is seen as a potential pre-existing cause of mental health problems by the RCP in 2011 (Royal College of Psychiatrists, 2011). However, as time goes on, psychological distress is positioned as causing negative social outcomes. Student Minds claims that 'Roughly 1 in 3 students experience clinical levels of psychological distress. This can contribute to decreased performance and interpersonal problems. In turn, this can lead to academic failure and dropout, job difficulties, and negative social outcomes' (2019, p. 3). The effect is, once again, to flip the pyramid of needs so that psychological needs must be fulfilled not only to secure material needs, but to avoid future material difficulties. Possessing good mental health is also positioned in the UMHC as necessary in order to learn and as forming part of the 'core transactional relationships' or key offerings of universities (Hughes & Spanner, 2019, p. 7). The Charter goes on, 'Creativity, problem solving and good quality academic learning, are all higher order cognitive functions that benefit from good mental health' (p. 7). First mental health must be promoted before not only learning can take place, but before skills can be effectively developed, and material problems broached.

This expansive language has been partially fed by the growth of the wellness industries who have encouraged views of mental health as something requiring pursuit and uncharacteristic of most people (H. J. Jackson & Haslam, 2022), touched on above in relation to technological interventions. It has also come as a result of increasing scepticism towards diagnosis, leading to lower valuations of specific conditions and the loosening of diagnostic criteria to encompass broader, and milder, 'spectrums' of disorder (H. J. Jackson & Haslam, 2022). The effect of the loosening of these boundaries is to open the sphere of psychological intervention to everyone. It also offers the ability to claim a steadily worsening situation. With a broad spectrum of emotion and experience available for claims-making, mental health advocates are able to allege the existence of a 'crisis' situation that appears increasingly intractable, relentless and unsolvable.

While mental health may not be soluble, constant vigilance is positioned as a solution. Universities and individuals within universities must constantly seek out and undertake rituals of self-care; they must make themselves aware of frameworks and regulations and embed these into the curriculum so that mental health becomes part of everything that the institution does. These expansive linguistic boundaries also permit a paradoxical dynamic of medicalization/de-medicalization. On the one hand, feelings become recoded as symptoms and placed under the umbrella of 'mental health'. On the other, a de-medicalization dynamic is accomplished through the language of holism and 'wellbeing' allowing for a watering down of what counts as 'support' and an expansion of those potentially involved and to whom responsibility can be given (or pushed).

Expanding victims

Inclusivity appears as a major focus of claims-making as well as in policy and grey literature. Student Minds makes 'intersectionality', or how 'different identities impact a student's experience of university life and support', an 'explicit priority' (Student Minds, 2019, p. 25), while the UMHC and Stepchange frameworks stress the necessity of inclusivity throughout their pages. Yet what is meant by inclusivity is discovering problems and extending the need for support to an increasingly expansive array of identities and groups. Groups said to be particularly at risk include LGBTQ+, women, the then-termed 'BAME' students and those from lower socioeconomic backgrounds. Demands are made and affirmed in policy that support be 'culturally competent' to speak to an increasingly diverse student body (Office for Students, 2019). Difference is therefore explicitly seen as a likely cause of increased mental health problems. For instance, the RCP claims 'In view of the increasing social and cultural diversity of UK students, it is possible that there will be a rise in symptom reporting and diagnosable conditions' (Royal College of Psychiatrists, 2011, p. 32). Yet there is a sense of universality in terms of a shared vulnerability. These vulnerabilities will differ, but what is needed is a translation of universal interventions into a language assumed to be accessible to diverse backgrounds.

The need for intervention and support is also extended to postgraduate students and staff. Initially concerned with the mental health of undergraduates (and largely those in their late teens and early twenties), the discourse shifts to include postgraduate students. The need for postgraduates to be 'master and commander of all aspects of their lives' and a tendency to manage problems on their own put them particularly at risk, argues a university mental health coordinator and UMHAN representative (Rutter, 2015). Targeting postgraduates is cited as a key inclusivity challenge in both the Stepchange (UUK, 2020, p. 25) and UMHC (Hughes & Spanner, 2019, p. 70) documents. Mental health problems of staff – sometimes as a result of supporting students' mental health – too form a particular site of concern. 'Studies of academic staff have highlighted the potential negative impacts of supporting ill students, ongoing uncertainty about role and boundaries, workload and job insecurity' the UMHC says (Hughes & Spanner, 2019, p. 6). It continues, 'Some authors have claimed that academics are more likely to be experiencing anxiety than medical or police personnel' and adds that too little research currently investigates the mental health of university staff. Yet there is a clear sense that part of this 'anxiety' stems from what was touched on in the previous section in terms of risk and responsibility being spread to academic staff. The UMHC continues:

> Evidence from research and the Charter consultations indicate that academics have become the frontline of student support [...]. However, many lack clarity about their role and boundaries, feel they lack the skills to appropriately respond and that gaps between academics and support services negatively impact on student and staff wellbeing. This lack of clarity creates risk for students, staff and universities.
>
> (p. 27)

Recall that this document goes on to note that many staff are wary of mental health training due to fears of potentially 'miss[ing] something' (Hughes and Spanner, 2019, p. 47) thus holding responsibility if things go wrong. However, the potential negative impacts of placing responsibility on academics are interpreted in terms of 'negative consequences for staff wellbeing' and 'negative impacts on their mental health' (pp. 44, 47). Despite the connection made to increasing job demands, not only in terms of responsibility for mitigating mental health risks but also in terms of workloads more generally, staff discontent is itself reconceived in mental health terms, for which more 'support' (and more frequent training) is again positioned as the solution (p. 47).

Recall from Chapter 3 that the project of governance is necessarily inclusive because there is nothing outside of it. Problems are matter-of-factly reconceived in mental health terms because these discourses take for granted subjectivity as the start and end point for impact on the world. 'Work on the transformation of the internal world of the neoliberal subject can only understand the subject as increasingly differentiated in its choice-making vulnerability, rather than as a potential collectivity' (Chandler, 2016b, p. 43). The focus remains on transformation, but of the internal rather than external world. These discourses are inclusive in the sense of an emphasis on our 'shared nature as vulnerable subjects' and operate in a society that must be continually 'learning' how to cope with uncertainty and risk (p. 43). The subject is the start and end point of intervention and no one can be left out.

Expanding the mission

Mental health offers opportunities for expansiveness that go beyond previous discourses like happiness and well-being, which it is able to subsume under its umbrella along with the full spectrum of human emotion. It has thus allowed not only for considerable concept but also mission creep as well. With such a vast purview, it is easy to argue that existing and new interventions must be expanded and made available to more people. More and more of the 'university community' must 'embed' mental health into their work and daily lives. More and more problems come to be subsumed into the mission of improving or promoting mental health.

However, the mission creep permitted by the fluid language of mental health and its corollary vocabularies is a peculiar one. Unlike the brazenness of self-esteem and some happiness and mindfulness advocates, claims-makers seemed more reluctant to promise solutions to broader social problems with their interventions, instead subsuming them into this new mission. In addition to the blurring and reversal of causes and effects discussed above, advocacy of tackling 'mental health inequalities' had the effect of subsuming greater swathes of the material world into the purview of 'mental health problems' and the achievement of 'genuine equality of mental health' to use Norman Lamb's words (Lamb in P. Brown, 2016, p. 3). For instance, the UMHC is keen to stress the importance of context for mental health:

> The idea of a whole-university approach has been motivated by our ever-increasing understanding of the factors that contribute to mental health and the importance played by context. Whether an individual has good or poor mental health is influenced by a wide range of societal and environmental factors, as well as by their thoughts, behaviours, experiences, biology and learning.
>
> (Hughes & Spanner, 2019, p. 10)

While this represents an attempt to avoid overmedicalization by bringing in social context, the effect is to reduce the significance of these social phenomena to their mental health effects. Context is ossified and turned into an aetiology for 'mental ill-health'. A similar effect is observable in relation to the wide acceptance and use of the 'social determinants of health' as a model for making sense of the broader aetiology of physical illness through which a wide range of structural inequalities gradually become medicalized (Wainwright, 2008a), important primarily in terms of their effects on health and positioned within the realm of healthcare. Lamb's HEPI report foreword also notes that 'Today's students are [...] under more pressure than ever to get a good degree to boost their prospects in a competitive economy' (Lamb in P. Brown, 2016, p. 4). Yet nothing is said about what might happen in a 'competitive economy' if large numbers of people have degrees. Instead, it is the mental health effects of this broader economic context that are singled out for scrutiny.

Again there appears a gap between the promised outcomes of liberal societies and liberal institutions – equality, opportunity, social mobility – and the reality of inequality, dwindling opportunity and, for many, the frustrated promise of getting ahead. Yet rather than thinking about how this gap might be bridged, claims-makers encourage the uptake of discursive framings and interventions that offer a means of attenuating oneself to living within it. This is not consciously reflected upon by claims-makers. Instead, the sense of crisis permeates any long-term thinking and renders the need to come up with a solution redundant. These bigger issues do not appear significant in and of themselves, but rather only insofar as they have a present negative impact on the mental health of young people. And for this 'more support is needed'.

Exhaustion

Part of the receptiveness to whole university approaches is almost certainly an attempt to counter the tendency to demand more support the more support is offered. In some ways, early claims-making, largely led by the counselling professions and their representatives, have become victims of their own success. As I have tried to show, expansion of the problem of mental health to mental health promotion, well-being, etc. also meant an expansion of responsibility for its amelioration. As Brewster and Cox (2022, p. 4) observe, 'This representation is key; by recontextualising mental health as a shared responsibility, it becomes what Fairclough (2009) describes as a "social problem". Responsibility for solving the issue is thus distributed rather than being solely an issue that has to be solved by UUK.' UUK's favoured 'whole university approach' subtly downplays claims for greater funding of specialized services in favour of less professionalized forms of peer support, curriculum embedding and the broad diffusion of risk across institutions, and in and beyond the sector as a whole. In this way, the sector attempts to benefit from the internal reframing of societal issues for which it has no answers while diffusing risks and side-stepping more expensive demands.

In this sense, the movement for mental health in HE may already be showing signs of exhaustion. However, it is worthwhile to consider precisely what is exhausted within earlier discourses. They may recede into the background, no longer capable of galvanizing support nor giving policymakers a new and fresh issue to be seen to be promoting. But they remain part of the ethnopsychology and push the next wave. In this sense, the concern for mental health in HE is unlikely to recede fully. It is possible that staying power can be fed by its existence as the ultimate expression of vulnerable subjectivity in the very heart of institutions that ostensibly feed the opposite. The broad capacity to locate problems in the safe arena of human subjectivity and to respond to them with 'care', the focus on a particularly liminal phase in the lives of young people, the ability to diffuse potentially contentious issues into a range of supports on offer, may also lend a staying power beyond what has come before. It offers a greater expansiveness than earlier discourses which permits it to comfortably subsume and supersede them, drawing at the same time validation from a largely unquestioned and implicit medical authority.[1]

Promising to lower teen pregnancy rates or reduce unemployment with classes in self-esteem is unlikely to galvanize the public or policymakers in the way it might have done thirty years ago. Yet this rise of mental health shows that the desire for emotional interventions has not become exhausted. If anything, it has become more insatiable. Claims-makers have been keen to avoid the optimism and over-promising of earlier discourses. They may make more modest proposals for the containment of risk, but the underlying belief system remains untouched. Conceptualizations of social problems in emotional terms with emotional solutions largely fail to deliver on their promises. But when this occurs, as a culture, we do not appear to question the manner in which the question has been posed. Instead, we question the capacity of the human subject all the more. The belief in the fundamental weakness of the human subject and its role in nearly everything that goes wrong becomes only further entrenched. This is all the better for the growing and diffuse ranks of conceptual entrepreneurs as they become the merchants of endless treatments for a disease that can't be cured.

Conclusion

The assumption of emotional vulnerability is a pervasive aspect of our ethnopsychology and increasingly necessary framing for social problems when the economic base has been rendered beyond critique. In many ways, it was only a matter of time before a challenge as great as higher learning was seen as a potential source of pathology. It reflects a kind of ultimate questioning of the role of reason in individual and social life. It is symbolically telling that the place that ostensibly fosters this reason should be positioned as so problematic and refashioned in emotional terms.

At a time when universities face uncertainty regarding their purpose and role in society, mental health discourses offer a means of connecting to students of varying backgrounds, needs and reasons for attending at the lowest common denominator. Tasked with solving social problems like inequality and revitalizing a sluggish economy, offering to bolster fragile mental health also offers a way to 'get something done'. Over time, it becomes an end in itself. Students are 'empowered' to lobby for an agenda that has already been set and largely agreed by management. Non-counselling staff are charged with uptake of the agenda and any pushback is itself reconceived within the pre-existing framework of mental health. Do not look to each other and informal networks. Seek training and 'support' from managers and others with the specialized skills to offer it.

The result is unlikely to be 'empowerment' beyond the power to implement and give legitimacy to a pre-existing agenda. Indeed, it may be the opposite. The injunction is not to be the 'self-governing neoliberal subject' in the sense of a reactivation of its liberal forebear. Rather, the ideal subject is presented as one with an increased dependency on professionals and an increasingly disembodied governance structure of rules and apps and guidance. These subjects do not recklessly take responsibility for their own welfare within their preexisting networks and relationships, but rather constantly seek out rules and regulations for the correct conduct of life. As Hayes (2017) adds, 'It merely creates diminished individuals who seek more therapeutic experiences' (p. 22). While this appears as the discursive invitation, whether or not subjects actually take up such invitations is a question that must be answered in future research.

There are clear differences between mental health and the waves described in earlier chapters. At least in terms of mental health in universities, there are few clear gurus who unambiguously 'own' the issue. There is little in the way of magic, though the emphasis on holism echoes the quasi-spiritual nature of earlier quests. There is a promise to re-enchant alienated and atomized experiences and impute them with meaning and purpose via mental health promotion, but it is a purpose that has been thoroughly internalized. Scientific claims feature heavily, but are less explicitly insisted upon. Claims-makers instead rely on the implicit authority of a medicalized framing. The 'magic bullet' framing is less obvious and 'prevention' becomes 'catastrophe avoidance'. There is also little in the way of 'revolution' promised, internal or otherwise. While partially concurrent with the rise of mindfulness, it betrays much more of a sense of cultural pessimism.

There are also many commonalities with earlier problematizations of apparently positive emotional signifiers. Claims-makers seek to drum up demand by ridiculing self-reliance as backward and dangerous. When successful, they portray uptake of interventions as indicative of the scale of the problem. Also similar is the fact that mental health gradually becomes not a default state, but rather something that must be consciously and actively pursued. It also becomes moral and behavioural and something that one is enjoined to adopt not only oneself but also to inculcate in others. Mental health comes to be portrayed as something that is uncharacteristic of the majority and which requires constant attention.

It is not simply that Maslow's pyramid has been inverted. Material security is pushed gradually out of bounds. Indeed, the failed promise of material progress and security is seen as the cause of a problem – dashed hopes of career dreams are just one more cause of mental ill-health. It's not the failed promise, but the feelings that this failure engenders that become the focus of problematization. All that remains of the hierarchy of human needs is psychic in nature. Instead of solving problems, these discourses dissolve them into a central mission: coping with the present in the age in which there is no alternative to and no way to move beyond the present. In a society in which there is no future capable of being affected radically by human will, people become passive reactors to conditions beyond their control.

It is possible that the discourse of mental health may be a long way from its eventual exhaustion, if it ever does exhaust. It provides an umbrella under which claims-makers for countless social problems can gather and clamour for attention, including those for other emotional signifiers they wish to problematize. Paired with other keywords and phrases, it forms part of a shifting de-medicalizing and re-medicalizing discourse. It has a stamp of approval of a quasi-medical framework, but can still comfortably accommodate myriad interventions from the clinical to mental health 'fitness' apps. Its apparently positive framing offers the possibility of building claims on a foundation of moral goodness rooted in the minds of individuals that is difficult to contest.

Conclusion

A good end to this book would offer a clear way out of the impasse. But that is precisely the issue. The human subject has been questioned not just ideally but materially too. In his brief Preface to *The German Ideology* (Marx & Engels, 1998b), Karl Marx refers tongue-in-cheek to a man who believed that people only drowned because they had convinced themselves of the reality of gravity. They need only be relieved of this superstition and all danger will dissipate. The persistence of narratives of diminished subjectivity hints at the possibility that what is happening is not just rhetorical. They are narrating a subject that is trapped between past and future. In the absence of a clear means of reconciling what is with what ought to be, these questions have been relocated inward, as problems endemic to human subjects themselves.

In other words, part of the reason why many problems have been redefined in subjective terms is because they apparently cannot be solved, at least not within the existing parameters of our economic and social systems. No amount of economic tinkering has ended inequality, nor economic crisis, nor the tendency for large swathes of human potential to go to waste within it all. Therapeutic redefinitions of social problems push issues further into human mind, where they also can't be solved. However, they can be overseen and their putative risks pathologized, medicalized and surveilled. In seeming to underscore the subjective over the objective and bring feeling back into politics, the therapeutic re-enchantment of the world that these discourses offer only obscures the highly rationalized forms of domination that they offer.

While it is important to denaturalize the vision of the human subject presented in these problem constructions, it is also important to grapple finally with how and whether it is possible to bridge the worlds of *is* and *ought*. If not intrinsic to human subjects, from where do seemingly perpetual tensions like inequalities, war, crisis and more emerge? Classical political economy, while undoubtedly deficient in myriad ways, had nonetheless offered the possibility to consider these phenomena from within the proper functioning of the economic system itself. Spurning the neoliberal consensus that locates problems in malfunctioning individuals rather than in a functioning system (whose *proper* functioning leads to problems) is one potential way forward. Discourses that naturalize the impasse can be de-naturalized and alternative ways of making sense of these problems might be forwarded in their place. At the very least, it is necessary to contest constructions of social problems that take as their point of departure some defect in the human mind. This is because, as I have tried to describe throughout this book, when this is where discussions start, it is also where they tend to end.

Interestingly, Marshall Berman, on whom I draw to make sense of some of the underlying impasse that these therapeutic discourses exemplify, makes a strikingly similar statement to Jon Kabat-Zinn's remark that mindfulness offers an answer to how we can feel 'at home in our own skin within the maelstrom' (2005, p. xxix). To be a modernist, Berman writes, 'is to make oneself somehow at home in the maelstrom, to make its rhythms one's own, to move within its currents in search of the forms of reality, of beauty, of freedom, of justice, that its fervid and perilous flow allows' (1982, p. 346). However, where therapeutic discourses hope to find some breathing space within the flux, Berman wants to feel at home enough in its movement to have the courage to look through the abyss to see what lies beyond.

In Chapter 2, I noted that the fluid nature of the modern world, so well described by Marx and Engels with their phrase, 'all that is solid melts into air' meant that subjectivity became increasingly historicized, rendered dynamic, and thrown open. The modern world is still fluid. But we are like Pascal trying to find some firm ground in the present only to be dismayed when once again it washes away. As Berman (1982, p. 27) says, our modern world might determine our fate, but the best philosophers have hoped to understand that fate, 'and once they understood it, to fight it.'

Methods Appendix

Chapters 5 & 6

I conducted a qualitative media analysis (Altheide & Schneider, 2013) of the rise and spread of mindfulness discourses from the United States, focusing largely on the adoption and expansion of claims within the UK context. While systematic sampling focused on newspaper archives, this was a starting point from which themes and developments were identified and explored through further theoretical sampling. I discuss some of the benefits and drawbacks of this approach in the next section in relation to the study of mental health. I explored the 'prehistory' of mindfulness claims by conducting searches in academic journal archives (Google Scholar, ProQuest and backchaining of identified prior publications across other archives). I also conducted searches for the keyword 'mindfulness' in archives of *The New York Times* (US) and *The Times* (UK) (via Times Digital Archive) from 1785 to 1980, I then analysed broader international news media discourses from 1980 to 1995 in the *Nexis* archive as well as uses of the keyword emerging in other media and other cultural artefacts emerging during that period.

Finally, I explored the spread and institutionalization of claims in the UK context through an in-depth analysis of a sample of 150 articles drawn from four UK broadsheets from 1990 until 2018. To compile this sample, a keyword search was performed for 'mindfulness' in *The Times*, *The Daily Telegraph*, *The Independent*, *The Guardian* and their Sunday editions between 1990 and 2018 – the most recent full year at the time of data gathering. A sample was selected by sorting results for each year by relevance (Nexis decides relevance by the number of times keywords appear and the proximity of the keyword to the headline) and selecting the first 5 per cent of articles per year. The results were imported into NVivo for detailed coding. Further theoretical sampling was conducted of commonly discussed or cited policy documents, books, presentations, commodities, individuals and organizations.

These particular newspapers were chosen as they are widely considered to represent the 'quality press' within the UK as well as a span of editorial viewpoints. As discussed in the introduction, newspapers were selected as the main sources as they allow for a broad sampling of different advocates and groups making claims about an issue, allowing them access to some of the broadest possible audiences. Knowing that they must convince broad audiences also means that their claims tend to conform to what they believe (or hope) will be strongly held cultural values. Widely repeated claims allude to success in this regard. While newspaper readership has declined in recent years, newspapers retain public trust over other media (Allcott & Gentzkow, 2017). Their broad reach continues to make them significant for agenda-setting, with the majority of news links shared on social media coming from mainstream news media sources, providing the 'lifeblood' of topical social media conversations (Newman, 2011, p. 6). Their ability to set the agenda that politics and other media tend to follow (Fawzi, 2018; Langer & Gruber, 2021; Weaver & Choi, 2017) lends them enduring centrality to claims-making campaigns towards the present and thus an ideal place from which to capture a variety of voices, views and commonly repeated claims. However, as stated above, this sample was a starting point and additional keyword searching and document gathering was carried out to further elucidate themes identified in the sample (Altheide & Schneider, 2013).

Chapters 7, 8, & 9

This section of the book on mental health in HE centres on a sample of 126 UK newspaper articles that appeared between 2005 and 2019 and which were drawn from four major broadsheets and their Sunday editions (*The Guardian, Observer, Times, Sunday Times, Independent, Independent on Sunday, Telegraph* and *Sunday Telegraph*) using the Nexis database as well as theoretical sampling of additional documents (books, policy documents, grey literature, charters, social media communications and additional newspaper articles across the entire Nexis database) as trends were identified during coding and analysis. Again, these were selected due to expectations of coverage of perceived major social issues and their representation, at least ostensibly, of left- to right-wing viewpoints.

A keyword search for '"mental health" AND "higher education" OR universities' was conducted in the aforementioned sources. This search was stratified by year with results sorted by relevance, which Nexis decides based on keyword frequency and proximity to the headline. Since mental health appeared with high frequency and often in relation to other issues, the first 100 articles appearing each year of greater than 300 words in which student mental health represented the main focus of the article were sampled. This produced an initial sample of 243 articles from which 50 per cent, stratified by year,[1] were sampled and, as with the study of mindfulness above, coded with attention to the most frequently appearing claims, their sources and the rhetoric used to support those claims.[2] The problems alleged by claims-makers and their stated causes were also coded, along with rationales for why action needed to be taken and the solutions offered (Best, 1987, 2021).

This sample gives a sense of some of the major claims and claims-makers involved in the problematization of mental health in universities in recent years. However, it also presents a number of limitations in that it does not give a detailed inventory of claims problematizing mental health and associated keywords (e.g. mental hygiene) in universities historically, which would require a much-expanded work. More significantly, it does not include a detailed analysis of shifts in this discourse as a result of the Covid-19 pandemic. This crisis, with its attendant restrictions and prohibitions on social life and education, dragged on from March 2020 and saw the acceleration of mental health claims (e.g. Hill, 2021; Loader, 2021). The dynamic of mental health claims, initially abating (McCrae, 2021) and then re-emerging in full force, hints at some of the ways that mental health can function as a kind of ideology (J. Davies, 2021). That is, in a climate in which political, religious and other vocabularies of justification for a course of action have waned, mental health appears to have emerged as one of the few fields on which debate could be played out. As Furedi (2021) commented at the time, 'It seems that the only legitimate grounds on which the UK government's lockdown policy can now be criticized is that of mental health.' Indeed, this is in keeping with the broader thrust of mental health discourses in which an ever-expanding array of grievances and perceived injustices come to be subsumed under the umbrella of 'mental health'. Indeed, mental health itself becomes a shorthand for its opposite, mental ill-health. However, a fuller fleshing out of this tendency within the context of the Covid-19 pandemic awaits future, more dedicated research.

Notes

Introduction

1   See Chapter 2 for specific examples.

Chapter 1

1   See for instance such turns in journalism studies (Wahl-Jorgensen, 2020), international relations (Clément & Sangar, 2018), geography (Bondi et al., 2007) and in the humanities and social sciences more generally (Lemmings & Brooks, 2014).

2   The text to which this footnote is appended notes that within capitalist circulation, tables begin to evolve 'grotesque ideas' from their 'wooden brains' (Marx, 1976, p. 163). The table's value, the product of human relations and brains, comes to appear separate from them, as a natural property of the table. Failing in their attempts to control this process in the attempted revolutions and rebellions of the mid-eighteenth century, human beings appear subordinate to and controlled by objects they themselves have created.

Chapter 2

1   See Rose (1999) for discussion of the term 'soul' within 'subjectivities' (e.g. p. xii).

2   See Heartfield (2006) and Žižek (2000) for an extended discussion of these phenomena in social and intellectual trends.

3   For a more detailed review of this book, see Frawley (2018c).

4   Since Aristotle admits that eudaimonia rests on certain conditions beyond our control, he found it necessary to acknowledge some truth in this story wherein the 'quality of one's life is entirely determined by what befalls him' and its message that one should thus 'look to the end' even if he thought happiness could be strived for within rather than judged after one's life ends (Burger, 2008, pp. 39–40).

5   The unwavering and even naive nature of his optimism is exemplified by his having written this text while in hiding during the French Revolution's Reign of Terror in 1794.

6   Interestingly, he seems to foresee, if dimly, a problem that would later become endemic when he criticizes the slowing of the project of extending rights by 'postponing the interests of political freedom to the freedom of commerce' (Condorcet, 1796, p. 202). This split between political and economic liberalism and its role in the undermining and inverting of the liberal project is discussed by Landa (2009).

7   Since I will come to him in a moment it may be worth mentioning that Marx also saw 'unequal individual endowment' as a given; they 'would not be different individuals if they were not unequal' (Marx, 1875, p. 4090).

8   While, of course, Malthus also talks of 'happiness', the overall tone is markedly more pessimistic.

9   Malik makes it clear however that Herder saw himself within the tradition of tolerant universalism encouraged by the Enlightenment and the eventual racialization of his stress on the uniqueness of peoples was not his intention (1996, p. 79).

Chapter 3

1   'In this way, he spurs on the development of society's productive forces, and the creation of those material conditions of production which alone can form the real basis of a higher form of society [...]' (Marx, 1976, p. 739).

2   Interestingly, Aristotle had foreseen the destructiveness of what had made up only a small portion of his own society, 'retail trade'. There are echoes of Aristotle in Marx's observation that hunger for commodities can be sated where hunger for wealth cannot. Yet Marx thought it is important to stress the progressive side of this phenomenon in modern societies in which wage labour forms their foundation rather than a small part. 'General wealth is produced in order to seize hold of its representative. In this way the real sources of wealth are opened up' (Marx, 1973, p. 224). That is, instead of being simply destructive by raising prices in the ancient world, in the modern world, money allows for wealth and culture to be multiplied almost as an accidental outcome. This gives people a taste of freedom and comfort that they will not relinquish easily when it is negated (even literally destroyed as in war and crisis) by the pursuit of abstract wealth (money).

3   That is, within the capitalist system, abstract wealth must be pursued for the capitalist to remain a capitalist (i.e. a firm cannot carry on without the augmentation of profit as its end). The emergence of complex financial instruments is another example of this.

4   See also Frawley (2015c) for an extended discussion of this tendency within discourses of 'happiness' as a social problem and Frawley (2020d) for a discussion of this phenomenon within Marx's work.

5 That is, to continue to make profits in order to reinvest a portion of those profits back into making production more efficient to remain competitive. However, over time machinery develops and these outlays become larger and larger in relation to the profit capitalists can expect to receive in return (Marx, 1976, p. 739).

6 This is true, but in the sense that it is as much an attempt to escape these as it is an entanglement in them (Frawley, 2015c).

7 However as Foucault (2008) points out, they were latent within them.

Chapter 4

1 See Frawley (2018b) for more details regarding methodology including the precise frequencies with which these themes appeared in samples of news media documents. While this method inevitably misses out a large amount of claims-making in that it focuses on and then gathers further data on the basis of commonly appearing claims (e.g. it misses less successful claims-making), it gives insight into which claims resonated and which fell away in one of the most mass of media available to claims-makers. Resonance gives insight into the cultural context with which such claims fit rhetorically and may not necessarily match those claims which the strongest scientific evidence supports. See, for example, the controversy over the shaky scientific foundations of Barbara Fredrickson's highly influential 'positivity ratios' which I describe in Frawley (2015a). Indeed, that claims can become widely repeated not only in the news media but also by policymakers and institutionalized into a range of policies apart from or in spite of shaky scientific foundations is significant to investigate sociologically. If not the strength of scientific evidence, what is it that made such claims so powerful? Moreover, there are many paths that policy and institutions can follow that are supported by as strong or stronger evidence than these discourses, yet they do not attain the same influence or uptake. Studying the process of claims-making including organization and rhetoric helps explain why this comes to be (see Best, 2017 for more information on this perspective and approach).

2 While, in an earlier attempt to make sense of the connections between these issues (Frawley, 2020a), I had conceived of the process as a series of cycles, the additional case studies of mindfulness (Nehring & Frawley, 2020b) and mental health (this volume) have made me realize that history is not simply repeating itself. Rather, the process of constructing similar problem formulations involves development and feedback. Instead of being 'cycles', these problem formulations appear to rise and fall in waves.

3 Figure produced by searching for the keywords (self-esteem, happiness, well-being OR 'well-being', 'mental health') in archival holdings for *The New York Times* (via ProQuest), *The Times* (via Times Digital Archive [1987–2019] and Nexis [2020–2022]), the *Sydney Morning Herald* (via Nexis) and *The Globe and Mail* (via ProQuest). These were chosen as they are newspapers

of record in their respective countries and have comparable data available at least since 1987. The Nexis database contains a large number of duplicate articles as results include morning and evening editions and web content. Duplicate articles were removed by searching within time periods producing less than 400 results at a time, within which Nexis will automatically remove duplicates. Results for each of these smaller searches (e.g. by week or month as needed) were then manually added together to produce totals for each year minus duplicate articles.

4   While I focus here on positive emotions as specific therapeutic discourses, it is possible that this process describes many therapeutic fads and I tend to refer to the two interchangeably to avoid clumsiness of wording and repetition.

5   It is important to note that this cycle is a heuristic device useful for making sense of similarities and connections between issues. Progression through these phases is not guaranteed; as I note in the final chapters on mental health, it is not clear whether this issue will exhaust. While I have used the term 'phases' to highlight the temporal dimension, aspects often overlap, particularly adoption and expansion. The importance of this exercise lies in drawing attention to the general tendencies to rise and fall and make expansive claims to act as magic bullets or at least catch-all devices for making sense of a wide range of social ills.

6   Mass media often encourage these framings as they are perceived as engaging to audiences. Savvy claims-makers pick up on this which makes such tales more common and more likely to be repeated. Steinem herself betrays this self-awareness when she writes, 'That's why a storyteller is magic, but a teller of facts is not. There is a reason why parables are the oldest form of teaching: they work' (1992, p. 34).

7   Financial gain only makes problem discovery more alluring. The problematization of emotion may be lucrative, but it is not simply a cynical money-making scheme. Whether or not people truly believe in what they are doing, what matters is why, at a particular time, these become such 'intuitively' powerful problem formulations.

8   Hewitt warns portrayals of psychic wounding risk constructing one as unable to fend for oneself (1998, p. 96). Indeed, this strategy has proved a double-edged sword (e.g. Million, 2013).

Chapter 5

1   This figure was created by searching four major UK broadsheets (*The Times, The Daily Telegraph, The Independent* and *The Guardian* including their Sunday editions/affiliations) for the keyword 'mindfulness' between 2001 (the first year in which all are included in full within the database) and the most recent full year. Duplicates were removed by searching shorter time periods to allow Nexis to produce only unique results (which it does for totals under 400).

2   For a detailed study of the diffusion of mindfulness across institutions, see
     Kucinskas (2018).

3   In many ways, mindfulness also calls to mind most acutely Berman's
     summation of Pascal's conviction that man was only ever 'truly himself'
     when 'locked in contemplation' (Berman, 1972, p. 64).

4   For instance, uses of mindfulness in the *NYT* and *The Times* largely are
     in passing until the 1950s when its usage in relation to meditation first
     appears. While 'mindfulness' as an English translation of *sati* in the Pali
     language or *smriti* in Sanskrit dates back to T. W. Rhys Davids' translation
     in the 1880s (Sutherland, 1881), the first use of the word in this sense
     does not appear in the *NYT* until 1956 when discussing the 'Eight
     Righteousnesses' central to those observing the Buddhist 'Middle Path'
     (Rosenthal, 1956). In the 1960s and early 1970s, mindfulness is bound up
     with the rising popularity of Buddhism and communal living experiments at
     the time, as for instance in a *NYT* article reporting on a 'prayer movement'
     blending prayer and meditation (Blau, 1971).

5   For critiques of these and similar trends, see Pupavac (2010b, 2010a).

6   For instance, while Denison practised a form of mindfulness meditation,
     she did not use the term as the flagship for the centre she would later found
     (the Dhamma Dena Desert Vipassana Center). Similarly, while mindfulness
     appears in the book and chapter titles of then-influential Buddhist literature,
     it was not often employed as a standalone term, particularly by leading
     Buddhist missionaries in the United States (Wilson, 2014, p. 29).

7   See Nehring et al. (2016) for a development of the concept of self-help
     entrepreneurship.

8   Interestingly, for this claims-maker, mental health also represents an
     additional causal step linking inequality and suffering.

9   Resilience or resilient appears in 17 per cent of articles sampled and is the
     sixth most commonly cited benefit out of fifty-three.

10   Indeed, Huffington founded *Thrive*, a global wellness company in 2016.

11   Pace of change and/or modern life and technology represented the seventh
     and twelfth most common problems mentioned out of seventy-one.

Chapter 6

1   For a discussion of these themes in relation to happiness, see Frawley (2018a).

2   Leaving aside what 'working' even means, as a variety of outcomes are
     claimed by both advocates and critics; see, for example, debate between
     David (2014a, 2014b) and Gardner et al. (2014).

Chapter 7

1   The association between emotions and intellect has been much debated
     since at least the nineteenth century (Dixon, 2012). As discussed below,

claims about the importance of attending to the mental health and emotions in general of university students emerged in the early twentieth century in association with the mental hygiene movement. One early claims-maker was American Psychiatrist and proponent of eugenics, Stewart Paton, who claimed in 1911 that '[…] the functional capacity of the brain and nervous system of each individual student' should be the business of the educator who should then 'prescribe the amount and character of mental discipline in each case' (Paton, 1911, p. 12). Paton was a pioneer in setting up university counselling services in the United States, having established the first recorded mental health service for students in a higher education setting at Princeton in 1910 (Kay & Schwartz, 2011).

2 In this article, a head of counselling services was interviewed and speculated that the rise in students seeking mental health support may be due to 'the burden of student debt, economic uncertainty, global political upheaval, apocalyptic climate change' (Sarner, 2017).

3 And indeed, the mind is increasingly seen in the same terms as the body, the former having become 'somatised', or reduced to neurobiological processes (De Vos, 2021).

4 Indeed, mental health appears to have been briefly bound up with claims emerging in the early 1990s by University vice-chancellors to increase state support for students suffering financial hardship thus allowing more students to enrol and remain enrolled (see e.g. Meikle, 1993).

Chapter 8

1 This figure refers to a search including *The Times*, *The Daily Telegraph*, *The Independent*, and *The Guardian* as well as their Sunday editions/affiliations. The first 100 articles sorted by relevance were read and those meeting criteria described in the Methods Appendix are reflected here.

2 For instance, these groups acted as advisers to the Alliance for Student-Led Wellbeing, of which Student Minds was a core member (Alliance for Student-Led Wellbeing, 2015).

3 On the other hand, the positioning may already have begun to form whereby support services are foregrounded in university advertising, but responsibility for 'severe' issues (and their associated putative risks) was positioned as belonging to the NHS. The objective, at least for universities, appears to have been a clearer delineation of responsibility should something go wrong.

4 See Bolton (2022) for an overview of admissions data since 1994.

5 While this claim appears incongruent with the others in this list, claims-makers often cited increases in numbers of students failing to complete exams or dropping out as potentially indicating the increasing scale of mental health problems.

6 The frequent repetition of this phrase in news media discourses was first brought to my attention by my PhD student, Robert Lenton.

7   Thomassen means societal collapse, but the argument might equally be made for institutions within that society.

8   Many of these warrants were institutionalized in the #Stepchange framework: 'For #Stepchange, motivation for action is justified in terms of risk, legal responsibility, and student achievement, emphasizing the importance and implications of the problem' (Brewster & Cox, 2022, p. 4).

Chapter 9

1   I thank my PhD student, Robert Lenton for the insights discussed in this paragraph which he suggested to me in personal correspondence and conversations.

Methods Appendix

1   The final sample is greater than 50 per cent of 243 articles due to rounding uneven numbers when selecting 50 per cent of articles by year.

2   For a detailed discussion of rhetoric in claims-making about emotion problems, see Frawley (2015c).

References

Abdallah, S., Wheatley, H., & Quick, A. (2017). *Measuring wellbeing inequality in Britain* (2017, March; Wellbeing Inequalities Report, p. 32). What Works Centre for Wellbeing.

Agate, J. (2018, March 6). Finding 'Appiness. *The Independent*.

Agnew, M. (2019, January 20). It is hard to accept. Life is always going to have a gap. *The Sunday Times*, 16, 17, 19, 21, 23.

Ahmed, S. (2010). The promise of happiness. In *The Promise of Happiness*. Duke University Press.

Ahmed, S. (2014). *The Cultural Politics of Emotion* (Second edition). Edinburgh University Press.

Albery, N. (1988, April 27). Prescribing happiness. *The Guardian*.

Ali, A. (2015, November 27). College pulls 'extremely offensive' mental health test. *The Independent*. https://www.independent.co.uk/student/news/bournemouth-and-poole-college-withdraws-and-apologises-for-extremely-offensive-mental-health-awareness-test-a6751721.html

Allcott, H., & Gentzkow, M. (2017). Social media and fake news in the 2016 election. *Journal of Economic Perspectives*, *31*(2), 211–36. https://doi.org/10.1257/jep.31.2.211

Alliance for Student-Led Wellbeing. (2015). *Alliance for Student-Led Wellbeing—ABOUT*. Alliance for Student-Led Wellbeing. https://web.archive.org/web/20151218124911/https://alliancestudentwellbeing.weebly.com/

Allin-Khan, R. [@DrRosena]. (2022, September 29). [Tweet]. Twitter. https://twitter.com/DrRosena/status/1575504766766960641?s=20&t=y3y7Gz-ojUDFJoI8MXqJJA

Altheide, D. L. (2009). *Terror Post 9/11 and the Media*. Peter Lang.

Altheide, D. L., & Schneider, C. J. (2013). *Qualitative Media Analysis* (Vol. *38*). Sage.

American Psychiatric Association (2022). *Psychiatry.org - Words Matter: Reporting on Mental Health Conditions*. Psychiatry.Org. https://psychiatry.org:443/news-room/reporting-on-mental-health-conditions

AMOSSHE (2001). *Responding to student mental health issues: 'Duty of Care' responsibilities for student services in higher education* (pp. 1–45). AMOSSHE. https://www.amosshe.org.uk/resources/Documents/AMOSSHE_Duty_of_Care_2001.pdf

Andrews, F. M. (1989). The evolution of a movement. *Journal of Public Policy*, *9*(04), 401. https://doi.org/10.1017/S0143814X00008242

'Anonymous Blogger' (2016, September 22). Mental health at university. *The Guardian*.

Anthony, A. (2014, January 19). The British amateur who debunked the mathematics of happiness. *The Observer*. https://www.theguardian.com/science/2014/jan/19/mathematics-of-happiness-debunked-nick-brown

Arendt, H. (1973). *The Origins of Totalitarianism* (New edition). Harcourt Brace Jovanovich.

Armstrong, A. (2017). The wooden brain: Organizing untimeliness in marx's capital | Mediations | Journal of the marxist literary group. *Mediations, 31*(1), 3–26.

Arnold, S. (2004, January 24). Don't tell me that dope isn't dangerous. *The Independent*, 18.

Ashton, G. (2013, September 26). Whatever a student's problems, there is always a way to find help. *Western Mail*, 11.

Austen, G. (1994, December 14). Now and Zen. *The Age*, 19.

Bache, I., & Reardon, L. (2013). An idea whose time has come? Explaining the rise of well-being in British politics. *Political Studies, 61*(4), 898–914.

Bache, I., & Reardon, L. (2016). *The Politics and Policy of Wellbeing: Understanding the Rise and Significance of a New Agenda*. Edward Elgar Publishing.

Bache, I., Reardon, L., & Anand, P. (2016). Wellbeing as a wicked problem: Navigating the arguments for the role of government. *Journal of Happiness Studies, 17*(3), 893–912.

Baird, S. (2014, May 10). How to support your friend with their mental health. *The Guardian*. https://www.theguardian.com/education/2014/may/10/students-how-to-help-a-friend-with-mental-health-illness

Balibar, É. (1994). Subjection and subjectivation. In J. Copjec (Ed.), *Supposing the Subject* (pp. 1–15). Verso.

Batchelor, S. (2016, February 6). Mindfulness takes lead over Buddhism in quest for nirvana. *The Times*.

Baumeister, R. F. (1996). Should schools try to boost self-esteem. *American Educator, 22*, 14–19.

Baumeister, R. F., Campbell, J. D., Krueger, J. I., & Vohs, K. D. (2003). Does high self-esteem cause better performance, interpersonal success, happiness, or healthier lifestyles? *Psychological Science in the Public Interest, 4*(1), 1–44.

Baxter, A. J., Scott, K. M., Ferrari, A. J., Norman, R. E., Vos, T., & Whiteford, H. A. (2014). Challenging the myth of an 'Epidemic' of common mental disorders: Trends in the global prevalence of anxiety and depression between 1990 and 2010. *Depression and Anxiety, 31*(6), 506–16. https://doi.org/10.1002/da.22230

Beane, J. A. (1991). Sorting out the self-esteem controversy. *Educational Leadership, 49*(1), 25–30.

Being (2022, August 23). *About Us*. Being.App. https://being.app/about-us

Belfast Telegraph (2018, February 18). Universities are facing winds of change, minister warns. *Belfast Telegraph Online*.

Bendelow, G., & Williams, S. J. (Eds.). (1998). *Emotions in Social Life: Critical Themes and Contemporary Issues*. Routledge.

Benford, R. D. (2013). Master Frame. In *The Wiley-Blackwell Encyclopedia of Social and Political Movements*. Blackwell.

Bennett, G. (1998). The Vanishing hitchhiker at fifty-five. *Western Folklore, 57*(1), 1. https://doi.org/10.2307/1500246

Bennett, R. (2015a, March 13). Support swells for manifesto. *The Times*. https://www.thetimes.co.uk/article/support-swells-for-manifesto-f00s0vkb6g9

Bennett, R. (2015b, August 13). When all that new-found freedom proves too much. *The Times*, 12–13.

Bennett, R. (2018, June 28). *Universities told to back mental-health charter for students*. https://www.thetimes.co.uk/article/students-can-opt-in-to-mental-health-warning-system-p9lmzfbvz

Berlin, I. (2002). *Freedom and Its Betrayal: Six Enemies of Human Liberty*. Chatto & Windus.

Berman, M. (1972). *The Politics of Authenticity*. Athenum.

Berman, M. (1982). *All That Is Solid Melts Into Air: The Experience of Modernity*. Penguin.

Berman, M. (1999). *Adventures in Marxism*. Verso.

Berns, N. (2011). *Closure: The Rush to End Grief and What It Costs Us*. Temple University Press.

Best, J. (1987). Rhetoric in claims-making: Constructing the missing children problem. *Social Problems*, *34*(2), 101–21. https://doi.org/10.2307/800710

Best, J. (1990). *Threatened Children: Rhetoric and Concern about Child-Victims*. University of Chicago Press.

Best, J. (1993a). But Seriously Folks: The Limitations of the Strict Constructionist Interpretation of Social Problems. *Reconsidering Social Constructionism: Debates in Social Problems*, 129–45.

Best, J. (1993b). *Threatened Children: Rhetoric and Concern about Child-Victims*. University of Chicago Press.

Best, J. (1999). *Random Violence: How We Talk about New Crimes and New Victims*. University of California Press.

Best, J. (2006a). *Flavor of the Month: Why Smart People Fall for Fads*. University of California Press.

Best, J. (2006b). *Flavor of the Month: Why Smart People Fall for Fads*. University of California Press.

Best, J. (2015). Beyond case studies: Expanding the constructionist framework for social problems research. *Qualitative Sociology Review*, *11*(2), 18–33.

Best, J. (2017). *Social Problems* (Third edition). W. W. Norton & Company.

Best, J. (2019). The bumblebee flies anyway: The success of contextual constructionism. *The American Sociologist*, *50*(2), 220–7. http://dx.doi.org/10.1007/s12108-018-9386-0

Best, J. (2021). *Social Problems* (Fourth edition). W. W. Norton & Company.

Best, J., & Loseke, D. R. (2018). Prospects for the sociological study of social problems. *The Cambridge Handbook of Social Problems*, *1*, 169.

Binkley, S. (2011). Happiness, positive psychology and the program of neoliberal governmentality. *Subjectivity*, *4*(4), 371–94.

Binkley, S. (2014). *Happiness as Enterprise: An Essay on Neoliberal Life*. Suny Press.

Binkley, S. (2016). Happiness as resource and resilience: An emotion for neoliberal times. In J. Pykett, R. Jones, & Whitehead (Eds.), *Psychological Governance and Public Policy* (pp. 37–55). Routledge.

Birchall, G. (2018, June 25). SUICIDE UNI SHOCK. *The Sun*.

Black, L. I., Barnes, P. M., Clarke, T. C., Stussman, B. J., & Nahin, R. L. (2018). Use of Yoga, Meditation, and Chiropractors Among U.S. Children Aged 4–17 Years. *NCHS Data Brief*, *324*, 1–8.

Blair, L. (2015, July 6). Mindfulness: How it can disappoint. *The Daily Telegraph*.

Blau, E. (1971, May 31). Nuns' prayer movement attracts laity. *The New York Times*.

Blumer, H. (1971). Social problems as collective behavior. *Social Problems*, *18*(3), 298–306.

Bodhi, B. (2011). What does mindfulness really mean? A canonical perspective. *Contemporary Buddhism*, *12*(1), 19–39. https://doi.org/10.1080/14639947.2011 .564813

Bolton, P. (2022). *Higher Education Student Numbers* (Briefing Paper No. 7857). House of Commons. https://researchbriefings.files.parliament.uk/documents/ CBP-7857/CBP-7857.pdf

Bondi, L., Davidson, J., & Smith, M. (2007). *Emotional Geographies*. Ashgate.

Booth, R. (2014a, May 7). Politicians joined by Ruby Wax as parliament pauses for meditation. *The Guardian*.

Booth, R. (2014b, August 26). Dark side of enlightenment: Mindfulness comes at a price for some, experts warn. *The Guardian*.

Booth, R. (2015a, July 15). Mindfulness study to track impact of meditation on 7,000 teenagers. *The Guardian*.

Booth, R. (2015b, October 19). Britain's most dangerous prisoners to get meditation lessons; About 60 inmates held in segregation units will be taught mindfulness-based techniques in an effort to calm their violent impulses. *The Guardian*. https://advance.lexis.com/document/?pdmfid=1519360&crid=e7d06 7ba-602e-4fc4-9c3d-2f453eb1ab7e&pddocfullpath=%2Fshared%2Fdocument %2Fnews%2Furn%3AcontentItem%3A5H61-FC81-JCJY-G1SC-00000-00&pd contentcomponentid=138620&pdteaserkey=sr0&pditab=allpods&ecomp=rbz yk&earg=sr0&prid=68449949-7d85-402a-a115-fafc2e881c9f

Booth, R. (2015c, October 20). Mindfulness in the mainstream: An old solution to modern problems. *The Guardian*. https://www.theguardian.com/ lifeandstyle/2015/oct/20/mindfulness-in-the-mainstream-an-old-solution-to- modern-problems

Booth, R. (2017, October 13). 'Way ahead of the curve': UK hosts first summit on mindful politics. *The Guardian*. https://www.theguardian.com/ lifeandstyle/2017/oct/13/politicians-meditate-commons-mindfulness-event

Booth, R. (2018, October 13). 'And breathe': Police try mindfulness to beat burnout; College of Policing to fund trial for more than 1,500 officers to combat stress-related sick leave. *The Guardian*. https://advance.lexis.com/doc ument/?pdmfid=1519360&crid=5998c4fd-c450-49a3-a951-d4e24248f5fb&pdd ocfullpath=%2Fshared%2Fdocument%2Fnews%2Furn%3AcontentItem%3A 5TGC-6051-F021-627P-00000-00&pdcontentcomponentid=138620&pdteaserk ey=sr1&pditab=allpods&ecomp=rbzyk&earg=sr1&prid=95c9dbd5-c406-4cc5- 98bf-deec01722a2d

Born This Way Foundation [@BTWFoundation]. (2015, October 24). *We're in the midst of an #EmotionRevolution. Join @ladygaga and spread the word! #IamNotJust*. https://twitter.com/BTWFoundation/ status/657951011647131648?s=20&t=-qDxPlk47qPmihKmbbOr5A

Bosotti, A. (2022, May 2). 'Stormy seas ahead' Prince Harry's Silicon Valley gig under threat of internal revolt. *Express Online*. https://advance.lexis.com/docu ment/?pdmfid=1519360&crid=2cff7303-f0fe-4422-9c8d-23c9ace39fb7&pddoc fullpath=%2Fshared%2Fdocument%2Fnews%2Furn%3AcontentItem%3A6

5C0-P8K1-DY4H-K27Y-00000-00&pdcontentcomponentid=408506&pdteaserk ey=sr1&pditab=allpods&ecomp=rbzyk&earg=sr1&prid=a50c14e8-a603-42b4- 8fa1-83b6442fb5a8

Boucher, S. (2005). *Dancing in the Dharma: The Life and Teachings of Ruth Denison*. Beacon Press. http://search.ebscohost.com/login.aspx?direct=true& scope=site&db=nlebk&db=nlabk&AN=191339

Bowditch, G. (2006, September 19). Ecosse: The colour of confidence. *The Sunday Times*.

Bowler, S. (2008). The object of medicine. In D. Wainwright (Ed.), *A Sociology of Health*. Sage.

Boyce, B. (2011). *The Mindfulness Revolution: Leading Psychologists, Scientists, Artists, and … - Google Books*. Shambhala. https://books.google.co.uk/books? id=S12Ak0szpPYC&printsec=frontcover&dq=mindfulness+revolution&hl=en& sa=X&ved=0ahUKEwjAma2P2_ffAhU6UxUIHXbIATcQ6AEIKDAA#v=onepage &q=%22a%20mindful%20consumer%20can%20help%22&f=false

Braithwaite, J. (2011). The regulatory state? In R. Goodin E. (Ed.), *The Oxford Handbook of Political Institutions* (pp. 266–88). https://doi.org/10.1093/ oxfordhb/9780199548460.003.0021

Brewster, L., & Cox, A. M. (2022). Taking a 'whole-university' approach to student mental health: The contribution of academic libraries. *Higher Education Research & Development*, 1–15. https://doi.org/10.1080/07294360.2022.2043 249

Bristow, J. (2019). Mindfulness in politics and public policy. *Current Opinion in Psychology*, *28*, 87–91. https://doi.org/10.1016/j.copsyc.2018.11.003

Brown, C. G. (2016). Can 'Secular' mindfulness be separated from religion? In R. E. Purser, D. Forbes, & A. Burke (Eds.), *Handbook of Mindfulness: Culture, Context, and Social Engagement* (pp. 75–94). Springer International Publishing.

Brown, J. D. (1991). The professional Ex-: *The Sociological Quarterly*, *32*(2), 219–30. https://doi.org/10.1111/j.1533-8525.1991.tb00354.x

Brown, N. J. L., Sokal, A. D., & Friedman, H. L. (2013). The complex dynamics of wishful thinking: The critical positivity ratio. *American Psychologist*, *68*(9), 801–13. https://doi.org/10.1037/a0032850

Brown, P. (2016). *The Invisible Problem? Improving Students' Mental Health* (HEPI Report 88; p. 66). Higher Education Policy Institute.

Brownlie, J. (2014). *Ordinary Relationships: A Sociological Study of Emotions, Reflexivity and Culture*. Palgrave Macmillan.

Bruni, L. (2006). *Civil Happiness*. Routledge.

Brunila, K. (2012). From risk to resilience: The therapeutic ethos in youth education. *Education Inquiry*, *3*(3), 451–64. https://doi.org/10.3402/edui. v3i3.22046

Buchan, L. (2018, February 1). Students wait up to four months for mental health support at UK universities. *The Independent*. https://www.independent.co.uk/ news/uk/politics/students-mental-health-support-waiting-times-counselling- university-care-diagnosis-treatment-liberal-democrats-norman-lamb-a8124111. html

Bunting, M. (2005, December 5). Madeleine Bunting: Consumer capitalism is making us ill. *The Guardian*. https://www.theguardian.com/politics/2005/ dec/05/society.britishidentity

Bunting, M. (2013, April 8). Policy goes Zen. *The Guardian*, 12.

Bunting, M. (2014, May 6). Why we will come to see mindfulness as mandatory. *The Guardian*. https://www.theguardian.com/commentisfree/2014/may/06/mindfulness-hospitals-schools

Burger, R. (2008). *Aristotle's Dialogue with Socrates: On the Nicomachean Ethics*. University of Chicago Press.

Burkeman, O. (2016, January 9). Do we really need more guides to mindfulness? *The Guardian*.

Burnett, D. (2015, April 21). Mindfulness: Beware the hype. *The Guardian*.

Burnett, S. (2012). *The Happiness Agenda: A Modern Obsession*. Palgrave Macmillan.

Busby, E. (2018a, August 15). A-level results day: Universities should do more to tackle growing student mental health crisis. *The Independent*. https://advance.lexis.com/document/?pdmfid=1519360&crid=d0aa734a-c3e8-4fc5-b020-6c2e7c34bed7&pddocfullpath=%2Fshared%2Fdocument%2Fnews%2Furn%3AcontentItem%3A5T1W-FH21-JCJY-G1Y7-00000-00&pdcontentcomponentid=382507&pdteaserkey=sr37&pditab=allpods&ecomp=yzynk&earg=sr37&prid=344ff9e6-8067-47be-80d9-0c2c2037cbbf

Busby, E. (2018b, September 15). Prioritising student mental health is 'non-negotiable', minister tells university bosses. *The Independent*. https://www.independent.co.uk/news/education/education-news/student-mental-health-universities-minister-sam-gyimah-freshers-week-wellbeing-suicides-a8539146.html

Busby, E. (2019, November 5). Black students with mental illness failed by universities. *The Independent*, 20.

Cabanas, E. (2018). Positive psychology and the legitimation of individualism. *Theory & Psychology, 28*(1), 3–19. https://doi.org/10.1177/0959354317747988

Cabanas, E., & Illouz, E. (2019). *Manufacturing Happy Citizens. How the Science and Industry of Happiness Control Our Lives*. Polity.

Cabanas, E., & Sanchez-González, J. C. (2012). The roots of positive psychology. *Papeles Del Psicólogo, 33*(3), 172–82.

Castle, C. (2017, July 22). Mental-health support at university. *The Daily Telegraph*, 9.

Cavendish, C. (2014, May 11). Calm down, class, and focus your mindfulness. *The Sunday Times*.

CBC News. (2018, January 17). U.K. names minister to tackle 'silent epidemic' of loneliness. *CBC News*.

Chan, R. Y. (2016). Understanding the purpose of higher education: An analysis of the economic and social benefits for completing a college degree. *Journal of Education Policy, Planning and Administration (JEPPA), 6*(5), 1–41.

Chandler, D. (2013). 'Human-Centred' development? Rethinking 'Freedom' and 'Agency' in discourses of international development. *Millennium, 42*(1), 3–23. https://doi.org/10.1177/0305829813492184

Chandler, D. (2014). *Resilience: The Governance of Complexity*. Routledge.

Chandler, D. (2016a). Development as adaptation. In D. Chandler & J. Reid (Eds.), *The Neoliberal Subject: Resilience, Adaptation, Vulnerability* (pp. 75–98). Rowman & Littlefield.

Chandler, D. (2016b). Resilience. In *The Neoliberal Subject: Resilience, Adaptation and Vulnerability* (pp. 27–50). Rowman & Littlefield.

Chandler, D., & Reid, J. (2016a). Introduction: The neoliberal subject. In
D. Chandler & J. Reid (Eds.), *The Neoliberal Subject: Resilience, Adaptation,
Vulnerability* (pp. 1–8). Rowman & Littlefield.

Chandler, D., & Reid, J. (2016b). *The Neoliberal Subject: Resilience, Adaptation
and Vulnerability*. Rowman & Littlefield International.

Chateau, F. (1993, September 14). When the going gets too tough to handle. *The
Guardian*, 18.

Chynoweth, C. (2013, November 10). Meditate with the marines. *The Sunday
Times*.

Clayton, B. (2017, August 17). We need a mental health league table for
universities. *The Independent*. https://www.independent.co.uk/voices/a-level-
results-mental-health-universities-not-good-enough-anxiety-stress-a7898536.
html

Clément, M., & Sangar, E. (2018). *Researching Emotions in International
Relations: Methodological Perspectives on the Emotional Turn*. Palgrave.

Cockerell, J. (2015, March 17). Labour rap mental health report. *Press Association
Mediapoint*.

Coldwell, W. (2012, September 19). Lonely in freshers week? You're not the only
one. *The Guardian*. https://www.theguardian.com/education/2012/sep/19/
lonely-in-freshers-week

Coleman, J. (2001). *The New Buddhism: The Western Transformation of an
Ancient Tradition*. Oxford University Press.

Condorcet, M. de (1796). *Outlines of an Historical View of the Progress of the
Human Mind*. Lang and Usticke.

Confino, J. (2014, May 14). Google's head of mindfulness: 'goodness is good for
business'. *The Guardian*. https://www.theguardian.com/sustainable-business/
google-meditation-mindfulness-technology

Cosgrove, L., & Karter, J. M. (2018). The poison in the cure: Neoliberalism and
contemporary movements in mental health. *Theory & Psychology, 28*(5),
669–83. https://doi.org/10.1177/0959354318796307

Coyne, J. C., Tennen, H., & Ranchor, A. V. (2010). Positive psychology in cancer
care: A story line resistant to evidence. *Annals of Behavioral Medicine, 39*(1),
35–42.

Crane, R. S., Kuyken, W., Hastings, R. P., Rothwell, N., & Williams, J. M. G.
(2010). Training teachers to deliver mindfulness-based interventions: Learning
from the UK experience. *Mindfulness, 1*(2), 74–86. https://doi.org/10.1007/
s12671-010-0010-9

Crewe, C. (2013, June 4). Ruby Wax: I don't want to pay for any more shrinks.
The Times.

Cribb, J., Waters, T., Wernham, T., & Xu, X. (2021, July 5). *Young adults well
protected from increased hardship through the pandemic but a risk that many
will bear scars of the recession for years to come*. The IFS. https://ifs.org.uk/
publications/15509

Crispin, J. (2021, June 2). Stressed-out amazon workers can now access
'mindfulness' training. Gee, thanks. *The Guardian*. https://advance.lexis.com/
document/?pdmfid=1519360&crid=3c6f7d3c-e3b8-4fc9-bd5f-6b50e64d25f9
&pddocfullpath=%2Fshared%2Fdocument%2Fnews%2Furn%3AcontentIte
m%3A62TR-VG81-JBNF-W3W2-00000-00&pdcontentcomponentid=138620&
pdteaserkey=sr4&pditab=allpods&ecomp=rbzyk&earg=sr4&prid=35464638-
848a-46e1-9564-7ebb989ccb3d

Curtis, P. (2005, May 17). Not drinking, drowning. *The Guardian*.

Daneshkhu, S. (2007, June 13). Call for happiness to be taught in schools. *Financial Times*, 3.

David, D. (2014a). And yet it moves! A reply to 'Rectifying misconception: A comprehensive response to gardner, moore, and marks comments on "Some concerns about the psychological implications of mindfulness: A critical analysis"'. *Journal of Rational-Emotive & Cognitive-Behavior Therapy, 32*(4), 345–51. https://doi.org/10.1007/s10942-014-0199-y

David, D. (2014b). Some concerns about the psychological implications of mindfulness: A critical analysis. *Journal of Rational-Emotive & Cognitive-Behavior Therapy, 32*(4), 313–24. https://doi.org/10.1007/s10942-014-0198-z

Davies, J. (2021). *Sedated: How Modern Capitalism Created Our Mental Health Crisis*. Atlantic Books. https://www.amazon.co.uk/Sedated-Modern-Capitalism-Created-Mental-ebook/dp/B08Q3MLH77/ref=sr_1_1?dchild=1&keywords=james+davies+sedated&qid=1627983552&sr=8-1

Davies, W. (2018). *Nervous States: How Feeling Took Over the World*. Penguin Random House.

Davis, I. (1988, January 22). Ministry for feeling good – Self love is something they feel strongly about in California, so strongly that now they have set up a special task force. *The Times*.

Dawson, G. (2021). Zen and the mindfulness industry. *The Humanistic Psychologist, 49*(1), 133–46. https://doi.org/10.1037/hum0000171

De La Fabián, R., & Stecher, A. (2017). Positive psychology's promise of happiness: A new form of human capital in contemporary neoliberal governmentality. *Theory & Psychology, 27*(5), 600–21. https://doi.org/10.1177/0959354317718970

De Maistre, J. (1993). *St Petersburg Dialogues: Or Conversations on the Temporal Government of Providence* (R. Lebrun A., Trans.). McGill-Queens University Press.

De Vos, J. (2021). A critique of digital mental health via assessing the psychodigitalisation of the COVID-19 crisis. *Psychotherapy and Politics International, 19*(1), e1582.

Deatherage, G. (1975). The clinical use of 'Mindfulness' meditation techniques in short-Term psychotherapy. *Journal of Transpersonal Psychology, 7*(2), 133–43.

Demarzo, M. M. P., Cebolla, A., & Garcia-Campayo, J. (2015). The implementation of mindfulness in healthcare systems: A theoretical analysis. *General Hospital Psychiatry, 37*(2), 166–71. https://doi.org/10.1016/j.genhosppsych.2014.11.013

Denham, J. (2013a, March 22). Are universities doing enough to support students with mental health problems? *The Independent*.

Denham, J. (2013b, June 4). Are students turning to gambling in the face of increased money troubles? *The Independent*.

Department for Education (2019, April 2). *One of the largest mental health trials launches in schools*. GOV.UK. https://www.gov.uk/government/news/one-of-the-largest-mental-health-trials-launches-in-schools

Department for Education, & Morgan, N. (2014, October 30). *Nicky Morgan announces children's social work reforms*. GOV.UK. https://www.gov.uk/government/speeches/nicky-morgan-announces-childrens-social-work-reforms

Department of Health and Social Care [@DHSCgovuk] (2019, January 21). *There's no such thing as #BlueMonday However, 1 in 4 of us are affected by mental health and the damage this can do, every day of the year, is very real. We've pulled together a collection of tweets from organisations across the UK who provide support.* https://t.co/hp25q6BcOM [Tweet]. Twitter. https://twitter.com/DHSCgovuk/status/1087367374804840448

Derbyshire, D. (2014, February 23). Should we be mindful of mindfulness? *The Observer.* https://www.theguardian.com/society/2014/feb/23/should-we-be-mindful-of-mindfulness-nhs-depression

Dineen, T. (2001). *Manufacturing Victims: What the Psychology Industry is doing to People.* Robert Davies.

Disabled Students. (2013, May 21). *20 per cent of students consider themselves to have a mental health problem.* National Union of Students. https://web.archive.org/web/20201024173047/http://www.nus.org.uk/en/news/20-per-cent-of-students-consider-themselves-to-have-a-mental-health-problem/

Dixon, T. (2012). Educating the emotions from gradgrind to goleman. *Research Papers in Education, 27*(4), 481–95. https://doi.org/10.1080/02671522.2012.690240

Dooris, M., & Doherty, S. (2010). Healthy universities: Current activity and future directions - findings and reflections from a national-level qualitative research study. *Global Health Promotion, 17*(3), 06–16. https://doi.org/10.1177/1757975910375165

Doughty, E. (2015, March 22). Present, sir: Benefits of a mindful classroom. *The Daily Telegraph,* 13.

Douglas, M. (1992). *Risk and Blame: Essays in Cultural Theory.* Routledge. http://ebookcentral.proquest.com/lib/swansea-ebooks/detail.action?docID=170075

Dowling, T. (2013, May 25). Anxieties mount over students' mental health. *Liverpool Echo,* 20.

Dunn, J. L. (2004). The politics of empathy: Social movements and victim repertoires. *Sociological Focus, 37*(3), 235–50.

Dunn, J. M. (2010). *Benefits of Mindfulness Meditation in a Corrections Setting* (p. 37). Upaya Chaplaincy Program.

Dyckhoff, C. (2013, July 24). Graduate blues: Why we need to talk about post-university depression. *The Independent.*

Ecclestone, K. (2012). From emotional and psychological well-being to character education: Challenging policy discourses of behavioural science and 'vulnerability.' *Research Papers in Education, 27*(4), 463–80. https://doi.org/10.1080/02671522.2012.690241

Ecclestone, K. (2013). Confident individuals: The implications of an 'Emotional Subject'. In M. Priestley & G. Biesta (Eds.), *Reinventing the Curriculum: New Trends in Curriculum Policy and Practice* (pp. 75–98). A&C Black.

Ecclestone, K. (2017). Behaviour change policy agendas for 'vulnerable' subjectivities: The dangers of therapeutic governance and its new entrepreneurs. *Journal of Education Policy, 32*(1), 48–62. https://doi.org/10.1080/02680939.2016.1219768

Ecclestone, K. (2018). 'Therapeutic Entrepreneurialism' and the Undermining of Expertise and Evidence in the Education Politics of Wellbeing. In I. Bache & K. Scott (Eds.), *The Politics of Wellbeing: Theory, Policy and Practice* (pp. 225–52). Springer. https://doi.org/10.1007/978-3-319-58394-5_10

Ecclestone, K. (2020, February 4). Are universities encouraging students to believe hard study is bad for their mental health? *Times Higher Education.*

https://www.timeshighereducation.com/features/are-universities-encouraging-students-believe-hard-study-bad-their-mental-health

Ecclestone, K., & Brunila, K. (2015). Governing emotionally vulnerable subjects and 'therapisation'of social justice. *Pedagogy, Culture & Society, 23*(4), 485–506.

Ecclestone, K., & Hayes, D. (2019). *The Dangerous Rise of Therapeutic Education* (Routledge Education Classic Edition). Routledge.

Ecclestone, K., & Lewis, L. (2014). Interventions for resilience in educational settings: Challenging policy discourses of risk and vulnerability. *Journal of Education Policy, 29*(2), 195–216. https://doi.org/10.1080/02680939.2013.8066 78

Ecclestone, K., & Rawdin, C. (2016). Reinforcing the 'diminished' subject? The implications of the 'vulnerability zeitgeist' for well-being in educational settings. *Cambridge Journal of Education, 46*(3), 377–93. https://doi.org/10.108 0/0305764X.2015.1120707

Economic and Social Research Council (2018, June 9). *UK Research and Innovation launches new Mental Health Networks*. Economic and Social Research Council. https://webarchive.nationalarchives.gov. uk/20200930153705/https://esrc.ukri.org/news-events-and-publications/news/ news-items/uk-research-and-innovation-launches-new-mental-health-networks/

Edwards, R., Gillies, V., Lee, E., Macvarish, J., White, S., & Wastell, D. (2017). *The Problem with ACEs'. Submission to the House of Commons Science and Technology Select Committee Inquiry into the evidence-base for early years intervention* (No. EY10039). https://blogs.kent.ac.uk/parentingculturestudies/ files/2018/01/The-Problem-with-ACEs-EY10039-Edwards-et-al.-2017-1.pdf

Ehrenreich, B. (2010). *Bright-Sided: How Positive Thinking Is Undermining America*. Metropolitan Books.

Elias, N. (2000). *The Civilizing Process: Sociogenetic and Psychogenetic Investigations* (E. Dunning, J. Goudsblom, & S. Mennell, Eds.; E. Jephcott, Trans.; Rev. edition). Blackwell Publishers.

Elliott, L. (2007, August 27). Cameron should count on happiness. *The Guardian*, 24.

Engstrom, S., & Whiting, J. (1996). *Aristotle, Kant, and the Stoics: Rethinking Happiness and Duty*. Cambridge University Press.

Ericson, R. V., & Doyle, A. (2003). *Risk and Morality*. University of Toronto Press.

Evans, B., & Reid, J. (2013). *Dangerously Exposed: The Life and Death of the Resilient Subject. 1*(2), 83–98.

Evans, B., & Reid, J. (2014). *Resilient Life: The Art of Living Dangerously*. Polity.

Evans, J. (2018). The end of history and the invention of happiness. In I. Bache & K. Scott (Eds.), *The Politics of Wellbeing: Theory, Policy, Practice* (pp. 25–48). Springer.

Farias, M., & Wikholm, C. (2015). *The Buddha Pill: Can Meditation Change You*. Watkins Publishing.

Fawzi, N. (2018). Beyond policy agenda-setting: Political actors' and journalists' perceptions of news media influence across all stages of the political process. *Information, Communication & Society, 21*(8), 1134–50. https://doi.org/10.1080 /1369118X.2017.1301524

Fay, L. (2017, September 16). Classrooms shouldn't become chill-out zones. *The Times*.

Fazackerley, A. (2018, October 9). Student mental health: Universities could be forced to involve parents. *The Guardian*.

Ferguson, K. (2018, June 25). *Number of university students committing suicide nearly doubles since 2000 with men twice as likely to take their own lives, new figures show*. MailOnline. https://www.dailymail.co.uk/news/article-5882733/Number-university-students-committing-suicide-nearly-doubles-2000.html

Fernández-Ríos, L., & Novo, M. (2012). Positive Psychology: Zeigeist (or spirit of the times) or ignorance (or disinformation) of history? *International Journal of Clinical and Health Psychology, 12*(2), 333–44.

Fineman, M. (2010). The vulnerable subject and the responsive state. *Emory Law Journal, 60*(2), 251–75.

Fineman, M. (2015). Social justice and the vulnerable state. *Inaugural Lecture at the Centre for Law and Social Justice, University of Leeds, 16*.

Finkelstein, D. (2009, April 11). The misery-guts are massing to criticise consumerism and inequality. But I doubt if the recession will be better. *The Times*, 4.

Fishel, J. (1992). Leadership for social change: John Vasconcellos (D-CA) and the promise of humanistic psychology in public life. *Political Psychology, 13*(4), 663–92. https://doi.org/10.2307/3791496

Fitzpatrick, A. (2017, February 17). *Dr Nicola Byrom: 'We all have mental health and we all need to look after it'*. Varsity Online. http://www.varsity.co.uk/features/12151

Fitzpatrick, M. (2002). *The Tyranny of Health: Doctors and the Regulation of Lifestyle*. Routledge.

Forbes, D. (2019). *Mindfulness and Its Discontents*. Ferwood Publishing.

Foucault, M. (2008). *The Birth of Biopolitics: Lectures at the Collège de France, 1978–79* (M. Senellart, Ed.). Palgrave Macmillan.

Frankenberg, R., Robinson, I., & Delahooke, A. (2000). Countering essentialism in behavioural social science: The example of 'the vulnerable child'ethnographically examined. *The Sociological Review, 48*(4), 586–611.

Frawley, A. (2015a). Happiness research: A review of critiques. *Sociology Compass, 9*(1), 62–77.

Frawley, A. (2015b). Happiness research: A review of critiques. *Sociology Compass, 9*(1), 62–77. https://doi.org/10.1111/soc4.12236

Frawley, A. (2015c). *Semiotics of Happiness: Rhetorical Beginnings of a Public Problem*. Bloomsbury.

Frawley, A. (2018a). 'Unhappy News': Process, rhetoric, and context in the making of the happiness problem. *Sociological Research Online, 23*(1), 43–66.

Frawley, A. (2018b). 'Unhappy News': Process, rhetoric, and context in the making of the happiness problem. *Sociological Research Online, 23*(1), 43–66. https://doi.org/10.1177/1360780417744791

Frawley, A. (2018c, November 21). *Technocracy once more, with feeling*. Spiked Online. https://www.spiked-online.com/2018/11/21/technocracy-once-more-with-feeling/

Frawley, A. (2020a). Self-esteem, happiness and the therapeutic fad cycle. In D. Nehring, O. J. Madsen, E. Cabanas, C. Mills, & D. Kerrigan (Eds.), *Handbook of Global Therapeutic Cultures* (pp. 139–52). Routledge.

Frawley, A. (2020b). Self-esteem, happiness and the therapeutic fad cycle. In *The Routledge International Handbook of Global Therapeutic Cultures*, 139–52.

Frawley, A. (2020c). «Supporting the Sacred Journey»: Les histoires causales et le «problème» de la parentalité autochtone. *Lien Social et Politiques, 85,* 85–107.

Frawley, A. (2020d). *The future and how to get there: A leftist critique of the modern left.* Culture on the Offensive. https://web.archive.org/web/20200213131537/https://www.cultureontheoffensive.com/leftist-critique-of-the-left/

Frawley, A. (2020e, March 18). *Mental health 'experts' are shamelessly exploiting Covid-19.* UnHerd. https://unherd.com/thepost/mental-health-experts-are-shamelessly-exploiting-covid-19/

Frawley, A. (2022, July 26). How trauma politics hurt the poor. *Compact Magazine.* https://compactmag.com/article/how-trauma-politics-hurts-the-poor

Fredrickson, B. L., & Losada, M. F. (2005). Positive affect and the complex dynamics of human flourishing. *American Psychologist, 60*(7), 678.

Frizzell, N. (2015, October 29). Yes, you can crawl out of your first-year depression at university. *The Guardian.* https://advance.lexis.com/document/?pdmfid=1519360&crid=1632e202-b76d-4f04-abc1-f6d51147ea9a&pddocfullpath=%2Fshared%2Fdocument%2Fnews%2Furn%3AcontentItem%3A5H83-VB11-F021-60N1-00000-00&pdcontentcomponentid=138620&pdteaserkey=sr0&pditab=allpods&ecomp=rbzyk&earg=sr0&prid=92321abb-e919-48a1-95f9-d0ebe71e662a

Fukuyama, F. (1989). The end of history? *The National Interest, 16* (Summer), 1–18.

Furedi, F. (2001). *Paranoid Paranting: Abandon Your Anxieties and Be a Good Parent.* Allen Lane.

Furedi, F. (2002). The silent ascendency of therapeutic culture in Britain. In J. B. Imber (Ed.), In Therapeutic Culture: Triumph and Defeat. Routledge.

Furedi, F. (2004). *Therapy Culture: Cultivating Vulnerability in an Uncertain Age.* Routledge.

Furedi, F. (2009). *Wasted: Why Education Isn't Educating.* Continuum.

Furedi, F. (2021, October 3). *The making of a Covid mental-health crisis.* Spiked. https://www.spiked-online.com/2021/03/10/the-making-of-a-covid-mental-health-crisis/

Furnham, A. (2014, May 11). Relax: Mindful managers will save the office's living dead. *The Sunday Times.*

Gamson, W. (1990). *The Strategy of Social Protest.* Dorsey Press.

Gani, A. (2016, March 13). Tuition fees 'have led to surge in students seeking counselling'. *The Guardian.* https://www.theguardian.com/education/2016/mar/13/tuition-fees-have-led-to-surge-in-students-seeking-counselling

Gans, H. J. (2004). *Deciding What's News: A Study of CBS Evening News, NBC Nightly News, Newsweek, and Time.* Northwestern University Press.

Gardner, F. L., Moore, Z. E., & Marks, D. R. (2014). Rectifying misconceptions: A comprehensive response to 'Some concerns about the psychological implications of mindfulness: A critical analysis'. *Journal of Rational-Emotive & Cognitive-Behavior Therapy, 32*(4), 325–44. https://doi.org/10.1007/s10942-014-0196-1

Gay, P. (1959). *Voltaire's Politics: The Poet Realist.* Princeton University Press.

Gelles, D. (2015a). *Mindful Work: How Meditation Is Changing Business from the Inside Out.* Houghton Mifflin Harcourt.

Gelles, D. (2015b, February 8). A Beautiful Mind. *The Sunday Times*.

Gervais, B. (1998, October 31). Self-esteem full-time job for families. *Hamilton Spectator*, N6. Nexis.

Gil, N. (2015, December 14). Majority of students experience mental health issues, says NUS survey. *The Guardian*. https://www.theguardian.com/education/2015/dec/14/majority-of-students-experience-mental-health-issues-says-nus-survey

Gil, N. (2016, March 3). Six things students can do to boost their mental health. *The Guardian*.

Gilligan, C. (2009). 'Highly vulnerable'? Political violence and the social construction of traumatized children. *Journal of Peace Research, 46*(1), 119–34. https://doi.org/10.1177/0022343308098407

Gold, J. (2017, February 20). *'Post-election stress disorder' strikes on both sides*. *CNN*. http://edition.cnn.com/2017/02/20/health/post-election-stress-partner/index.html

Goleman, D. (1971). Meditation as meta-therapy: Hypotheses toward a proposed fifth state of consciousness. *Journal of Transpersonal Psychology, 3*, 1–25.

Goleman, D. (1986, May 13). Relaxation: Surprising benefits detected. *The New York Times*. https://www.nytimes.com/1986/05/13/science/relaxation-surprising-benefits-detected.html

Goleman, D. (2011). A mindful consumer can help change the world. In B. Boyce (Ed.), *The Mindfulness Revolution*. Shambhala Publications.

Goode, E., & Ben-Yehuda, N. (2009). *Moral Panics: The Social Construction of Deviance* (2nd edition). Wiley-Blackwell.

Gov.uk (2018, September 16). *Minister Gyimah: Universities must ensure their mental health services are fit for purpose*. The Education Hub. https://educationhub.blog.gov.uk/2018/09/16/minister-gyimah-universities-must-ensure-their-mental-health-services-are-fit-for-purpose/

Greenfield Bloomberg, R. (2016, September 11). Arianna Huffington wants to sell your boss on office naps. *Chicago Daily Herald*.

Griffin, A. (2018, February 24). Can you have a healthy relationship with your phone? Mindfulness could be the key to stopping technological misery. *The Independent*.

Griffiths, H., & Best, J. (2016). Social problems clusters as contexts for claimsmaking: Implications for the study of off-campus housing. *Sociological Spectrum, 36*(2), 75–92. https://doi.org/10.1080/02732173.2015.1091756

Griffiths, S. (2007, September 9). Children – The new battleground. *The Sunday Times*, 11.

Griffiths, S. (2013, August 12). Wanted: A cure for the university blues. *The Sunday Times*, 12.

Grossman, H. (2015). *Marx, Classical Political Economy and the Problem of Dynamics* (R. Kuhn, Trans.; Kindle). Socialist Alternative.

Grossman, P. (2019). On the porosity of subject and object in 'mindfulness' scientific study: Challenges to 'scientific' construction, operationalization and measurement of mindfulness. *Current Opinion in Psychology, 28*, 102–7. https://doi.org/10.1016/j.copsyc.2018.11.008

Grove, J. (2017, January 27). Happiness expert advises UK's first 'positive university'. *Times Higher Education (THE)*. https://www.timeshighereducation.com/news/happiness-expert-advises-uks-first-positive-university

Guldberg, H. (2009). *Reclaiming Childhood: Freedom and Play in an Age of Fear*. Taylor & Francis.

Guldberg, H. (2012). *Ignore these pedlars of panic – the kids are all right*. https://www.spiked-online.com/2012/01/16/ignore-these-pedlars-of-panic-the-kids-are-all-right/

Gurkan, E. (2014, July 22). I couldn't stop crying, then counselling changed my life | Students | The Guardian. *The Guardian*. https://www.theguardian.com/education/mortarboard/2014/jul/22/university-counselling-really-helped-me

Haidrani, L. (2013, February 20). Mental health: Don't suffer in silence. *The Independent*.

Haidt, J. (2005). *The Happiness Hypothesis: Finding Modern Truth in Ancient Wisdom*. Basic Books.

Hall, D. E. (2004). *Subjectivity: The New Critical Idiom*. Routledge.

Hall, L. (2015). *Mindfulness: What it is, the benefits, and how it can be applied in the workplace* (HR Network Paper No. 113). Institute for Employment Studies. https://www.employment-studies.co.uk/system/files/resources/files/mp113_0.pdf

Hall, R. (2018, June 19). Wellbeing at university: Why support is a priority. *The Guardian*.

Hall, R. (2019, October 3). Teach us how to look after our mental health, say university students. *The Guardian*. https://www.theguardian.com/education/2019/oct/03/teach-us-how-to-look-after-our-mental-health-say-university-students

Halliwell, E. (2010a, January 5). Buddhism beats depression. *The Guardian*. https://www.theguardian.com/commentisfree/belief/2010/jan/05/religion-buddhism

Halliwell, E. (2010b, September 8). Mindfulness: Beyond the science. *The Guardian*.

Hamburgh, R. (2016, January 7). Can money buy happiness? *The Guardian*. https://www.theguardian.com/money/2016/jan/07/can-money-buy-happiness

Hanh, T. N. (1975). *The Miracle of Mindfulness: An Introduction to the Practice of Meditation* (M. Ho, Trans.). Beacon Press.

Happify (2022). *Happify* (1.77.0-b8d7f5359285) [English; Android]. Twill Inc.

Happinessplanner.com (2022). *The Happiness Planner®*. The Happiness Planner®. https://thehappinessplanner.com/

Harvard University (2020). *Managing Fears and Anxiety around the Coronavirus (COVID-19)*. Harvard University Health Services. https://www.harvard.edu/coronavirus/wp-content/uploads/sites/5/2021/02/coronavirus_HUHS_managing_fears_A25.pdf

Haslam, N. (2016). Concept creep: Psychology's expanding concepts of harm and pathology. *Psychological Inquiry, 27*(1), 1–17. https://doi.org/10.1080/1047840X.2016.1082418

Haslam, N., Tse, J. S. Y., & De Deyne, S. (2021). Concept creep and psychiatrization. *Frontiers in Sociology, 6*, 806147. https://doi.org/10.3389/fsoc.2021.806147

Hathaway, B. (2015, October 25). Yale and Lady Gaga host teens to talk about emotions. *YaleNews*. https://news.yale.edu/2015/10/25/yale-and-lady-gaga-host-teens-talk-about-emotions

Hawksley, R. (2014, September 28). Traffic noise? It's a pleasant sound. *The Sunday Telegraph, 17*, 19.

Hayes, D. (Ed.). (2017). Beyond the mcDonaldization of higher education *Beyond McDonaldization: Visions of Higher Education* (1st edition, pp. 1–18). Routledge.

Hearing, A. (2016, April 2). Universities need to do more to tackle mental health issues among students, survey finds. *Independent.Co.Uk*.

Heartfield, J. (2006). *The 'Death of the Subject' Explained*. Sheffield Hallam University Press.

Hedges, C. (2009). *The End of Literacy and the Triumph of Spectacle*. Nation Books.

Hegel, G. W. F. (1988). *Lectures on the Philosophy of Religion: One Volume Edition*. University of California Press.

Hendriks, T., Warren, M. A., Schotanus-Dijkstra, M., Hassankhan, A., Graafsma, T., Bohlmeijer, E., & de Jong, J. (2018). How WEIRD are positive psychology interventions? A bibliometric analysis of randomized controlled trials on the science of well-being. *The Journal of Positive Psychology*, 1–13.

Hennum, N. (2014). Developing child-centered social policies: When professionalism takes over. *Social Sciences*, *3*(3), 441–59.

Heritage, R. (2017, August 30). What students need to know about university and mental health. *The Independent*.

Herodotus. (2013). *The Histories* (G. Rawlinson, Trans.). Roman Roads Media. https://files.romanroadsstatic.com/materials/herodotus.pdf

Herridge, C. (2021, November 9). Anonymous app offers support to veterans suffering with mental health. *CBS News*. https://www.cbsnews.com/news/sound-off-app-veterans-mental-health/

Hewitt, J. P. (1998). *The Myth of Self-Esteem: Finding Happiness and Solving Problems in America*. St Martin's Press.

Hilgartner, S., & Bosk, C. L. (1988). The rise and fall of social problems: A public arenas model. *American Journal of Sociology*, *94*(1), 53–78.

Hill, A. (2021, July 15). Young mental health referrals double in England after lockdowns. *The Guardian*. http://www.theguardian.com/society/2021/jul/15/young-mental-health-referrals-double-in-england-after-lockdowns

Holden, J. P. (2021, July 5). Young's job worries due to mental health. *The Herald*, 5.

Horwitz, A. V. (2013). *Anxiety: A Short History*. JHU Press.

Horwitz, A. V., & Wakefield, J. C. (2007). *The Loss of Sadness: How Psychiatry Transformed Normal Sorrow into Depressive Disorder*. Oxford University Press.

Horwitz, A. V., Wakefield, D., Jerome C., & Wakefield, J. C. (2012). *All We Have to Fear: Psychiatry's Transformation of Natural Anxieties into Mental Disorders*. Oxford University Press USA - OSO. http://ebookcentral.proquest.com/lib/swansea-ebooks/detail.action?docID=916045

House of Being (2022). *Being: My mental health friend* (2.0.4) [Android].

House, R., & Loewenthal, D. (2018). *Childhood, Well-Being and a Therapeutic Ethos* (1st edition). Routledge.

Howe, S. (2018, January 22). We must act now to secure future of the NHS. *The Western Mail*, 28–9.

Howse, C. (2013, July 2). Money buys happiness? I wouldn't bank on it. *The Telegraph*, 24.

Hromek, R., & Roffey, S. (2009). Promoting social and emotional learning with games: 'It's fun and we learn things'. *Simulation & Gaming*, *40*(5), 626–44. https://doi.org/10.1177/1046878109333793

Huffington, A. (2013, March 18). *Mindfulness, Meditation, Wellness and Their Connection to Corporate America's Bottom Line*. HuffPost. https://www.huffpost.com/entry/corporate-wellness_b_2903222

Huffington, A. (2014). *Thrive: The Third Metric to Redefining Success and Creating a Life of Well-Being, Wisdom, and Wonder*. Harmony Books.

HuffPost UK. (2022). *Ed Pinkney | HuffPost*. HuffPost UK. https://www.huffingtonpost.co.uk/author/ed-pinkney

Hughes, G., & Spanner, L. (2019). *The University Mental Health Charter* (p. 92). Student Minds.

Humphrey, N., Lendrum, A., Wigelsworth, M., & Greenberg, M. (2016). Editorial introduction. *Cambridge Journal of Education, 46*(3), 271–5. https://doi.org/10.1080/0305764X.2016.1195947

Humphrey, N., Lendrum, A., Wigelsworth, M., & School of Education, U. of M. (2010). *Social and Emotional aspects of Learning (SEAL) Programme in Secondary Schools: National Evaluation*. Department for Education.

Hurst, G. (2017, April 9). More freshers have mental health woes. *The Times*.

Hyland, T. (2017). McDonaldizing spirituality: Mindfulness, education, and consumerism. *Journal of Transformative Education, 15*(4), 334–56. https://doi.org/10.1177/1541344617696972

ItsKoko.com. (2016, April 27). *About*. Koko. https://web.archive.org/web/20160427230558/http://itskoko.com/about

Jackson, H. J., & Haslam, N. (2022). Ill-defined: Concepts of mental health and illness are becoming broader, looser, and more benign. *Australasian Psychiatry*, 10398562221077898. https://doi.org/10.1177/10398562221077898

Jackson, S. W. (2001). PRESIDENTIAL ADDRESS: The wounded healer. *Bulletin of the History of Medicine, 75*(1), 1–36.

Jacobs, E. (2021, August 12). BetterUp rides the mental health tech boom. *Financial Times*.

Jeffries, S. (2002, March 12). I giggle, therefore I am. *The Guardian*. https://www.theguardian.com/education/2002/mar/12/schools.uk

Jeffries, S. (2008, July 19). Will this man make you happy? *The Guardian*, 12.

Jenkin, M. (2014, February 14). Mind over cancer: Can meditation aid recovery? *The Guardian*.

Jones, M. (2014, October 6). How cambridge university almost killed me. *The Guardian*. https://www.theguardian.com/education/2014/oct/06/cambridge-university-student-depression-eating-disorders

Jupp, E., Pykett, J., & Smith, F. (Eds.). (2017). *Emotional States: Sites and Spaces of Affective Governance*. Routledge, Taylor & Francis Group.

Kabat-Zinn, J. (1982). An outpatient program in behavioral medicine for chronic pain patients based on the practice of mindfulness medicine: Theoretical considerations and preliminary results. *General Hospital Psychiatry, 4*, 33–47.

Kabat-Zinn, J. (2003). Mindfulness-based interventions in context: Past, present, and future. *Clinical Psychology: Science and Practice, 10*(2), 144–56. https://doi.org/10.1093/clipsy.bpg016

Kabat-Zinn, J. (2005). *Full Catastrophe Living: Using the Wisdom of Your Body and Mind to Face Stress Pain and Illness*. Bantam Dell.

Kabat-Zinn, J. (2011). Some reflections on the origins of MBSR, skillful means, and the trouble with maps. *Contemporary Buddhism, 12*(1), 281–306. https://doi.org/10.1080/14639947.2011.564844

Kay, J., & Schwartz, V. (2011). *Mental Health Care in the College Community*. John Wiley & Sons.

Kehily, M. J. (2010). Childhood in crisis? Tracing the contours of 'crisis' and its impact upon contemporary parenting practices. *Media, Culture & Society, 32*(2), 171–85. https://doi.org/10.1177/0163443709355605

Kerr, H. (2013, May). *Mental Distress Survey Overview*. https://docplayer. net/28281501-Mental-distress-survey-overview-prepared-by-helen-kerr-research-officer.html

Kidd, P. (2017, October 18). Zen-like MPs find peace in the Westminster bubbles. *The Times*.

Kim, H., H. (2018, January 29). *The Meditation Industry*. Sage Business Researcher. http://businessresearcher.sagepub.com/. doi: 10.1177/237455680404.n1

Kingdon, J. W. (2003). *Agendas, Alternatives, and Public Policies*. Longman.

Kirby, J. (2010, March 22). Can't buy happiness. *The Sunday Times*, 9.

Kirby, J. (2022, July 12). Mindfulness in secondary schools 'fails to prevent mental health problems'. *The Independent*.

Kitayama, S., & Cohen, D. (Eds.). (2007). *Handbook of Cultural Psychology*. Guilford Press.

Kleeman, J. (2004, October 6). Trendspotting: 20 minutes to eat two raisins. *The Guardian*.

Knapton, S. (2017, June 8). Loneliness is deadlier than obesity, study suggests. *The Telegraph*. https://www.telegraph.co.uk/science/2017/08/06/loneliness-deadlier-obesity-study-suggests/

Knowles, D. (2002). *Routledge Philosophy GuideBook to Hegel and the Philosophy of Right*. Taylor & Francis Group. http://ebookcentral.proquest.com/lib/swansea-ebooks/detail.action?docID=180103

Kokocares.org. (2022, August 23). Koko: Emotional support tools for online communities & social platforms. *KokoCares*. https://www.kokocares.org/

Kornfield, J. (1979). Intensive insight meditation: A phenomenological study. *The Journal of Transpersonal Psychology, 11*(1), 41.

Kozma, G. (2010, December 13). A suitable case for treatment. *The Times*.

Kristjánsson, K. (2012). Positive psychology and positive education: Old wine in new bottles? *Educational Psychologist, 47*(2), 86–105. https://doi.org/10.1080/00461520.2011.610678

Kucinskas, J. (2018). *The Mindful Elite: Mobilizing from the Inside Out*. Oxford University Press.

Kucinskas, J. (2021). The transmission of spirituality in broader landscapes of power. In B. Steensland, J. Kucinskas, & A. Sun (Eds.), *Situating Spirituality: Context, Practice, and Power* (pp. 314–34). Oxford University Press.

Lambert, V. (2013, August 12). Lessons from the fast lane. *The Daily Telegraph*.

Landa, I. (2009). *The apprentice's sorcerer: Liberal Tradition and Fascism*. Brill.

Langer, A. I., & Gruber, J. B. (2021). Political agenda setting in the hybrid media system: Why legacy media still matter a great deal. *The International Journal of Press/Politics, 26*(2), 313–40. https://doi.org/10.1177/1940161220925023

Lantin, B. (2005, September 5). Carefree image, but plenty to be anxious about. *Daily Telegraph*.

Lasch, C. (1979). *The Culture of Narcissism: American Life in an Age of Diminishing Expectations*. Abacus.

Laurance, J. (2005, May 9). Unhappiness is 'Britain's worst social problem'. *The Independent*, 5.

Layard, R. (2003, September 3). Don't worry, be happy (and pay your taxes). *The Independent on Sunday*, 26.

Layard, R. (2005). *Happiness: Lessons from a New Science*. Penguin.

Le Fanu, J. (2001, August 26). Joyfulness may be purely a matter of hormones. *The Sunday Telegraph*, 4.

LeBel, T. P., Richie, M., & Maruna, S. (2015). Helping others as a response to reconcile a criminal past: The Role of the Wounded Healer in Prisoner Reentry Programs. *Criminal Justice and Behavior*, *42*(1), 108–20. https://doi.org/10.1177/0093854814550029

Lee, E. (2003). *Abortion, Motherhood, and Mental Health: Medicalizing Reproduction in the United States and Great Britain*. Transaction Publishers.

Lee, E. (2017). Constructing abortion as a social problem: 'Sex selection' and the British abortion debate. *Feminism & Psychology*, *27*(1), 15–33. https://doi.org/10.1177/0959353516678010

Lee, E., Bristow, J., Faircloth, C., & Macvarish, J. (2014). *Parenting Culture Studies*. Palgrave Macmillan.

Leggett, W. (2022). Can Mindfulness really change the world? The political character of meditative practices. *Critical Policy Studies*, *16*(3), 261–78. https://doi.org/10.1080/19460171.2021.1932541

Lemmings, D., & Brooks, A. (Eds.). (2014). *Emotions and Social Change: Historical and Sociological Perspectives*. Routledge.

Leslie, E. (2004). *Hollywood Flatlands: Animation, Critical Theory and the Avant-Garde*. Verso.

Lewis, C. (2019). Love Socialism Hate Brexit: We're going on tour and want to meet you. *LabourList*. https://labourlist.org/2019/04/love-socialism-hate-brexit-were-going-on-tour-and-want-to-meet-you/

Lightfoot, L. (2018). Universities outsource mental health services despite soaring demand; Critics say shifting counselling resources into 'wellbeing' is perverse and dangerous when depression and suicide among students are at worrying levels. *The Guardian*. https://advance.lexis.com/document/?pdmfid=1519360&crid=119a2f8d-cd15-4acb-b322-dacf9756dd23&pddocfullpath=%2Fshared%2Fdocument%2Fnews%2Furn%3AcontentItem%3A5STM-F031-JCJY-G1K6-00000-00&pdcontentcomponentid=138620&pdteaserkey=sr0&pditab=allpods&ecomp=rbzyk&earg=sr0&prid=d090cced-ac6a-42e1-8914-63b807aafbef

Lister, S. (2010, December 1). School teaches boys to meditate to reduce stress. *The Times*. https://www.thetimes.co.uk/article/school-teaches-boys-to-meditate-to-reduce-stress-3hggms0rwpk

Little, W. (2018, January 31). Mindfulness courses at work? This should have us all in a rage. *The Guardian*.

Lloyd, G. E. R. (1968). *Aristotle: The Growth and Structure of His Thought*. Cambridge University Press.

Lloyds Banking Group. (2022). *Mental Health UK partnership*. https://www.lloydsbankinggroup.com/who-we-are/responsible-business/mental-health-uk-partnership.html

Loader, G. (2021, July 15). Mind Cymru: Covid mental health 'crisis' for young people. *BBC News*. https://www.bbc.com/news/uk-wales-57854193

Locke, J. (2003). *Two Treatises on Government and A Letter Concerning Toleration* (I. Shapiro, Ed.). Yale University Press.

Loseke, D. R. (2003). *Thinking about Social Problems* (2nd edition). Aldine De Gruyter.

Loseke, D. R. (2009). Examining emotion as discourse: Emotion codes and presidential speeches justifying war. *The Sociological Quarterly, 50*(3), 497–524. https://doi.org/10.1111/j.1533-8525.2009.01150.x

Löwy, M., & Sayre, R. (2002). *Romanticism against the Tide of Modernity*. Duke University Press.

Lupton, D. (1995). The imperative of health: Public health and the regulated body. *The Imperative of Health*, 1–192.

Lupton, D. (2012). *Medicine as Culture: Illness, Disease, and the Body* (3rd edition). SAGE.

Lutz, C. A., & Abu-Lughod, L. (Eds.). (1990). *Language and the Politics of Emotion*. Cambridge University Press.

Lydall, R. (2017, January 26). University to observe students' Facebook and Twitter posts in mental health drive. *London Evening Standard*, 7.

Lyons, M. (2021, September 12). *How mental health in college students is changing*. https://www.betterup.com/blog/mental-health-in-college-students

Lyttelton, A. (1973). Introduction. In *Italian Fascisms: Readings in Fascist, Racist and Elitist Ideology* (pp. 11–36). Jonathan Cape Ltd.

MacLeod, M. (2005, May 25). Is happiness a con? *The Independent*, 39.

Macvarish, J., & Lee, E. (2019). Constructions of parents in adverse childhood experiences discourse. *Social Policy and Society, 18*(3), 467–77. https://doi.org/10.1017/S1474746419000083

Macvarish, J., Lee, E., & Lowe, P. (2014). The 'First Three Years' movement and the infant brain: A review of critiques: The 'First Three Years': Review of critiques. *Sociology Compass, 8*(6), 792–804. https://doi.org/10.1111/soc4.12183

Malik, K. (1996). *The Meaning of Race*. Macmillan.

Malthus, T. (2013). *An Essay on the Principle of Population*. Digireads.com Publishing.

Manthorpe, J., & Stanley, N. (2002). *Students Mental Health Needs Problems and Responses*. Jessica Kinglsey Publishers.

MAPPG (2015). *Mindful Nation UK: Report of the mindfulness all-party parliamentary group*. https://web.archive.org/web/20151106114628/http://themindfulnessinitiative.org.uk/images/reports/Mindfulness-APPG-Report_Mindful-Nation-UK_Oct2015.pdf

Marks, V. (2015, March 14). Present, sir: Benefits of a mindful classroom. *The Daily Telegraph*.

Marsh, S. (2009, July 15). Self-help or self-delusion. *The Times, 34*, 35.

Marsh, S. (2017a, February 9). Suicide is at record level among students at UK universities, study finds. *The Guardian*.

Marsh, S. (2017b, May 23). Number of university dropouts due to mental health problems trebles. *The Guardian*.

Marshall, C. (2013, May 21). One in eight students considers suicide'. *Scotland on Sunday*.

Marx, K. (1875). Critique of the gotha programme, 1875. In F. Engels (Trans.), *The Complete Works of Karl Marx* (pp. 4076–108). Kindle.

Marx, K. (1969). *Theories of Surplus Value*. Progress Publishers.

Marx, K. (1973). *Grundrisse* (M. Nicolaus, Trans.). Penguin Books.

Marx, K. (1976). *Capital: A Critique of Political Economy Volume One* (B. Fowkes, Trans.). Penguin Books.

Marx, K. (1994). A contribution to the critique of hegel's philosophy of right: Introduction. In J. O'Malley & R. A. Davis (Eds.), *Marx: Early Political Writings* (pp. 57–70). Cambridge University Press.

Marx, K. (2008). *The 18th Brumaire of Louis Bonaparte*. Wildside Press LLC.

Marx, K. (2019). *The Political Writings*. Verso.

Marx, K., & Engels, F. (1998a). *The German Ideology*. Prometheus Books.

Marx, K., & Engels, F. (1998b). *The German Ideology*. Prometheus Books.

Marx, K., & Engels, F. (2009). *The Economic and Philosophic Manuscripts of 1844 and the Communist Manifesto*. Prometheus Books.

Matthews, V. (2014, September 13). The right attitude for a head start. *The Daily Telegraph*, 13.

Matthiesen, N. (2018). Control and responsibility: Taking a closer look at the work of ensuring well-being in neoliberal schools. *Integrative Psychological and Behavioral Science, 52*(3), 438–48. https://doi.org/10.1007/s12124-018-9418-x

Maudsley Learning (2022). Student mental health skills for academics. Maudsley Learning. https://maudsleylearning.com/courses/student-mental-health-skills-for-academics-and-tutors/

Mayhew, L. (2004, April 5). The eating cure: Forget drugs. Diet is the way forward in treating mental illness, says Lucy Mayhew. *The Guardian*, 10.

Mazlish, B. (1972). The tragic farce of marx, hegel, and engels: A note. *History and Theory, 11*(3), 335. https://doi.org/10.2307/2504684

McAteer, M. (1987, April 7). Buddhist forecast gets a serene start. *The Toronto Star*, M13.

McCardle, L. (2014, September 16). New minister on message. *Children Now*.

McCarthy, J., Smith, J., & Zald, M. (1996). Accessing public, media, electoral, and governmental agendas. In D. McAdam, J. McCarthy, & M. Zald (Eds.), *Comparative Perspectives on Social Movements: Political Opportunities*. (pp. 291–311). Cambridge University Press.

McCombs, M., & Valenzuela, S. (2020). *Setting the Agenda: Mass Media and Public Opinion*. Polity Press.

McCrae, N. (2021, January 14). What happened to the mental health crisis among younger people? *Areo*. https://areomagazine.com/2021/01/14/what-happened-to-the-mental-health-crisis-among-younger-people/

McLellan, D. (1969). *The young hegelians and Karl Marx*. Macmillan.

McMahon, B. (2014, January 11). How mindfulness can help your children. *The Times*. https://www.thetimes.co.uk/article/how-mindfulness-can-help-your-children-vk2fw0n8p57

McTiernan, A. (1994, January 18). Giving children the best possible start. *Irish Times*, 10. Nexis.

Mecca, A., Smelser, N. J., & Vasconcellos, J. (1989). *The Social Importance of Self-Esteem*. University of California Press.

Meikle, J. (1993, August 25). Students to get 'beat the blues' advice. *The Guardian*, 5.

Mental Wealth. (2008). Mental Wealth. *Mental Wealth*. https://web.archive.org/web/20080203095130/http://www.mentalwealth.org.uk:80/.

Mental Wealth UK (2011). *Mental Wealth UK | Promoting Positive Wellbeing on Campuses and Beyond*. Mental Wealth UK. https://web.archive.org/web/20111001124518/http://www.mentalwealthuk.com/

Mentinis, M. (2013). The entrepreneurial ethic and the spirit of psychotherapy: Depoliticisation, atomisation and social selection in the therapeutic culture of the 'crisis'. *European Journal of Psychotherapy & Counselling, 15*(4), 361–74.

Million, D. (2013). *Therapeutic Nations: Healing in an Age of Indigenous Human Rights*. University of Arizona Press.

Mills, C. (2014). *Decolonizing Global Mental Health*. Routledge.

Mills, C. W. (2000). *The Sociological Imagination*. Oxford University Press.

MindMapperUK. (2022). Youth mental health. *MindMapper UK*. https://www.mindmapperuk.com

MindUP. (2022). Our mission. *MindUP*. https://mindup.org/our-mission/

Mirowski, P. (2003). Review of Vilfredo Pareto and the Birth of Modern Microeconomics [Review of *Review of Vilfredo Pareto and the Birth of Modern Microeconomics*, by L. Bruni]. *History of Economic Ideas, 11*(3), 120–2.

Mooney, B. (2006, July 8). Let joy be unconfined. *The Times*.

Morris, R. (2022, August 23). Origin story of Kokobot. *KokoCares*. https://www.kokocares.org/origin-story

Moyers, B. (1993). *Healing and the Mind*. Doubleday.

Murphy, C. (2019, November 3). Time to put your mind at ease. *The Sunday Times*, 5.

Myers, K. (2012). Marking time: Some methodological and historical perspectives on the 'crisis of childhood'. *Research Papers in Education, 27*(4), 409–22. https://doi.org/10.1080/02671522.2012.690237

MYRIAD Project. (2022). *Publications*. MYRIAD: My resilience in adolescence. https://myriadproject.org/engagement-activities/the-do-nothing-campaign/

Nairn, R. G. (2007). Media portrayals of mental illness, or is it madness? A review. *Australian Psychologist, 42*(2), 138–46. https://doi.org/10.1080/00050060701280623

NAMI [@NAMICommunicate]. (2020). It's okay to feel sad, angry, or scared because of the #COVID19 outbreak. However you feel is valid. https://twitter.com/NAMICommunicate/status/1238178955728953346?s=20&t=d0FIY4Dh-EvOe6UrQhXF_Q

National Institute for Clinical Excellence (2004). *Depression: Management of depression in primary and secondary care* (Clinical Guideline 23; p. 63). National Institute for Clinical Excellence. https://web.archive.org/web/20060513205559/http://www.nice.org.uk/pdf/CG023NICEguideline.pdf

National Union of Students. (2015). *Mental Health Poll*. http://appg-students.org.uk/wp-content/uploads/2016/03/Mental-Health-Poll-November-15-Summary.pdf

Nehring, D., Alvarado, E., Hendriks, E., C., & Kerrigan, D. (2016). *Transnational Popular Psychology and the Global Self-Help Industry*. Palgrave Macmillan.

Nehring, D., & Frawley, A. (2020a). Mindfulness and the 'psychological imagination'. *Sociology of Health & Illness, 42*(5), 1184–201.

Nehring, D., & Frawley, A. (2020b). Mindfulness as a self-help fad. *The Routledge International Handbook of Global Therapeutic Cultures*.

Nehring, D., Madsen, O. J., Cabanas, E., & Kerrigan, D. (2020). *The Routledge International Handbook of Global Therapeutic Cultures*. Routledge.

Nelson, B. J. (1984). *Making an Issue of Child Abuse: Political Agenda Setting for Social Problems*. University of Chicago Press.

Nesbitt, J. (1993, March 8). A Valium Nation? *St. Louis Post-Dispatch*, E1. Nexis.

New Zealand Government. (2019, July 5). *The Wellbeing Budget 2019*. Beehive. Govt.Nz. https://www.beehive.govt.nz/feature/wellbeing-budget-2019

Newman, N. (2011). *Mainstream Media and the Distribution of News in the Age of Social Discovery* (p. 58). Reuters Institute for the Study of Journalism.

Nirell, L. (2014, August 5). How successful marketing leaders (Like Arianna Huffington) Unplug. *The Huffington Post*.

Nolan, J. L. (1998). *The Therapeutic State: Justifying Government at Century's End*. NYU Press.

Northen, S. (2012, January 17). Whatever happened to happiness? *The Guardian*, 32.

Norton, S. (2015, March 14). Mindfulness Once the preserve of Buddhists, mindfulness is now big business in the City. *Independent Magazine*.

NUS Connect (2014, November 7). *Partnership with Student Minds launched at Zone Conference @ NUS Connect*. NUS Connect. https://www.nusconnect. org.uk/articles/partnership-with-student-minds-launched-at-zone-conference–2

Office for Students (2019). *Insight Bulletin 5 Mental Health – Are all students being properly supported?* (Insight 5). Office for Students. https://www. officeforstudents.org.uk/media/b3e6669e-5337-4caa-9553-049b3e8e7803/ insight-brief-mental-health-are-all-students-being-properly-supported.pdf

Omar, S. M. (2012). Rethinking development from a postcolonial perspective. *Journal of Conflictology, 3*(1). https://doi.org/10.7238/joc.v3i1.1296

ONS. (2016). *Student suicides in those aged 18 years and above, by sex and usual place of residence indicator, deaths registered in England and Wales between 2001 and 2015*. https://www.ons.gov.uk/ peoplepopulationandcommunity/birthsdeathsandmarriages/deaths/adhocs/00 5991studentsuicidesinthoseaged18yearsandabovebysexand usualplaceofresidenceindicatordeathsregisteredinenglandandwalesbetween 2001and2015

ONS. (2018, June 25). *Estimating Suicide among Higher Education Students, England and Wales: Experimental Statistics*. https://www.ons.gov.uk/ peoplepopulationandcommunity/birthsdeathsandmarriages/deaths/articles/ estimatingsuicideamonghighereducationstudentsenglandandwales experimentalstatistics/2018-06-25

Orr, D. (2017, April 18). Talking about feelings does not make you a snowflake. *The Guardian*. https://advance.lexis.com/document/?pdmfid=1519360&c rid=caae2a29-e3eb-4655-b6a0-18a5bd599f45&pddocfullpath=%2Fshare d%2Fdocument%2Fnews%2Furn%3AcontentItem%3A5NBN-1911-F021- -62M2-00000-00&pdcontentcomponentid=138620&pdteaserkey=sr0&p ditab=allpods&ecomp=pbzyk&earg=sr0&prid=6ae7341f-136f-40c3-8d8a- cbdf9b7f692d

Owen, J. (2015, May 10). Let GPs offer 'mindfulness' say experts. *The Independent on Sunday*.

Pagden, A. (2013). *The Enlightenment: And Why it Still Matters*. Oxford University Press.

Page, L. (2014, April 4). Students: Where to get help for your mental health. *The Guardian*.

Paris, J. (2015). *Overdiagnosis in Psychiatry: How Modern Psychiatry Lost its Way While Creating a Diagnosis for Almost All of Life's Misfortunes.* Oxford University Press.

Partington, R., & correspondent, R. P. E. (2021, July 4). Young people fear poor mental health will affect post-Covid job prospects. *The Guardian.* https://www.theguardian.com/society/2021/jul/05/young-people-fear-poor-mental-health-will-affect-post-covid-job-prospects

Passmore, J. A. (2000). *The Perfectibility of Man* (2nd edition). Liberty Fund.

Passmore, J. (2019). Mindfulness in organizations (part 1): A critical literature review. *Industrial and Commercial Training, 51*(2), 104–13. https://doi.org/10.1108/ICT-07-2018-0063

Paton, S. (1911, July 10). Vocational training. *The New York Times,* 12.

Paton, S. (1912, October 19). Psychopathic hospitals. *The New York Times.*

Paton, S. (1915, September 7). The menace of insanity at large. *The New York Times.*

Pells, R. (2019, July 9). Number of university students claiming special circumstances for mental health problems 'Soars'. *The Independent.* https://www.independent.co.uk/news/education/education-news/number-of-university-students-mental-health-problems-illness-claiming-special-circumstances-cambridge-newcastle-sheffield-a7831791.html

Pender, J. (2002). Empowering the poorest? The world bank and the 'Voices of the Poor'. In *Rethinking Human Rights* (pp. 97–114). Springer.

Pérez-Álvarez, M. (2012). Positive psychology: Sympathetic magic. *Papeles Del Psicólogo, 33*(3), 183–201.

Perez-Alvarez, M. (2013). Positive psychology and its friends: Revealed. *Papeles del Psicólogo, 34*(3): 208–26.

Peyrot, M. (1984). Cycles of social problem development: The case of drug abuse. *The Sociological Quarterly, 25*(1), 83–95. https://doi.org/10.1111/j.1533-8525.1984.tb02240.x

Piper, R., & Emmanuel, T. (2019). *Co-producing Mental Health Strategies with Students: A Guide for the Higher Education Sector* (p. 99). Student Minds.

President and Fellows of Harvard College (2022). *Mindfulness for Students.* Harvard University Health Services. https://wellness.huhs.harvard.edu/mindfulness-for-students

Prime Minister's Office (2018, January 17). Press release: PM commits to government-wide drive to tackle loneliness. GOV.UK. https://www.gov.uk/government/news/pm-commits-to-government-wide-drive-to-tackle-loneliness

Pugh, R. (2016, June 14). What can mindfulness teach the police force? *The Guardian.*

Pupavac, V. (2004a). War on the couch: The emotionology of the new international security paradigm. *European Journal of Social Theory, 7*(2), 149–70. https://doi.org/10.1177/1368431004041749

Pupavac, V. (2004b). International therapeutic peace and justice in bosnia. *Social & Legal Studies, 13*(3), 377–401. https://doi.org/10.1177/0964663904045000

Pupavac, V. (2006). *Humanitarian Politics and the Rise of International Disaster Psychology.* Unpublished. https://doi.org/10.13140/2.1.1715.4883

Pupavac, V. (2008). Changing concepts of international health. *A Sociology of Health.* London: Sage, 173–90.

Pupavac, V. (2010a). From materialism to non-materialism in international development: Revisiting rostow's stages of growth and schumacher's small is beautiful. In J. S. Sörensen (Ed.), *Challenging the Aid Paradigm: Western Currents and Asian Alternatives* (pp. 47–77). Palgrave Macmillan UK. https://doi.org/10.1057/9780230277281_3

Pupavac, V. (2010b). The consumerism-development-security nexus. *Security Dialogue*, *41*(6), 691–713.

Purser, R. E. (2015). Clearing the muddled path of traditional and contemporary mindfulness: A response to monteiro, musten, and compson. *Mindfulness*, *6*(1), 23–45. https://doi.org/10.1007/s12671-014-0373-4

Purser, R. E. (2018). Critical perspectives on corporate mindfulness. In *Journal of Management, Spirituality & Religion* (Vol. 15, Issue 2, pp. 105–8). Taylor & Francis.

Purser, R. E. (2019). *McMindfulness: How Mindfulness Became the New Capitalist Spirituality*. Repeater.

Purser, R. E. (2020). Why should Buddhist Mindfulness get a Pass? *Religious Studies Review*, *46*(2), 165–7.

Purser, R., E., Forbes, D., & Burke, A. (2016). *Handbook of Mindfulness: Culture, Context, and Social Engagement*. Springer Berlin Heidelberg.

Pye, M. (2004). *Skilful Means: A Concept in Mahayana Buddhism*. Routledge.

Quelch, J. A., & Knoop, C.-I. (2018). *Compassionate Management of Mental Health in the Modern Workplace*. Springer.

Quimby, P. P. (1921). *The Quimby Manuscripts* (H. W. Dresser, Ed.; Ebook). Pantianos Classics.

Qureshi, H. (2009, May 2). Food for thought. *The Guardian*. https://www.theguardian.com/education/2009/may/02/ideal-exam-diet

Rana, R., Smith, E., & Walking, J. (1999). *Degrees of Disturbance: The New Agenda*. Association for University and College Counselling.

Ratcliffe, R. (2013, May 20). Students stay silent about mental health problems, survey shows. *The Guardian*. https://www.theguardian.com/education/2013/may/20/students-stay-silent-about-mental-health-problems

Reid, M. (2008, January 8). 'Mr Happy' gives lesson from the bright side. *The Times*.

Reilly, N. (2016, March 13). A fad too far? Rise of the mindfulness kids. *The Sunday Telegraph*.

Richards, H. (2005, October 11). Head start to happiness. *The Guardian*, 12.

Richtel, M. (2019, April 5). The Latest in Military Strategy: Mindfulness. *The New York Times*.

Rigby, H. (2018, December 31). Seeking inner peace in a violent, unequal world is not a selfish act. *The Guardian*. https://www.theguardian.com/commentisfree/2018/dec/31/inner-peace-twitter-yoga-retreat

Robertson, I. (1994, November 15). A breath of life and hope. *The Times*.

Rodger, J. (2018, June 25). Nearly 100 university students killed themselves last year—As numbers seeking counselling soar. *Birmingham Mail*.

Rose, N. (1999). *Governing the Soul: The Shaping of the Private Self* (2nd edition., [reprint]). Free Association Books.

Rose, N. (2020). Social suffering. *RSA Journal*, *166* (2(5582)), 30–3.

Rosenthal, A. M. (1956, June 5). The buddhist way. *New York Times*, 221.

Royal College of Psychiatrists (2003). *The Mental Health of Students in Higher Education* (No. CR112). Royal College of Psychiatrists. https://web.archive.org/web/20040731044804/http://www.rcpsych.ac.uk/publications/cr/council/cr112.pdf

Royal College of Psychiatrists. (2011). *Mental Health of Students in Higher Education: College Report CR166 Royal College of Psychiatrists* (No. CR166). https://www.rcpsych.ac.uk/docs/default-source/improving-care/better-mh-policy/college-reports/college-report-cr166.pdf?sfvrsn=d5fa2c24_2

Royal College of Psychiatrists. (2021, October 28). *The Climate Crisis will Take a far Greater Toll on Our Mental Health if COP26 Fails to Deliver, Says RCPsych.* https://www.rcpsych.ac.uk/news-and-features/latest-news/detail/2021/10/28/the-climate-crisis-will-take-a-far-greater-toll-on-our-mental-health-if-cop26-fails-to-deliver-says-rcpsych

Rubington, E., & Weinberg, M. (2011). *The Study of Social Problems: Seven Perspectives.* OUP USA.

Rutter, T. (2015, February 3). Postgrad, term two: How to get through the dark days. *The Guardian.* https://advance.lexis.com/document/?pdmfid=1519360&crid=b9ba62b5-61da-4e7d-9dcf-7fa4e461a068&pddocfullpath=%2Fshared%2Fdocument%2Fnews%2Furn%3AcontentItem%3A5F6Y-95R1-F021-643W-00000-00&pdcontentcomponentid=138620&pdteaserkey=sr0&pditab=allpods&ecomp=rbzyk&earg=sr0&prid=0d20a394-d0ae-467e-acc7-f002f06c89f5

Salvatore, S., O'Connor, E., Hinman, A., & Firfer, H. (Directors). (1999, June 12). Beating stress with mindfulness. In *CNN Your Health.* CNN; Nexis.

Sanderson, D. (2015, October 9). Universities 'failing on mental health'. *The Times.*

Sanghera, S. (2014, August 15). 'Mindfulness' has gone mainstream, but in the wrong context it's creepy. *The Times,* 41.

Sarner, M. (2017, October 28). Campus confidential: The counsellors on the frontline of the student mental health crisis. *The Guardian.*

Sauerborn, E. (2022). The politicisation of secular mindfulness – Extinction Rebellion's emotive protest practices. *European Journal of Cultural and Political Sociology,* 1–24. https://doi.org/10.1080/23254823.2022.2086596

Sayre, R., & Löwy, M. (2005). Romanticism and capitalism. In M. Ferber (Ed.), *A Companion to European Romanticism* (pp. 433–49). Blackwell.

Scherer, B., & Waistell, J. (2018). Incorporating mindfulness: Questioning capitalism. *Journal of Management, Spirituality & Religion, 15*(2), 123–40.

Schrank, B., Brownell, T., Tylee, A., & Slade, M. (2014). *Positive Psychology: An Approach to Supporting Recovery in Mental Illness. 24,* 10.

Schroeder, J. W. (2004). *Skillful Means: The Heart of Buddhist Compassion.* Motilal Banarsidass Publ.

Science and Technology Committee. (2018). *Evidence-based early years intervention.* House of Commons. https://publications.parliament.uk/pa/cm201719/cmselect/cmsctech/506/50605.htm

Screpanti, E. (2007). *Libertarian Communism: Marx, Engels and the Political Economy of Freedom.* Palgrave Macmillan.

Security Leak. (2018, January 5). 'We all need to be less scared of asking for help': Campus security on mental health. *The Guardian.* https://www.theguardian.com/higher-education-network/2018/jan/05/we-all-need-to-be-less-scared-of-asking-for-help-campus-security-on-mental-health

Seldon, A. (2007, June 25). It is worthwhile teaching children well-being. *Financial Times.*

Seldon, A. (2014, March 24). Breathe deep and mind how you go. *The Sunday Times.* https://www.thetimes.co.uk/article/breathe-deep-and-mind-how-you-go-wpt8psmztf6

Seligman, M. E. (1998). *Positive Psychology Network Concept Paper.* University of Pennsylvania Positive Psychology Center. https://web.archive.org/web/20141114133957/http://www.ppc.sas.upenn.edu/ppgrant.htm

Seligman, M. E. (1999). The president's address. *American Psychologist, August* (1998 Annual Report), 559–62.

Seligman, M. E. (2002). Authentic happiness: Using the new positive psychology to realize your potential for lasting fulfillment. *New York: The Free Press, 160,* 168–266.

Seligman, M. E. (2007). *The Optimistic Child: A Proven Program to Safeguard Children against Depression and Build Lifelong Resilience.* Houghton Mifflin Harcourt.

Seligman, M. E. (2011). *Flourish: A Visionary New Understanding of Happiness and Well-Being.* Free Press.

Seligman, M. E., & Csikszentmihalyi, M. (2000). Positive psychology: An introduction. *American Psychologist, 55*(1), 5–14.

Selva, J. (2017, February 13). *32 Mindfulness Trainings, (Online) Courses, Programs, Workshops & Degrees.* https://positivepsychologyprogram.com/mindfulness-training-courses-programs-workshops-degrees/

Shackle, S. (2019, September 27). 'The way universities are run is making us ill': Inside the student mental health crisis. *The Guardian.* http://www.theguardian.com/society/2019/sep/27/anxiety-mental-breakdowns-depression-uk-students

Shattock, E. H. (1958). *An experiment in mindfulness.* Rider & Company. http://archive.org/details/in.ernet.dli.2015.128318

Sherwood, H. (2015, October 28). Mindfulness at risk of being 'turned into a free market commodity'. *The Guardian.* https://www.theguardian.com/lifeandstyle/2015/oct/28/mindfulness-free-market-commodity-risk

Siegel, R. D., Germer, C. K., & Olendzki, A. (2009). Mindfulness: What is it? Where did it come from? In F. Didonna (Ed.), *The Clinical Handbook of Mindfulness* (pp. 17–36). Springer New York.

Simons, J. (2010, August 2). The happiest men in the world. *The Times,* 9.

Skenderi, S. (2016, February 5). The dangers of e-therapy. *The Vancouver Province.*

Skidelsky, W. (2011, January 2). Stars' meditation technique gains mental health experts' approval | Mental health | The Guardian. *The Guardian.* https://www.theguardian.com/society/2011/jan/02/mindfulness-meditation-meg-ryan-goldie-hawn?CMP=gu_com

Slack, B. (2012, August 14). Coping with university: Don't worry, they'll have lots of support. *The Independent.* https://www.independent.co.uk/student/into-university/clearing/coping-with-university-don-t-worry-they-ll-have-lots-of-support-8031609.html

Smellie, A. (2015, May 2). Relax, kids, this stress relief is all in the mind. *The Daily Telegraph.*

Smelser, N. J. (1989). Self-esteem and social problems: An introduction. In A. Mecca, N. J. Smelser, & J. Vasconcellos (Eds.), *The Social Importance of Self-Esteem* (pp. 1–23). University of California Press.

Smith, J. (2016, February 3). Student mental health: A new model for universities. *The Guardian.*

Smith, R. (2010). Beyond growth or beyond capitalism. *Real World Economics Review, 53,* 28–36.

Smucker, J. A., Boyd, A., & Mitchell, D. O. (2012). Floating signifier. In A. Boyd & D. O. Mitchell (Eds.), *Beautiful Trouble: A Toolbox for Revolution* (pp. 234–5). OR Books.

Snow, D. A., & Benford, R. D. (1988). Ideology, frame resonance, and participant mobilization. *International Social Movement Research, 1*(1), 197–217.

Snow, D. A., & Benford, R. D. (1992). Master frames and cycles of protest. *Frontiers in Social Movement Theory, 133*, 155.

Sonnemaker, T. (2020, January 29). *Airbnb Quietly Acquired Koko, an AI-powered Content Moderation Startup, in 2018 as It Looked to Avoid the Pitfalls Faced by Social Media Platforms around Toxic Content.* Business Insider. https://www.businessinsider.in/tech/enterprise/news/airbnb-quietly-acquired-koko-an-ai-powered-content-moderation-startup-in-2018-as-it-looked-to-avoid-the-pitfalls-faced-by-social-media-platforms-around-toxic-content/articleshow/73745088.cms

Sotirakopoulos, N. (2016). *The Rise of Lifestyle Activism: From New Left to Occupy.* Palgrave Macmillan.

Spector, M., & Kitsuse, J. I. (2017). *Constructing Social Problems.* Routledge.

Stanley, E. (2022). *MMFT® Online.* Elizabeth A. Stanley, PhD. https://elizabeth-stanley.com/courses/mmft-online/

Stearns, P. N., & Stearns, C. Z. (1985). Emotionology: Clarifying the history of emotions and emotional standards. *The American Historical Review, 90*(4), 813–36.

Steerpike. (2022, July 28). Prince Harry presiding over 'toxic boys' club,' former employees claim | The Spectator. *The Spectator.* https://www.spectator.co.uk/article/prince-harry-presiding-over-toxic-boys-club-former-employees-claim

Steinem, G. (1992). *Revolution from Within: A Book of Self-esteem.* Little, Brown and Company.

Stella. (2015, October 25). Is mindfulness bad for your health? *The Sunday Telegraph.*

Stevens, J. (2019, July 1). Why the hippy message of Glastonbury's Healing Field sounds like common sense. *The Guardian.* https://www.theguardian.com/music/2019/jul/01/why-the-hippy-message-of-glastonbury-healing-field-sounds-like-common-sense

Stinchcombe, A. L. (1965). Social structure and organizations. In J. March G. (Ed.), *Handbook of Organizations* (pp. 142–93). Routledge. https://doi.org/10.1016/S0742-3322(00)17019-6

Stogdon, C. (2018, June 16). Take control of your monsters with mindfulness. *The Daily Telegraph*, 7.

Stone, D. A. (1989). Causal stories and the formation of policy agendas. *Political Science Quarterly, 104*(2), 281–300.

Strauss Cohen, I. (2021, March 13). *Suffering With Mental Health Doesn't Make You Ungrateful.* Psychology Today. https://www.psychologytoday.com/us/blog/your-emotional-meter/202103/suffering-mental-health-doesnt-make-you-ungrateful

Street-Porter, J. (2006, May 4). Brutal buildings just breed brutal people. *The Independent*, 38.

Stress Reduction Tapes. (2022). *About Us – Mindfulness Meditation.* Guided Mindfulness Meditation. https://www.mindfulnesscds.com/pages/about-us

Student Minds. (2018). *Looking after Your Mental Wellbeing.* Student Minds. https://www.studentminds.org.uk/lookingafteryourmentalwellbeing.html

Student Minds. (2019). *Student Minds Annual Report 2018-2019*. Student Minds.

Student Minds. (2022). *What We Do*. Student Minds. https://www.studentminds. org.uk/whatwedo.html

Sugarman, J. (2007). Practical rationality and the questionable promise of positive psychology. *Journal of Humanistic Psychology, 47*(2), 175–97. https://doi. org/10.1177/0022167806297061

Summerfield, D. (2012). Afterword: Against 'global mental health'. *Transcultural Psychiatry, 49*(3–4), 519–30. https://doi.org/10.1177/1363461512454701

Sutherland, J. C. (Ed.). (1881). The hibbert lectures. *The Academy 1869-1902, 472*, 377.

Suzukamo, L. B. (1996, February 9). Mind over pain. *Saint Paul Pioneer Press*, 1A. Nexis.

Swain, H. (2016, January 26). Mindfulness: The craze sweeping through schools is now at a university near you. *The Guardian*. https://www.theguardian.com/ education/2016/jan/26/mindfulness-craze-schools-university-near-you-cambridge

Sweeting, H., Thomson, H., Wells, V., & Flowers, P. (2021). Evolution of 'whole institution' approaches to improving health in tertiary education settings: A critical scoping review. *Research Papers in Education*, 1–29. https://doi.org/10. 1080/02671522.2021.1961302

Swindells, K. (2019, May 8). Students are turning to memes for mental health support because university pressure is so bad. *The Independent*.

Teng, B. (2016, November 29). *I'm a Therapist. Here's How I Help Patients Traumatized by the Election*. Vox. https://www.vox.com/first-person/2016/11/29/13763816/trump-election-trauma-therapist

The Express (2021, July 5). 25% of young people suffer job anxieties. *The Express*, 45.

The Guardian (2014a, May 6). On our networks this week: Exploring forest schools: Unveiling the results of our mental health survey: Launch of a new global students section. *The Guardian*. https://advance.lexis.com/document/ ?pdmfid=1519360&crid=8e31140a-5562-48dd-b1cf-a377c16bd5de&pddocful lpath=%2Fshared%2Fdocument%2Fnews%2Furn%3AcontentItem%3A5C 4N-8VY1-DYRX-X00H-00000-00&pdcontentcomponentid=138620&pdteaserk ey=sr0&pditab=allpods&ecomp=rbzyk&earg=sr0&prid=b4bcd1a4-ee35-41da-b713-f9532044be03

The Guardian (2014b, October 7). *Mental Health: A University Crisis*. The Guardian. https://web.archive.org/web/20141007044242/https://www. theguardian.com/education/series/mental-health-a-university-crisis

The Guardian (2016, February 18). Mindfulness: How to live well by paying attention. *The Guardian*.

The Independent (2022, August 22). Layla Haidrani. *The Independent*. https:// www.independent.co.uk/author/layla-haidrani

The Irish Times (1996, November 26). Campus counsel too thin. *The Irish Times*. https://www.irishtimes.com/news/education/campus-counsel-too-thin-1.110143

The Mental Wealth Project (2010, April 11). *The Mental Wealth Project – Home*. The Mental Wealth Project. https://web.archive.org/web/20100411074426/ http://www.mentalwealthuk.com/

The Times (2003, September 6). Happier people are more popular, less prone to divorce, fall prey to less illness, and live longer. *The Times*.

The Times (2017, August 17). The first lesson at university is learning to look after yourself. *The Times*.

Thera, N. (1968). The power of mindfulness. *Buddhist Publication Society, 121,* 1–29.

TheTabOfficial (2016, November 29). *The Universities Spending the Least on Mental Health Counselling.* UK. https://thetab.com/uk/2016/11/29/revealed-universities-spending-least-mental-health-counselling-26717

Thomas, B., & Sahota, J. (2018, September 23). Student minds charity is pushing universities to improve their mental health services. *The Times.* https://advance.lexis.com/document/?pdmfid=1519360&crid=85fc30d9-cd68-4bcc-a8b6-c1c5cd09727b&pddocfullpath=%2Fshared%2Fdocument%2Fnews%2Furn%3AcontentItem%3A5TB3-8NH1-F021-6059-00000-00&pdcontentcompo nentid=382503&pdteaserkey=sr1&pditab=allpods&ecomp=yzynk&earg=sr1& prid=dd37f087-4f02-421b-bae3-703fd37761c1

Thomas, K. (2018, August 14). Mental health at university: Know where to find support. *The Guardian.*

Thomassen, B. (2015). Thinking with liminality: To the boundaries of an anthropological concept. In A. Horvath, B. Thomassen, & H. Wydra (Eds.), *Breaking Boundaries: Varieties of Liminality* (pp. 39–58). Berghahn Books, Incorporated.

Thomson, A. (2015, July 4). If you're a pushy parent you are guilty of a form of abuse. *The Times,* 4–5.

Thorley, C. (2017). *Not By Degrees: Improving Student Mental Health in UK's Universities* (p. 77). Institute for Public Policy Research.

Tobin, C. (2016, February 12). So you feel like dropping out of university. What are the options? *The Guardian.*

Topping, K. J., Trickey, S., & Cleghorn, P. (2019). *A Teacher's Guide to Philosophy for Children.* Routledge.

Toynbee, P. (1998, November 25). Micawber was right; money doesn't buy happiness but poverty makes you miserable. *The Guardian,* 2.

Toynbee, P. (2003, July 3). Money and happiness. *The Guardian,* 27.

Tran, H. (2013). Online agenda a new frontier setting for theory development. In T. J. Johnson (Ed.), *Agenda Setting in a 2.0 World: New Agendas in Communication* (pp. 205–29). Taylor & Francis Group. http://ebookcentral. proquest.com/lib/swansea-ebooks/detail.action?docID=1323322

Tsaliki, L., & Chronaki, D. (Eds.). (2020). *Discourses of Anxiety over Childhood and Youth across Cultures.* Palgrave Macmillan. https://doi.org/10.1007/978-3-030-46436-3

Tucker, E. (2007). *Haunted Halls: Ghostlore of American College Campuses.* University Press of Mississippi. http://ebookcentral.proquest.com/lib/swansea-ebooks/detail.action?docID=515661

Tucker, N. (2018, December 9). … have a breakdown at oxford university. *The Sunday Times, 50,* 51.

Turner, C. (2018a, June 8). Universities' main purpose is no longer learning, minister says as he calls for mental health focus. *The Telegraph.*

Turner, C. (2018b, June 29). Universities may be fuelling the mental health crisis, leading psychiatrist warns. *The Telegraph.* https://advance.lexis.com/docume nt/?pdmfid=1519360&crid=d5a202fd-bae9-4fac-bcd0-72d37af2f75d&pddocfu llpath=%2Fshared%2Fdocument%2Fnews%2Furn%3AcontentItem%3A5S

NV-MHG1-JCJY-G48R-00000-00&pdcontentcomponentid=389195&pdteaserk
ey=sr8&pditab=allpods&ecomp=tb72k&earg=sr8&prid=c4d34238-d1c6-4b19-
88b8-cd5ff3bb0c7d

Turner, V. (1967). *The Forest of Symbols: Aspects of Ndembu Ritual* (Vol. 101). Cornell University Press.

Turner, V. (1974). Liminal to liminoid, in play, flow, and ritual: An essay in comparative symbology. *Rice Institute Pamphlet-Rice University Studies*, *60*(3).

Twenge, J. M., Campbell, W. K., & Gentile, B. (2012). Increases in individualistic words and phrases in american books, 1960–2008. *PLoS ONE*, *7*(7), e40181. https://doi.org/10.1371/journal.pone.0040181

UC Berkeley. (1989, September 29). Poor self-esteem plays a role in causing social problems, University of California scientists find. *Business Wire*. Nexis.

University Mental Health Advisers Network (UMHAN). (2021). *About UMHAN*. UMHAN. https://www.umhan.com/pages/2-about-umhan

U.S. Department of Justice. (1998). *Programs in Correctional Settings: Innovative* State *and* Local Programs. Bureau of Justice Assistance, Office of Justice Programs.

Useem, B., & Zald, M. N. (1982). From pressure group to social movement: Organizational dilemmas of the effort to promote nuclear power. *Social Problems*, *30*(2), 144–56.

UUK. (2020). *Stepchange: Mentally Healthy Universities* (p. 36). https://www.universitiesuk.ac.uk/sites/default/files/field/downloads/2021-07/uuk-stepchange-mhu.pdf

Uzelac, E. (1989, March 12). The I'm-OK, You're-OK task force. *St. Louis Post-Dispatch*, 1D.

Vailes, F. (2017, September 21). Freshers' week: How tutors can help students cope. *The Guardian*. https://advance.lexis.com/document/?pdmfid=1519360&crid=3a40087b-8868-400f-ac1a-1f0bbb0dd36f&pddocfullpath=%2Fshar ed%2Fdocument%2Fnews%2Furn%3AcontentItem%3A5PHV-FVG1-F021--6338-00000-00&pdcontentcomponentid=138620&pdteaserkey=sr0&pd itab=allpods&ecomp=rbzyk&earg=sr0&prid=72d14b0a-215f-469a-b2c1-d8647332f45c

Van Dam, N. T., van Vugt, M. K., Vago, D. R., Schmalzl, L., Saron, C. D., Olendzki, A., Meissner, T., Lazar, S. W., Kerr, C. E., Gorchov, J., Fox, K. C. R., Field, B. A., Britton, W. B., Brefczynski-Lewis, J. A., & Meyer, D. E. (2018). Mind the hype: A critical evaluation and prescriptive agenda for research on mindfulness and meditation. *Perspectives on Psychological Science*, *13*(1), 36–61. https://doi.org/10.1177/1745691617709589

Vaughan, R. (2018, August 13). Mental health crisis among students 'must be top priority'. *I-Independent Print Ltd*, 6.

Vernon, P. (2014, October 19). Mindfulness: It's so very now. *The Sunday Telegraph*.

Waggoner, D., & Goldman, P. (2005). Universities as communities of fate: Institutional rhetoric and student retention policy. *Journal of Educational Administration*, *43*(1), 86–101. https://doi.org/10.1108/09578230510577317

Wahl-Jorgensen, K. (2020). An emotional turn in journalism studies? *Digital Journalism*, *8*(2), 175–94. https://doi.org/10.1080/21670811.2019.1697626

Wainwright, D. (Ed.). (2008a). *A Sociology of Health*. Sage.

Wainwright, D. (2008b). Illness behaviour and the discourse of health. In *A Sociology of Health* (pp. 76–96). Sage.

Wainwright, D., & Calnan, M. (2002). *Work Stress: The Making of a Modern Epidemic*. Open University Press.

Wakeford, J. (2017, September 7). It's time for universities to put student mental health first. *The Guardian*. https://www.theguardian.com/higher-education-network/2017/sep/07/its-time-for-universities-to-put-student-mental-health-first

Walden, C. (2016, August 17). You've got to be out of your mind to do this. *The Daily Telegraph*.

Walker, E. T. (2014). *Grassroots for Hire: Public Affairs Consultants in American Democracy*. Cambridge University Press.

Walker, R. (2018, November 25). 'It stops the scary stuff': Pupils thrive with mindfulness lessons. *The Observer*. https://www.theguardian.com/lifeandstyle/2018/nov/25/schools-deprived-areas-embrace-mindfulness

Walsh, R. N., Goleman, D., Kornfield, J., Pensa, C., & Shapiro, D. (1978). Meditation: Aspects of research and practice. *Journal of Transpersonal Psychology, 10*(2), 113–33.

Watts, R., Woolcock, N., Joiner, S., & Stannard, J. (2018, December 24). Universities spend millions but mental health crisis only grows. *The Times*.

Wax, R. (2017, January 10). Ruby Wax: 'I wanted to find a method to defuse my depression'. *The Guardian*.

Weale, S. (2018, May 10). UK universities call for joined-up mental health care for students. *The Guardian*. https://www.theguardian.com/society/2018/may/11/uk-universities-call-for-joined-up-mental-health-care-for-students

Weale, S. (2022a, April 18). Tony Blair calls for drastic increase of young people in higher education. *The Guardian*. https://www.theguardian.com/education/2022/apr/18/tony-blair-calls-for-drastic-increase-of-young-people-in-higher-education

Weale, S. (2022b, July 12). Mindfulness in schools does not improve mental health, study finds. *The Guardian*.

Weare, K. (2010). Mental health and social and emotional learning: Evidence, principles, tensions, balances. *Advances in School Mental Health Promotion, 3*(1), 5–17. https://doi.org/10.1080/1754730X.2010.9715670

Weare, K., & Ormston, R. (2022). *Initial Reflections on the Results of the Large RCT of Mindfulness in Schools* MYRIAD *(My Resilience in Adolescence) Project* (p. 10). The Mindfulness Initiative. https://www.themindfulnessinitiative.org/Handlers/Download.ashx?IDMF=edd4fc28-aef1-42c8-95c5-3b2c082da1c1

Weaver, D. H., & Choi, J. (2017). The media agenda: Who (or What) sets it? In K. Kenski & K. H. Jamieson (Eds.), *The Oxford Handbook of Political Communication* (pp. 359–76). Oxford University Press.

Wessely, S. (2019). Foreword. In N. Barden & R. Caleb (Eds.), *Student Mental Health and Wellbeing in Higher Education: A Practical Guide* (pp. xvi–xix). Sage.

Western Interstate Commission for Higher Education. (1973). *The Ecosystem Model: Designing Campus Environments* (HE 004 827; p. 28). Western Interstate Commission for Higher Education.

What Works Centre for Wellbeing. (2017, February 23). *Trust, Wellbeing and Measuring Inequality*. What Works Wellbeing. https://whatworkswellbeing.org/blog/trust-wellbeing-and-measuring-inequality/

White, G. M. (1992). Ethnopsychology. In T. Schwartz, G. M. White, & C. A. Lutz (Eds.), *New Directions in Psychological Anthropology*. Cambridge University Press. https://doi.org/10.1017/CBO9780511621857.002

Whyte, J. (2013). *Quack Policy: Abusing Science in the Cause of Paternalism*. London: Institute of Economic Affairs.

Williams, J. (2013). *Consuming Higher Education: Why Learning Can't Be Bought*. Bloomsbury.

Williams, M., Coare, P., Marvell, R., Pollard, E., Houghton, A.-M., & Anderson, J. (2015). *Understanding Provision for Students with Mental Health Problems and Intensive Support Needs* (No. 00099–3782). HEFCE. https://eprints.lancs.ac.uk/id/eprint/80492/1/HEFCE2015_mh.pdf

Williams, M., & Penman, D. (2011). *Mindfulness: An Eight Week Plan for Finding Peace in a Frantic World*. Rodale.

Wilson, J. (2014). *Mindful America: Meditation and the Mutual Transformation of Buddhism and American Culture*. OUP USA.

Winfrey, O. (2009, January 1). Here we go! *O, The Oprah Magazine*, *10*, 25, 148.

Woodham, A. (2001, June 26). Meditation to repair stress. *The Times*.

Woods, J. (2013, January 1). It's the moment for mindfulness. *The Telegraph*. https://www.telegraph.co.uk/lifestyle/wellbeing/9772911/Nows-the-moment-for-mindfulness.html

Woolcock, N. (2017, May 3). Mindfulness lessons 'can harm children'. *The Times*.

Wright, C. (2013). Against flourishing: Wellbeing as biopolitics, and the psychoanalytic alternative. *Health, Culture and Society; Pittsburgh*, *5* (1),n/a. http://dx.doi.org/10.5195/HCS.2013.151

Wright, K. (2008). Theorizing therapeutic culture: Past influences, future directions. *Journal of Sociology*, *44*(4), 321–36.

Yang, J. (2013). 'Fake Happiness': Counseling, potentiality, and psycho-Politics in china: Counseling, Potentiality, and Psycho-Politics in China. *Ethos*, *41*(3), 292–312. https://doi.org/10.1111/etho.12023

Yang, J. (2015). *Unknotting the Heart: Unemployment and Therapeutic Governance in China*. Cornell University Press.

Yorke, H. (2018, June 27). Universities urged to invest in mental health services as minister launches new charter to promote student wellbeing. *The Telegraph*.

Yorkshire Post. (2009, March 17). Law students take first prize in new challenge. *Yorkshire Post*. https://advance.lexis.com/document/?pdmfid=1519360&crid=3b3e0ce0-8072-471a-b2f3-d7aaf9f7a998&pddocfullpath=%2Fshared%2Fdocument%2Fnews%2Furn%3AcontentItem%3A7VHJ-WDS0-YC1P-V14K-00000-00&pdcontentcomponentid=250237&pdteaserkey=sr0&pditab=allpods&ecomp=qbxnk&earg=sr0&prid=ea3dedc8-0842-4d27-aeaa-837791461e12

Young, D. (2014). *Enterprise for All: The Relevance of Enterprise in Education* (URN BIS/14/874). BIS. https://assets.publishing.service.gov.uk/government/uploads/system/uploads/attachment_data/file/338749/EnterpriseforAll-lowres-200614.pdf

Young-Powell, A. (2014, February 18). Students to laugh, tweet and bounce on university mental health day. *The Guardian*.

Zeffman, H. (2018, June 25). Mental health 'biggest issue for students'. *The Times*, 2.

Žižek, S. (2000). *The Ticklish Subject: The Absent Centre of Political Ontology*. Verso.

Index